PUBLIKATIONEN
DER BAYERISCHEN AMERIKA-AKADEMIE
Band 18

PUBLICATIONS
OF THE BAVARIAN AMERICAN ACADEMY
Volume 18

---

SERIES EDITORS
Bavarian American Academy

NOTE ON THE EDITORS

Klaus Lösch is Senior Lecturer in American Studies at Friedrich-Alexander-University Erlangen-Nuremberg and a member of the Bavarian American Academy.

Heike Paul is Professor and Chair of American Studies at Friedrich-Alexander-University Erlangen-Nuremberg. She is also Deputy Director of the Bavarian American Academy and Vice President of the German Association for American Studies (GAAS) / Deutsche Gesellschaft für Amerikastudien (DGfA).

Meike Zwingenberger is Executive Director of the Bavarian Center for Transatlantic Relations / Stiftung Bayerisches Amerikahaus gGmbH in Munich.

# Critical Regionalism

Edited by

KLAUS LÖSCH
HEIKE PAUL
MEIKE ZWINGENBERGER

in collaboration with

JASMIN FALK

Universitätsverlag
WINTER
Heidelberg

Bibliografische Information der Deutschen Nationalbibliothek
Die Deutsche Nationalbibliothek verzeichnet diese Publikation in der Deutschen Nationalbibliografie; detaillierte bibliografische Daten sind im Internet über *http://dnb.d-nb.de* abrufbar.

UMSCHLAGBILD
© Klaus Lösch

ISBN 978-3-8253-6679-7


Imprimé en Allemagne · Printed in Germany
Druck: Memminger MedienCentrum, 87700 Memmingen

Gedruckt auf umweltfreundlichem, chlorfrei gebleichtem und alterungsbeständigem Papier.

Den Verlag erreichen Sie im Internet unter:
www.winter-verlag.de

# Table of Contents

# Critical Regionalism: An Introduction

*Klaus Lösch and Heike Paul*

## I.

Regionalism has always been premised on both, particularization and generalization. In the United States, it suggests geographical and cultural differences among distinct parts of the country as, in sum, part(s) of the nation; regions *add up* to the nation as a whole. But what may count as a region and in which discourse? Some regions have always been crucial for American studies; they were at the center of early Americanist scholarship and thus foundational for the development of American studies and its "field imaginary" (Pease 10), i.e. for the scholarship that addressed the United States in its unity (and to a lesser degree in its diversity) and that made it the object of a new discipline. Henry Nash Smith's book on the American West (*Virgin Land: The American West as Symbol and Myth*, 1950) is perhaps the single most important work in this context since it also demonstrates how the notion of regions (in this case: the West) is considered as symbolically meaningful for the nation as a whole. This region and its history are seen as representative of the nation and its becoming, a pars pro toto, so to speak, in conjunction with notions of a manifest destiny which are being transposed into a kind of geographical determinism. The local specificity of a region is not explicitly addressed by Nash Smith and other scholars of his cohort, and 'region' is therefore not being used as (literal) signifier of the local but rather in an allegorical way. By inversion and in contrast to the discourse(s) on the West, the South has often figured as that which the nation is *not*: a supposedly national place or region representative of the whole. The South as region has often been projected as the 'other' America. In their respective variations, regional fictions of the West and the South (with, of course, some overlap between them) have for a long time dominated Americanist scholarship; both also competed, if you will, in establishing a privileged perspective on the United States along an East/West or a North/South axis. The West, in particular, has been repeatedly conceptualized as a kind of region that is more of a space of transition and of nation-building than an actual place (in the sense of belonging and rootedness) with scholars not even agreeing on 'where' exactly it is located. More recent scholarship in the field of new western history (works such as Patricia Nelson Limerick's *The Legacy of Conquest*, Clyde Milner's new history of the West, and Neil Campbell's *The Rhizomatic West*) has drawn upon this observation and has used it to engender a more self-reflexive approach – an approach that has also helped to think about regions anew – and more critically. These works are part of a genealogy of critical regionalism.

Within literary studies, a closer look at regions and regionalisms (in contradistinction to their allegorization and as an attempt at defining regional identities) has been at the center of the writings of the various regional movements (such as the Southern Agrarians). So-called local color fiction and regionalist literature are the object of regionalist scholarship; the latter turns against all forms of an allegorical reading of regions and affirms the historical, cultural, and political specificity of regional landscapes and locales. To give but one example: Charles Reagan Wilson, a representative scholar of regionalism, has focused on the "regional consciousness" in his work (mostly on the South). Not only do regionalists in literary (and in cultural) studies make claims about regional specificity, they may even claim this specificity in opposition (in the framework of a counter-discourse, so to speak) to the national rather than seeing it as/or at its core. Robert Dorman's *Revolt from the Provinces* has chronicled this 'other' kind of regionalism that not only affirms and highlights local and regional cultural and political distinctions but also relates the region to the nation in quite an antagonistic manner. In extending this kind of critique that may be seen as anti-modern and/or anti-capitalist critique, region has often become associated somewhat imprecisely with a kind of "ruralized regionalism" where the region is considered as the locus of origin that guarantees authentic practices of an unalienated life in reaction to anxieties induced by modernization and globalization. Regionalism, in this classical partial understanding, has been viewed as championing a "pastoral ideal," i.e. an ethically superior way of life which we may want to protect or should return to. Of course, this vision is quite exclusive in a literal sense: "Never met a stranger" is a phrase Mary E. Grey uses as a starting point for identifying and interrogating queer absences and presences in rural America – and the list of the excluded could go on. In that sense, region and regional identity are positioned as categories of difference and markers of identity alongside race, gender, sexuality, and class and intersect with them; region is thus seen as a highly relevant difference that needs to be addressed, represented, and recognized by others. In such contexts, positive thoughts on the region may appear to be nostalgically tinged.[1]

In a constructivist paradigm, the region is no less an "imagined community" (Anderson) than the nation, and any essentialist understanding of it as a defining factor in individual and collective identity formation must be analyzed as an expression of people's longing for a localized version of ontological security, i.e. for a home and a homeland at hand, so to speak. Against this background, regional difference cannot simply be considered marginal and be absorbed in an overarching national identity. Recent debates in the context of globalization have also called into question the adequacy of a center-periphery model on various levels including that between city and country, between urban centers and rural

[1] With regard to the relation between the regional and the rural, see the introduction in Kley and Paul 2015.

regions. In American studies scholarship we may think of Leo Marx's *The Machine in the Garden: Technology and the Pastoral Ideal in America* (1964, 2000) as an early case in point and Marx's later modification of the initial argument in order to account for more ambivalent representations of regions and their political implications. It is Marx's notion of an older pastoralism revisited that provides a critical intervention into discourses of the region and the nation that are structured along binary oppositions.[2]

## II.

*Critical regionalism* connects the dominant ways of analyzing the region in the field of American studies and does the work of revisioning those approaches against the backdrop of globalization. Thus, critical regionalism draws upon the national, the subnational, and the transnational dimension in the study of regions and prompts a series of questions: How to define a region? Turning away from the allegorical mode, can we conceive of it as territorial in the literal sense at all? Many contributors to this volume do not. And even if so, does it exist *only* as a territory in the sense of a spatial entity? Such a semantics of region would sit uneasily with a contemporary concept of culture that has been quite radically deterritorialized. What, then, is the relationship of region and culture? On a local-global continuum, is the region closer to the local or to the global? Or does it keep the middle ground to mediate between both? Does it entail a particular set of spatial practices? These are some of the questions the essays in this volume address.

*Critical regionalism* is not a new paradigm; rather, it is a set of fresh approaches in various disciplines, some of them part of an interdisciplinary American studies framework and of area studies scholarship in general. It investigates the construction of regions and their inter-relation which may be evoking analogies, convergences, or antagonisms. Moving beyond essentialist modes of conceptualizing, describing, and scrutinizing regional identities (both as self-representations and as representations by others), critical regionalism follows a comparative perspective that pays attention to cultural specificity on the one hand and to processes of cultural exchange and transfer on the other, i.e. it tries to elucidate the hidden connections between the local/regional and the global which are mostly being glossed over in self-conscious constructions of regional identities. In privileging an approach to regions that highlights the constitutive dialectic of the local and the global, it emphasizes questions of power and authority. Thus, regions

2 In a similar vein, publications such as *Regionalists on the Left* attest to the fact that a regionally tinged political agenda need not necessarily be nostalgic, back-ward looking, and conservative.

have to be conceptualized not as autonomous entities but as part of intricate global structures implying interdependencies of all kinds.

The agenda of *critical regionalism* may be viewed as one particular trajectory of more recent revisionist regionalist scholarship in general. The term itself has entered cultural studies debates via contemporary architectural criticism (after critical regionalism was coined by Alexander Tzonis and Lianne Lefaivre in 1981) and has been programmatically used by Kenneth Frampton in his manifesto *Towards a Critical Regionalism: Six Points for an Architecture of Resistance* (1983). Frampton argues for a new placeboundedness in the architecture of late capitalism and – drawing on Paul Ricoeur – against a universalization that is seen as destructive (16). He identifies "the freestanding high-rise and the serpentine freeway" as the "two symbiotic instruments of Megalopolitan development" (17) that share a global ubiquity. Sharply criticizing a normative utilitarianism ("utility established as meaning generates meaninglessness," ibid.), Frampton calls for the re-attachment of architectural design to particular local, regional, and cultural elements, not in a seemingly innocent nostalgic but in a self-reflexive way: "It may find its governing inspiration in such things as the range and quality of the local light, or in a *tectonic* derived from a peculiar structural mode, or in the topography of a given site" (21).

Of course, *critical regionalism* in its wider sense is not only interested in cultural factors and their symbolic effects but also in forms of political participation and in economic aspects of the local "linking cultural and socioeconomic localized identities, especially as these stand in antagonistic, if also negotiated, relationships with late capitalist globalization" (Limón 167). Thus, critical regionalism may be seen as a discourse that articulates a topical cultural critique which tries to resist late capitalism as a hegemonic (i.e. naturalized) order. In this perspective, a late capitalist logic fabricates regions along the lines of a "corporate geography" that only allows for a kind of regional difference that can be used in commercials for commercial interests, as Cheryl Herr points out (3). In this vein, regions themselves become commodities being circulated in global processes of production and consumption. In contradistinction, critical regionalism explores alternative regionalisms that may offer different (diasporic) configurations of regions and regional structures and that may produce different genealogical accounts of how regions 'become' regions in the first place.

These accounts invariably touch upon the construction of region on the one hand and the aims of regional studies on the other focusing on that which the region etymologically has at its root: rule and power. In American studies, this may have us envision a broad trajectory that returns us to Turner's geographical determinism echoing 19$^{th}$ century evolutionary theory, then has us look at the ways in which the geopolitical constellation of the cold war translates colonialist semantics into a new framework for area studies in which regions simultaneously do and do not 'exist', to, finally, more recent studies that enforce a sense of an economic determinism which pertains to regions at various levels. In a diachronic perspective it thus becomes obvious that the semantics of regions are quite contingent, and one may even see region as an empty signifier that is made to signify various hierarchies in historically specific discourses. Therefore, it is necessary to painstakingly contextualize the term and to try to analyze the overt and the covert agendas underlying its usage. This caveat is especially pertinent when we study evaluative collocations such as 'the wild West' or 'the dirty South,' to give but two examples. And, last but not least, in dealing with aesthetic discourses that claim (or deny) a specific regional register, it is important to dig into their respective agendas and focus on the power dynamics they (a) represent and (b) engage in.

Frampton's manifesto has found echoes in various disciplines. In his own it has been either highly acclaimed or severely criticized. In a recent critique, Keith Eggener posits that Frampton's program has "marginalized and conflated the diverse architectural tendencies it has championed" (Eggener 229) and that his critical regionalism has produced a new hegemonic architectural order that again involves othering, but of a different kind. Notwithstanding this criticism, Frampton's theses have strongly resonated in the humanities, among them American studies. Wendy Katz and Timothy Mahoney's *Regionalism and the Humanities* addresses regionalism after the spatial turn in literary and cultural studies; the contributors to their volume highlight revisionist regionalism (as in the works of the New Western historians) as well as 'new regionalisms' (see Wilson). In an attempt to refresh regionalist studies, Douglas Reichert Powell defines region as "a loosely and variously defined zone that cuts across the boundaries of the academic landscape" (Reichert Powell 6) and thus emphasizes interdisciplinarity. In a cultural studies framework Cheryl Herr (also a contributor to this book) has been the first to apply the term critical regionalism for cultural and literary analyses, and, in a similar context, Heike Paul has argued for a critical regionalist perspective as a quintessential post-exceptionalist American studies framework (Paul).

The present volume is to be situated within the context of these recent interventions. One of its core tenets is that critical regionalism is a current, productive, and highly relevant approach in cultural studies-scholarship, and the essays in this volume attest to this.

## III.

The contributions to this collection apply a perspective informed by critical regionalism to cultural, historical, political, social, and literary analyses. They address various geographical regions, specific figurations of place and region as well as a series of transregional (and transnational) trajectories; they deal with distinct groups within American society and their cultural productions in terms of (region-based or region-related) minority discourses, and representations of the effects of an exploitative approach to the making and unmaking of regions.

**Cheryl Temple Herr** sees critical regionalist scholarship addressing instances of crises. It is the "bees in crisis" and the contemporary practices of "migratory bee keeping" in the United States that are at the center of her article. She analyzes the larger implications of the cross-country trucking of bee hives for scheduled pollinations in various regions of the country and argues that these practices reveal the thorough commodification of bees and the destruction of their habitat as an effect of global markets that rely on bee pollination for profit. Herr draws on a critical regionalist and ecocritical perspective in order to address these grievances and to reflect more broadly on "the circumstances behind the [hegemonic] administration of space" for animals and humans alike. In his essay "Ruins, Places, and Photography: Towards a Cultural Aesthetics of Catastrophe," **Miles Orvell** offers a typology of ruin that encompasses ruins as part of a temporal cycle, as the result of a singular, catastrophic event, and as part of an apocalyptic narrative/vision. Orvell revisits an archive of 150 years of ruin photography and time and again points to the role of photography as documentation of ruin landscapes, to its aesthetic transformations, and its uses as a medium of political intervention. **Claudia Sadowski-Smith** sees border regions in their local as well as transnational quality as an exemplum for critical regionalism. It is the indigenous peoples of North America (whose land is often cut across by the borders of current nation states), whom she sees at the forefront of a critical regionalism that intervenes in hegemonic spatialities and insists on regional sovereignty: border crossing, in her argumentation, is part and parcel of a critical regionalist practice. **Silvia Spitta** also zooms in on the border, promoting "trans-border studies" as a critical regionalist paradigm; she addresses recent performance work and art productions of and on the US-Mexico borderlands by the architect Teddy Cruz, the writers Eduardo Antonio Parra and Humberto Félix Berumen and the artist Heriberto Yépez. All of them, she suggests, take a critical angle toward hegemonic discourses of 'border control.' Picking up from there, **Carmen Brosig**'s essay extends the transnational scope further. In her discussion of the region of Aztlan, the mythical homeland of Mexican-Americans evoked by the Chicano movement, she identifies constructions of transnational solidarity in the wake of protests against the war in Vietnam by Mexican Americans in the United States. The nexus of Chicano cultural nationalism and anti-Vietnam-War protests, established in a move of anticolonial cross-mapping is to be found in Chicano literature, poster art, and other forms of political commitment that are suggestive of transregional and transnational connections between two forms of colonial oppression. **Birgit Bauridl** uses a critical regionalist paradigm in order to identify and reflect on the symbolic construction of "Graf," a US military training area in Southern Germany. In her exploration of the multiple meanings of that site and the various, at times competing cultural and spatial practices that 'produce' it, she views it as a prism of larger diachronic and synchronic processes of cultural mobility and transfer and as a regional turntable of transnational and transcultural processes with wide-ranging impact. In her article "Sisterhood Is Regional?: US-American Women's Activism between the Global and the Local," **Katharina Gerund** investigates the role and function of the region and of regionalism for the activism of second wave feminists. Taking Betty Friedan's "suburban feminism" and Robin Morgan's declared "global feminism" as two manifestations of the feminist spectrum ranging from place-bound particularity of feminist organization on the one hand to unbound universalism on the other, Gerund suggests that critical regionalism offers a fresh perspective on spatial feminist genealogies and the ways in which these are attached to local, regional, and global agendas and claims. In line with recent regionalist and feminist scholarship, **Amy Doherty Mohr** discusses Willa Cather's work in the context of critical regionalism and looks more closely at the crossmapping, of domestic affiliations with international contexts. As Mohr points out, Cather's novels, particularly *One of Ours*, present an ironic revisiting of the domestic space at home and abroad (in Europe) in time of war and, in doing so, ironizes (and mobilizes) notions of masculinity and of patriotism. A very different literary reading is at the center of **Rachael Price**'s piece on Larry McMurtry's *The Last Picture Show* and its poignant anti-pastoralism. The novel shows the situation of a Texas oil town in rapid decline, which is reflected in all of the dysfunctional personal and intimate relationships the novel portrays. Conspiciously counter-playing desert and garden imagery as the two dominant tropes of the (South)West, both are ultimately shown as insufficient for characterizing the state of the rural Southwestern town in a late capitalist scencario that puts it at the mercy of global forces seemingly located *elsewhere*. Finally, **Tanja Aho** discusses the reality television series *Here Comes Honey Boo Boo* (aired on TLC, 2012-2014) against hegemonic cultural practices of "rednexploitation" by taking recourse to Eve Kosofsky Sedgwick's concepts of paranoid and reparative reading and applying them to different representations of Southernness in popular culture. Drawing on a 'low theory' of television, Aho disentangles bottom-up, viewer responses from an overall mis-recognition of the series and its region- and class-specific cultural work.

This volume brings together selected key-note presentations and student papers from the Bavarian American Academy's Summer Schools of 2013, 2014, and 2015. The Bavarian American Academy with its regional institutional setting in Germany and its commitment to transatlantic dialogue and exchange may be itself an ideal site from which to articulate a critical regionalist perspective. Its Summer School program, bringing together renowned faculty and doctoral students from the United States and Europe since 2006, has evolved around key issues in American studies to be fruitfully considered in a transatlantic framework. "Critical Regionalism" has been the overall theme of 2013 and 2014 with a bit of a reprise in 2015. This volume captures some of the trajectories of our discussions. The editors would like to thank the participants for engaging with this topic under the arc of the BAA and for contributing their work to the present volume. Thanks also go to Jasmin Falk at the BAA for her diligent editorial work.

## Works Cited:

Campbell, Neil. *The Rhizomatic West: Representing the American West in a Transnational, Global, Media Age*. Lincoln: University of Nebraska Press, 2008. Print.

Dorman, Robert. *Revolt of the Provinces: The Regionalist Movement in America, 1920-45*. Chapel Hill: University of North Carolina Press, 2010. Print.

Eggener, Keith L. "Placing Resistance: A Critique of Critical Regionalism." *Journal of Architectural Education* 55.4 (2002): 228-37. *JSTOR*. Web. 7 June 2016.

Frampton, Kenneth. "Toward a Critical Regionalism: Six Points for an Architecture of Resistance." *The Anti-Aesthetic: Essays on Postmodern Culture*. Ed. Hal Foster. Port Townsend, Washington: Bay Press 1983. 16-30. Print.

Gray, Mary L. *Out in the Country: Youth, Media, and Queer Visibility in Rural America*. New York: New York University Press, 2009. Print.

Herr, Cheryl Temple. *Critical Regionalism and Cultural Studies: From Ireland to the American Midwest*. Gainesville: University Press of Florida, 1996. Print.

Katz, Wendy, and Timothy Mahoney (eds.). *Regionalism and the Humanities*. Lincoln: Nebraska University Press, 2008. Print.

Kley, Antje, and Heike Paul (eds.). *Rural America*. Heidelberg: Winter, 2015. Print.

Lefaivre, Liane, and Alexander Tzonis. *Architecture of Regionalism in the Age of Globalization: Peaks and Valleys in the Flat World*. London: Routledge, 2012. Print.

Limerick, Patricia. *The Legacy of Conquest: The Unbroken Past of the American West*. New York: Norton, 1987. Print.

Limón, José E. "Border Literary Histories, Globalization, and Critical Regionalism." *American Literary History* 20.1-2 (2008): 160-82. Print.

Marx, Leo. *The Machine in the Garden: Technology and the Pastoral Ideal in America*. 1964. New York: Oxford University Press, 2000. Print.

Milner II, Clyde A. *A New Significance: Re-Envisioning the History of the American West*. New York: Oxford, 1996. Print.

Nash Smith, Henry. *Virgin Land: The American West as Symbol and Myth*. Cambridge: Harvard University Press, 1950. Print.

Paul, Heike. "Critical Regionalism and Post-Exceptionalist American Studies." *Towards a Post-Exceptionalist American Studies*. *REAL*. Ed. Winfried Fluck and Donald Pease. 30 (2014): 397-424. Print.

Pease, Donald. "New Americanists: Revisionist Interventions into the Canon." *Revisionist Interventions into the Americanist Canon*. Durham: Duke University Press, 1994. 1-37. Print.

Reichert Powell, Douglas. *Critical Regionalism: Connecting Politics and Culture in the American Landscape*. Chapel Hill: University of North Carolina Press, 2007. Print.

Steiner, Michael C. *Regionalists on the Left*. Norman: Oklahoma University Press, 2015. Print.

Turner, Frederick Jackson. "The Significance of the Frontier in American History." 1893. *American Studies at the University of Virginia*. Web. 17 June 2016. <http://croads.virginia.edu/~hyper/turner/chapter1.html>.

Wilson, Charles Reagan (ed.). *The New Encyclopedia of Southern Culture: Myth, Manners, Memory*. Vol. 4. Chapel Hill: North Carolina University Press, 2006. Print.

# Critical Regionalism and Cultural Studies: Bees in Crisis

*Cheryl Temple Herr*

## Critical Regionalists

Critical regionalism as an architectural practice and cultural discourse has several points of origin. In most discussions of critical regionalism, Alexander Tzonis, Kenneth Frampton, and Fredric Jameson have prominence. More recent texts by Mary Hufford, Douglas Reichert Powell, Michael Trujillo, and José Limón have continued to extend this approach to the study of culture. By and large, each of these individuals has written in a critical regionalist mode in order to address a moment of crisis. We can make the claim, then, that perceived cultural crisis drives critical regionalism in its primary formulations and, as it happens, for its precursors.

One such precursor was Lewis Mumford. His multidisciplinary writings from the 1920s through the 70s worried about the future of community, the expansionist ideology of modernity, warfare in the 20th century, and the designed obsolescence that characterizes what he called megatechnics. Throughout the literature of architectural critical regionalism, people return to Mumford's work for inspiration. For practical purposes, however, it was the invitation received in 1978 by architect Alexander Tzonis to write an essay on the work of young German architects that jump-started the architectural movement called critical regionalism. Tzonis turned to Mumford's regionalist critique of the International Style to begin his investigation into these German architects and "eine andere Architektur" (Lefaivre and Tzonis 6). Tzonis has stated, "[t]he task of critical regionalism is to rethink architecture through the concept of region. Whether this involves complex human ties or the balance of the ecosystem, it is opposed to mindlessly adopting narcissistic dogmas that undermine community, economy, and the environment" (Lefaivre and Tzonis 20).

During the early 1990s, I wrote a book about Ireland and the American (US) Midwest called *Critical Regionalism and Cultural Studies*. At the time, under the sign of the Single European Act, I tried to develop a critical regionalist model for cultural studies, adapting architectural theory to encounter literary, historical, and visual texts, to think through the global agricultural crisis that had begun in the 1980s. I wanted to widen the purview of critical regionalism to cover artifacts beyond but also including the built environment. Thinking back and forth across the Atlantic, across somewhat symmetrical terrains, proved to be a productive way to think about family farming in the era of agribusiness. Turning back to critical regionalism's dialectic of diversity and globalization, I looked at filiated rural regions' production of narratives that essentially filled in the blanks in each other's stories. What emerged was a complex inter-zone that gestured beyond the structures of administered society. Artists, it seemed, and many of them architects, had prepared the terrain for a critical cross-regionalism eager for material change and sustainable agricultures.

## The Problem: Bees in Crisis

For the purposes of this paper, the crisis is one that we are all familiar with – the phenomenon of bee colony collapse. In this case, a critical regionalist approach should carry us into the history and representation of regional social forces behind this worldwide problem and perhaps offer useful insights about the way forward.

A helpful starting point is the fact that at the end of April 2013, fifteen of the EU member states approved a restriction on neonicotinoid pesticides. Spurred on by European initiatives, American beekeepers are now lobbying Congress to take action against these invasive and systemic pesticides. The Cummings Report, issued periodically on Project Apis to cover the condition of bees in the California almond orchards, stated in mid April that this year's "pollination force" was "relatively poor." Pollination prices rose to $200 per hive as it became obvious that the "near perfect almond bloom" would be under-pollinated. As anticipated, hives were quite susceptible to viruses and mites, and many brood boxes lost up to half of the colony while waiting to pollinate the almond crop. Altogether, honey bee pollination in California's early spring was spotty (Cummings). In this paper, I undertake a quick glance at two or three regions within the United States in terms of their bee history and current beekeeping practices.

First and foremost, it is not the case that apiculture was at one time pristinely productive and has suddenly become problematic. The history of the bee in America is much more complicated than this. For instance, there have always been bee pathogens. American beekeepers have long had to watch for problems like foulbrood and wax moths. It is the current *combination* of pathogens, pesticides, and other stressors that have caused unprecedented problems in cultivating honey bees (Jacobsen 139). Beyond the assault of neonics, honey bees have suffered from continuing loss of meadowlands and floral diversity. Over the years bee colonies have sometimes dwindled or simply absconded, but starting in 2006 the number of colonies that abruptly disappeared in the United States (also in various parts of Europe) has been substantial, widespread, and seemingly unmistakable.

Further and to a degree that feels distinctively American, bees have become super-stressed by the now-routine practices of extensive migratory beekeeping. Consider the annual itinerary of a large-scale beekeeper. In *The Beekeeper's Lament*, Hannah Nordhaus provides the template of John Miller's annual bee runs (Nordhaus 18-22).

- January 19: feed 2,700 hives in Newcastle, CA
- January 20: ship 7,000 hives from Idaho to California
- January 26-February 10: place hives in California almond orchards
- March 9-13: collect hives. Feed bees. Ship 3,000 hives to Newcastle, 3,000 hives to Washington State apple orchards, and 1,600 hives to Stockton, CA cherry orchards
- End of April: re-collect hives, divide hives, and re-queen them
- May: truck hives to North Dakota
- Harvest honey in September
- Store bees for winter in special cellars in Idaho

My own discussions with midwestern beekeepers confirm that this strenuous agenda is relatively routine for the industry.

Many problems unfurl from the practice of trucking bees. For instance, in *Fruitless Fall*, Rowan Jacobsen notes,

> [i]t's not in a beehive's nature to be at full strength in February. The European honey bee would normally spend December and January in semi-hibernation. To have a full, eight-frame hive of bees by the beginning of February, beekeepers need to trick their bees into believing that spring has come in December and that food is abundant. They need to park the bees somewhere relatively warm for November, December, and January, and feed, feed, feed. Only then will the queen start laying so that a phalanx of foragers will be ready for the February almonds. (127)

Nonetheless, the practice of parking bees is widespread enough to have a name: "feedlot beekeeping" (Jacobsen 127). Despite the cost in bees, all of the experts agree with Nordhaus that "[t]his annual bee migration […] [is] the glue that holds much of our [America's] agricultural system together" (Nordhaus 22).

A map posted on the internet by the Beekeepers Association in Person County, North Carolina shows three typical commercial routes in the complex and, given the peak oil situation, increasingly expensive solution to American agriculture's lust for bees (<http://www.personcountybeekeepers.org/wordpress/wp-content/uploads/2011/10/Pollination21.jpg>). One route runs from California's sunflowers, apples, cherries, almonds, melons, avocados, cucumbers, and kiwis north to Washington State's apples, cherries, cranberries, pears, and plums. From the Pacific Northwest, the same bee colonies circle to the midwestern crops of sunflowers, cucumbers, and cherries before the cycle begins again. A second route connects Florida with the Midwest, the Midwest with Maine's blueberry harvest, and returns the busy pollinators from New England to Florida. Yet a third route connects the South with the Northeastern states in an endless circle of fructification. These routes are not the only ones possible, but they impressively map American agriculture as a site of restless industrial churning. And how does being trucked around feel to the subjects themselves? Search the internet for "trucking bee hives," and YouTube brings up numerous videos taken on American highways showing massive numbers of bees being whipped against the netting holding their colonies on the truck.

## Bees in America

How did we arrive at this constellation of beekeeping practices in the United States? What were the historical pressures and cultural circumstances that have made honey bees the medium – a peculiarly architectural medium – through which rural regional desires in the United States are currently met? Certainly, there is little or nothing in what we might call the bee's nature that leads to migratory beekeeping. To the contrary, bees are often celebrated for their ability to become one with their immediate stable environment. In a strikingly original book called *Insect Media*, Finnish theorist Jussi Parikka explains that he is investigating distributed intelligence among insects as a "milieu approach to the world" (Parikka xxvi). Parikka draws on nineteenth- and twentieth-century understandings of 'instinct' to underwrite his attention to bee behavior and environment. From Henri Bergson he takes the view that instinct is "not merely [...] an automated response [that] a primitive animal (such as an insect) gives to a stimulus but in addition involves 'discernment and attunement' to the animal's environment" (Parikka 20). From William James, Parikka draws the proposal "that instincts are not abstract schemes an animal might have but instead 'functional correlatives of a structure.'" And Parikka extends these definitions to regard insect instincts as "prelinguistic modes of intertwining the body with its surroundings" in a mise-en-scène in which all is motion and potentiality rather than reductive response (Parikka 23). Thus in order to achieve its rich possibilities, the instinctual capacity of a bee colony will "intimately" conform to the materiality of the immediate setting (Parikka 30). The cascade of minute adjustments implied in this formulation resonates with Tzonis' views on the architectural ecology of critical regionalism. According to this mode of understanding, bees organize material environments into habitat while not really distinguishing between their own individual embodiment and that of the collective (Parikka 33). As a 'superorganism,' the bee colony is woven into its surroundings in a way that human beings obviously have trouble imagining but that is also within the trajectory of critical regionalist desire. Left to their own devices, bees would probably stay put, only gradually spinning off new hives. And it is precisely a lack of cross-species imagination that enables bee farmers to wrest bee boxes (already one remove from nature) from meadows and propel them at high speeds across American highways.

A robust corollary to this point is that honey bees as we know them are not even native to the North American continent. Tammy Horn explains, "[e]ven though honey bees [...] were not native to North America, as soon as colonists *imagined* that America could be 'a land of milk and honey,' they set in motion the events to make America so" (5). In the decades of European settlement that preceded the sugar economy's impact on America, bees and their keepers arrived from Sweden, England, the Netherlands, France, and Germany. Historical records locate the earliest American bees, a dark variety then known as German bees, in 1620. On the 47 million acres that William Penn purchased from Charles II, one could find a wide array of "proficient" German Protestant beekeepers (Horn 29). Many records note native Indians' complaints about "the white man's flies," the arrival of which on Indian land always preceded land takeovers (Horn 27-28). At the same time, Native Americans soon learned to appreciate honey as a supplement to their traditional maple syrup.

Along with the German bees out there on the westward-moving frontier were honey hunters. "Forests in Sweden, England, and Germany were tightly controlled by the state, but colonists were free to find bee trees in America" (Horn 30). After meeting their own modest needs for sweetening, these transplanted honey hunters soon sold their newly claimed product on a fairly large-scale commercial basis to town-dwellers. Horn notes, "[f]rom Texas to Iowa" the bee hunter "became a type [...] the man pushing the boundaries of the frontier, one foot in the wild, one foot in civilization" (73).

## James Fenimore Cooper

One of America's earliest popular writers of historical romances, James Fenimore Cooper (1789-1851), was well aware of the honey hunter character type. Cooper's 1848 fiction *Oak Openings* represents the frontier in 1812, nine years after the Louisiana Purchase. Most of Cooper's fame comes from his Leatherstocking tales, including *The Last of the Mohicans*. So it is that very little criticism has been written on *Oak Openings*, but Scott Michaelsen's 1999 volume *The Limits of Multiculturalism: Interrogating the Origins of American Anthropology* offers a compelling interpretation; in this narrative Cooper subtly criticizes the racism of both 1812 and 1848:

> The most remarkable feature of the novel is the constant, recurrent ethnological (that is, comparative) focus across specifically *cultural* lines that few anthropologists ever – and no other contemporaneous ones – permit themselves to cross: that is, the border between First and Third World, between Anglo and Amerindian. (Michaelsen 125)

Michaelsen compares Cooper's *Oak Openings* to Francis Parkman's *The History of the Conspiracy of Pontiac* (1851) because both works deal with "the rise of pan-Indian resistance on the white frontier" (125). I want to reinforce this claim by attending to Cooper's repeated efforts to describe the biome – the specific region –

that supplies both setting and theme and that, in relation to the historical challenges of 1813, accounts for the action.

Cooper is fascinated by the landscape named in the title to his novel, a 300 square mile region that extends into both Ohio and Michigan. This zone features oak woodlands and prairie wetlands that before European settlement were surrounded by the Great Black Swamp. Coming from the densely wooded swamp into clearings dotted with oaks, early wagon trains could move easily through this park-like landscape. For many years, European settlers assumed that the oak openings were natural formations. The prevalent belief was that the natives who had lived in this area had not altered the so-called wilderness in any way. As we know, during the 1950s and even later, ecologists tended to imagine 'wilderness' as something pristine, entirely natural, and unaffected by Native American inhabitants. However, in 1954, ethnographer Omer Stewart published work that documented the systematic burning of various American landscapes by indigenous hunter-gatherers. Fire allowed these inhabitants to shape regional landscapes to their needs. Stewart claimed,

> [t]he irony is that some of these 'virgin' ecosystems evolved with the presence and influence of Indians over thousands of years. The […] oak forest margins in the Great Lakes region that [H. C.] Cowles included in his designation of 'mature, climax' forest were in fact an expanded artifact of former Ojibwa burning practices. (38)

The fact is that many locations had long been actively managed by native tribes. The wilderness was not the easy Eden, the "steady state system," so often assumed. What seemed to incoming Europeans to be the "balance of nature" had been constructed to feature "maximum species diversity and biomass production" (Stewart 38). Perhaps needless to say, "[t]he forces that degrade and rejuvenate ecosystems, such as insects, floods, fires, diseases, tree windfalls, and detritus accumulation, were frequently not factored into this [previously held] idyllic image" (9; see also Williams). Indeed, the genial face that the oak openings presented to Europeans had been carefully constructed before they arrived.

Stewart makes the case that the regular (one to three year) intentional burns (identified after the fact by fire scars in tree rings and fossil evidence) were the principal forces constructing the so-called wilderness that Cooper depicts in *Oak Openings*. These burns diversified the midwestern habitat and determined what types of vegetation flourished, how animal life was managed, and how much of America was constructed as prairie. The oak savannahs in question were not fixed features but biological zones that Native Americans had long managed to their own ends. The clearings that provide the setting for Cooper's novel of 1812 had already been controlled by indigenous tribes in order to optimize hunting and foraging, to minimize pests, to enable travel and warfare, and to encourage waterfowl and other species to populate the area. Stewart argued that what looked to early settlers like an undisturbed balance of nature has been revised with what he calls "a non-equilibrium paradigm whereby the dynamics of natural communities are found to have [had] multiple persistent states and are subject to physical disruptions from a wide range of natural and human forces and events" (44).

Towards the outset, the narrator of *Oak Openings* describes just such a space: "The prairie alluded to was one of those small natural meadows, or pastures, that are to be found in Michigan, and may have contained four or five thousand acres of open land. The heavy timber of the swamp [still] [...] jutted into it" (J. Cooper chapter 1) Soon the narrative turns back to the challenge of describing this area:

> The northern portions of the noble peninsula of Michigan are somewhat low and swampy, or arc too broken and savage to tempt the native hunters from the openings and prairies that then lay, in such rich profusion, further south and west. With the exception of the shores, or coasts, it was seldom that the northern half of the peninsula felt the footstep of man. With the southern half, however, it was very different; the 'openings,' and glades, and water-courses, offering almost as many temptations to the savage, as they have since done to the civilized man. (chapter 2)

The beautiful region is depicted as distinctly Edenic. Later still, the narrator mentions Prairie Round (aka Prairie Ronde Township in S. Michigan, currently 14,000 acres of grassland), a spot brimming with natural beauty and also for a reason unknown to the narrator recently burned so "as to leave the entire expanse covered with young grasses and flowers, the same as if it were a well-kept park" (chapter 19). The novel represents the burning as accidental and contingent. The point is that Cooper himself is not sure whether lightning or human beings (or possibly both) have affected this terrain.

The French naming of Prairie Ronde reminds us that Cooper's narrative takes place during the early part of the War of 1812. One of the three main theaters in this conflict followed the US-Canadian border along the Great Lakes, the St. Lawrence River, and Lake Champlain. Here, American forces tackled the British and forestalled an Indian confederacy by 1813 when they came to control Lake Erie. The so-called Siege of Detroit in 1812, an early engagement in the war, saw the British and their Indian allies taking the city from the United States. In short, honeyhunting for his Detroit customers in this region has put Cooper's hero, Ben Boden, at risk of antagonizing otherwise relatively peaceable Native Americans. Yet the fact that Ben has good relations with the French is clear from his jolly nickname, *le Bourdon*.

The narrator of *Oak Openings*, having run to ground in describing the terrain, says,

> [w]e have now less to do with the cause, than with its consequences. These were most agreeable to the eye, as well as comfortable to the foot, the grass

> nowhere being of a height to impede movement, or, what was of still more importance to *le Bourdon's* present pursuit, to overshadow the flowers. Aware of this fact, he had led his companions all that distance, to reach this scene of remarkable rural beauty, in order that he might make a grand display of his art, in presence of the assembled chiefs of that region. (chapter 19)

Indeed, Ben and his comrades are in the control of chiefs who have gathered for a pan-tribal assembly, no doubt about the impending war, and he is eager to extricate his group from the scene before trouble comes to pass. In this clearing, Ben is very likely to be able to find enough bees to enable his triangulation of their hive. He needs a straight shot and a clear view.

At this pivotal moment, when Ben's skills are on the line, Cooper still ruminates, once again evoking these fascinating park-like spaces. He observes:

> As a whole, it was clear of the forest; quite as much so as if the axe had done its work there athousand years before, though wood was not wanting. On the contrary, enough of the last was to be seen, in addition to that which formed the frame of this charming landscape, to relieve the view from all appearance of monotony, and to break it up into copses, thickets, trees in small clusters, and in most of the varieties that embellish native scenery. One who had been unexpectedly transferred to the spot, might well have imagined that he was looking on the site of some old and long-established settlement, from which every appliance of human industry had been suddenly and simultaneously abstracted. (chapter 19)

We perceive once more that Cooper is not fully aware of Native American burns and that this region's indeterminate and almost European attractions puzzle him. Is this spot the ultimate sign of 'the free hand of nature'? Cooper is not certain and cannot let go of the quandary.

In her introduction to *Oak Openings*, Susan Fenimore Cooper lays out the origin of this late fiction. In June 1847, her father had traveled to Detroit and "the beautiful open groves of southern Michigan," retracing steps taken when he was a youth. During this trip he met a farmer who was hunting for a swarm of bees, and Cooper conversed with him as they searched. They discussed the practice of felling ancient trees for honey, which Cooper objected to, and the farmer said that his practice was to call the bees down from the tree onto which they had alighted.

> And taking up his tin pail, he began to move about over a little spot of waste land, where many flowering plants grew at will; here he soon found a honey-bee sipping from the cup of a rose raspberry; he professed to know at once the face of one of his own bees, "to say nothin' of the critter's talk," as he termed the buzzing of the wings. A glass taken from the pail was placed over it, a few drops of sweet honey having been previously thrown into it; the captive bee,

> after moving about uneasily for a while, began to sip the honey; when its little bag was quite full, it was set at liberty, the course it took being carefully followed as far as the eye could reach.

The farmer repeats the process "at an opposite point of the compass from that where he had first stood" and again watches the bee's flight. After a dozen tries, the farmer is satisfied that he knows where the "natural hive" is located: "an old, half-charred oak stub, some forty feet in height, with a single limb near the top." Grabbing a new hive (presumably a skep), the farmer sprinkles honey and flowers near its doorway to lure the bees. "[W]hen the sun set, the bees had of their own accord taken possession of their new abode; by moonlight they were rowed across the lake, and placed on the shelf in the farmer's garden, beside the mother swarm they had left a few days earlier on their adventurous journey to the Châlet" (S. Cooper 381-82).

As we have seen, Cooper repeatedly depicts the oak clearings not only for their readily apparent transcendental qualities but also as theatrical settings. Here, Ben's bee hunting becomes a spectacle so powerful that it temporarily deflects the chiefs' attention from the political purpose for their assembling. The apparently pristine oak openings are in the earliest phases of European refiguring, and the growing conflict – both environmental and political – is unsettling the area of future settlement.

So it is that in the novel Boden is in southern Michigan taking honey from bees that have preceded and are the immanent sign of Euro-settlement. Along the Detroit River, using his bark canoe, Ben supplies his customers with the finest and purest honey – wild honey being favored (then as now) over domesticated varieties. He finds this newly configured commodity – hundreds of pounds of it at a time – by bee-lining. On two occasions, Cooper describes Ben's skills. When he performs for the Native Americans, he aims to mystify them, and he succeeds. The narrator reminds us that when red men came upon honey it was only by chance and not by calculation or "that far-sighted and persevering industry, which enables the white man to lay in a store large enough to supply a neighbourhood, in the course of a few weeks' hunting" (chapter 19). To the Indians gathered there,

> [i]t was curious, and it was inexplicable! Could the pale-faces compel bees to reveal the secret of their hives, and was that encroaching race about to drive all the insects from the woods and seize their honey, as they drove the Indians before them and seized their lands? Such was the character of the thoughts that passed through the minds of more than one chief, that morning, though all looked on in profound stillness. (chapter 19)

The chiefs are described as if they were at a magic show, attempting to account for something truly supernatural. Extending his self-promotion even further, Ben insists that he tells the bees where to go and when. He asserts, "[t]he bees obey *me*, as your young men obey *you*. I am their chief, and they *know* me" (chapter 19). To extricate himself and his companions, Boden pretends that he can consult bees for knowledge of the future. To prove all of these boasts, Ben not only locates a hive but also identifies a bear den, the inhabitants of which are promptly slain by the gathered Indians. While they are thus distracted, Ben makes his escape.

In *The Prairie* a bee hunter named Paul Hover is a minor character; in *Oak Openings* Ben Boden's actions prescribe the novel's course and its representation of a distinctive American region. To carry out a critical regionalist reading of this novel I would ideally want to set up some further comparisons with historical romances written before the early twentieth century. Cross-regional depictions of bee culture as the frontier was closing would ideally unfold into representations of migratory bee-keeping as it became the industry norm.

## Gene Stratton-Porter

Although the space of this essay does not permit this larger investigation, I do want to isolate quickly another historical moment and regional destination in the westward trek of bees as captured by Gene Stratton-Porter in *The Keeper of the Bees* (1925). The central figure is an ailing veteran of World War I named Jamie, who leaves a G.I. rest home to see the Pacific Ocean before he dies. Jamie meets and quickly takes the place of an aged bee master, whose two-acre home plot on the Pacific Coast Highway is covered in flowers and bee skeps. Historian John Baur has written of the many late nineteenth-century Americans who, in varying degrees of ill health, moved to California to regain their physical resilience. That westward movement, especially in the late nineteenth and early twentieth century, has a lot to do with the history of American honey bees.

Baur notes that one John S. Harbison ushered in the "golden age of California honey" (1870-1900). The dry climate and general fructification prompted Harbison to ship 110 hives to San Diego. It was reported in 1891 that the combination of drought and flora made the area "the very Paradise of the honey-bee" (Baur 349). Invalids and the elderly could do this work, as could women. The apiary journal of the period, *Gleanings in Bee Culture*, praised the southern California climate as perfect for both bees and asthmatic or catarrh-ridden beekeepers. Tubercular Midwesterners made for the west coast. And yet, it was social growth in southern California that soon displaced the drought-tolerant white sage and other native bee-favored plants, to replace them with shade trees and urban settlements. Baur supplies the history:

> American honey production had never been on a large scale until the late nineteenth century. Then southern California led in making it a comparatively large-scale activity. Natural it was that the most individualistic branch of so self-reliant an occupation as agriculture would develop without benefit of com-

> mercial advertising, and on territory not usually owned by private concerns, but [rather] government land. The health seeking rancher in southern California was a frontiersman, and beekeeping was the most rugged and probably the earliest rampart of this farm frontier. The apiarist went where the land was wild and empty. Virtually by necessity he sought out the hillsides and hidden, protected valleys where thrived numerous wild plants ideally suited to honey production. (349)

At that historical moment, "the fruit farmer and stockman had not yet destroyed the natural vegetation which was the beeman's destined profit. When these later and more prosaic men arrived, honey declined in price and production and the apiarist disappeared as a significant builder of California" (Baur 349).

Keeping Baur in mind, we can see that Stratton-Porter's bee master, like Jamie, has followed in the footsteps of that health-seeking generation. These people oversaw much of California's agricultural development. Some became independent beekeepers. Others took the agri-business route. From 1950 onwards, the bee industry went global. "[D]uring this period of globalization," writes Tammy Horn, "American beekeepers would have to redefine how they operated given the number of pesticides, new imports, land zoning, regulations, federal quarantines, and chemicals" (200).

The primary force in the American bee industry today is the Almond Board of California. Horn explains,

> [t]he Almond Board of California, created in 1950 by the U.S. Congress, promoted the relationship between almonds and honey bees. With extensive research paid for by almond companies, growers were able to learn the optimal grid patterns for orchards and the formulas of hives per acre that would ensure adequate pollination of their almond trees. For every ninety-five trees, two hives should be planted to ensure maximum pollination. (205)

This grid system of planting has since given way to diamond patterns to allow for more trees per acre. Currently, there are 740,000 acres of almond trees in California's Central Valley. They produce 80% of the world's almonds, and they all bloom in February. Beetles, bats, and ground bees help the pollination process, but honey bees carry the heaviest load (Nordhaus 6-7). The Almond Board hosts an informative website, which states:

> The blossoms of all California Almond varieties are self-incompatible, requiring cross-pollination with other varieties to produce a crop. The single most important factor determining a good yield is pollination during the bloom period. More than a million colonies of honey bees are placed in California Almond orchards at the beginning of the bloom period to pollinate the crop. California beekeepers alone cannot supply this critical need, which is why

> honey bees travel across the country and from other countries to the San Joaquin Valley each year. Over many years, the Almond Board of California has funded research to help understand bee colony health, behavior and requirements for pollination. Diseases and issues that limit bee health, such as colony collapse disorder, have also been studied.

After listing the studies of bee behavior and various assaults on bee life that the Almond Board has undertaken, the website boasts that it has created a database of bee farmers willing to make contractual arrangements regarding the supply of healthy hives during pollination season. Although mention is not made of pollination brokers, it's important now to factor this relatively new agent into the array of bee-related human industrial positions.

Finally, the website poses the key question: "Are you asking yourself, 'What is sustainability, and why do I need to know about it?'" The Board then defines "sustainability": "Sustainable almond farming utilizes production practices that are economically viable and are based upon scientific research, common sense and a respect for the environment, neighbors and employees."

## "Honey Flowing in All Directions"

My work on critical regionalism, honey bees in America, and the global markets that rely on bee pollination obviously takes sustainability as a positive value. So far, what I've demonstrated to myself is that there is no ideal past – no fully functional and self-sustaining natural landscape – for us to recover but rather a series of dynamic regional situations caught up in historical conflict, evolving agricultural economies, and changing land management. In the current moment, we have decidedly failed to protect honey bees and their homes and habitats. We have seen them and their epiphenomena as commercial products rather than natural resources, as stock to be directed or as commodities to be re-engineered or replaced rather than as embodied and embedded signs of regional health or dysfunction.

Recall that it was in 1978 that Alexander Tzonis turned to critical regionalism as a point of departure for architectural and environmental analysis. At precisely the same moment, artist Joseph Beuys was thinking profound thoughts about honey. At the art exhibition Documenta 6 in 1977, Beuys built his important installation "Honigpumpe am Arbeitsplatz" ("Honey Pump in the Workplace"). I view this artwork as an exemplary spatial construction that critiques the conceptions of nature located in Cooper, in Stratton-Porter, and in the discourse of the Almond Board. The museum description reads: "A pump driven by two strong motors forces honey over a 17 meter high pipe into a distribution network" (Staeck). The two tons of honey that circulated through plastic tubing for 100 days represented in Beuys's cosmology not only warmth, love, energy, action, and the human circulatory system, but also a sweetened form of labor. The work was also, for Beuys,

> a symbol for the Free International University; and then, in and around this honey pump, people will be able to experience the core idea implicit in the honey pump directly, both as symbol and as machine, but also in a spiritual sense, by communicating their ideas there for a hundred days, speaking with others, making connections. So, this honey pump is therefore inconceivable simply as an object, as a machine or sculpture. And since the Free International University is also engaged very intensively with the circulation of capital, this is a very good symbol for this work: an organic, material circulation, or an organic circulation of money like a human being's blood circulation, with catabolic and synthesizing processes, where something is credited again and again, put into circulation, but not a penny more or less returns to the point of creation. Once the blood has completed its process, it is credited, or released back into the system, in a primary process of renewal. (46)

Here we see Beuys attending not to monumentalized sculpture – to capital-A Art – but to 'forces' and 'substances,' 'processes' and 'perception.' We know that for Beuys the substances most worthy of attention constantly change, and these material transformations are distributed throughout his own artful making. In a comparable fashion, honey bees spread themselves into the niches – forever shrinking – not yet taken up by human industry, human construction. Much as bees engineer their own workplaces, so the American territory that honey bees have occupied has in some ways always been built rather than natural, constructed by all manner of human beings intent on managing their environment. Above all, critical regionalism scrutinizes the circumstances behind this administration of space. Critical regionalism also produces counter-discourses that try to imagine building differently. We will certainly fail to meet all of our goals for sustainability, but thinking in a critical-regionalist fashion helps us, like characters out of Samuel Beckett, to fail better.

## Works Cited

Baur, John E. "The Health Seekers and Early Southern California Agriculture." *Pacific Historical Review* 20 (November 1951): 347-63. Print.

Beuys, Joseph. *What Is Art? Conversation with Joseph Beuys*. Ed. Volker Harlan. West Sussex: Clairview, 2004. Print.

Cooper, James Fenimore. The Project Gutenberg EBook of *Oak Openings*. Web. 25 November 2015. <www.gutenberg.org/files/4215/4215-h/4215-h.html>.

Cooper, Susan Fenimore. *Introductions to Novels by James Fenimore Cooper*. Web. 9 June 2016. <http://external.oneonta.edu/cooper/susan/susan-oakopenings.html>.

Cummings Report. Project Apis m. 18 March 2013. Web. Not available anymore.

Horn, Tammy. *Bees in America: How the Honey Bee Shaped a Nation*. Lexington: University of Kentucky Press, 2006. Print.

Jacobsen, Rowan. *Fruitless Fall: The Collapse of the Honey Bee and the Coming Agricultural Crisis*. New York: Bloomsbury, 2008. Print.

Jameson, Fredric. "The Cultural Logic of Late Capitalism." *Rethinking Architecture: A Reader in Cultural Theory*. Ed. Neil Leach. London: Routledge, 1997. 238-46. Print.

Lefaivre, Liane, and Alexander Tzonis. *Critical Regionalism: Architecture and Identity in a Globalized World*. Munich, London, New York: Prestel, 2003. Print.

Limón, José E. "Border Literary Histories, Globalization, and Critical Regionalism." *American Literary History* 20: 1-2 (2008): 160-82. Print.

Michaelsen, Scott. *The Limits of Multiculturalism: Interrogating the Origins of American Anthropology*. Minneapolis: University of Minnesota Press, 1999. Print.

NC Beekeepers Association, Person County. Web. 9 June 2016. <www.personcountybeekeepers.org/wordpress/wp-content/uploads/2011/10/Pollination21.jpg>.

Nordhaus, Hannah. *The Beekeeper's Lament: How One Man and Half a Billion Honey Bees Help Feed America*. New York: Harper Perennial, 2011. Print.

Parikka, Jussi. *Insect Media: An Archaeology of Animals and Technology*. Posthumanities 11. Minneapolis: University of Minnesota Press, 2010. Print.

Staeck, Klaus (ed.). *Joseph Beuys – Honey is Flowing in all Directions*. Göttingen: Steidl, 1997. Print.

Stewart, Omer Call. *Forgotten Fires: Native Americans and the Transient Wilderness*. Ed. Henry T. Lewis and M. Kat Anderson. Norman: University of Oklahoma Press, 2009. Print.

Stratton-Porter, Gene. *The Keeper of the Bees*. Bloomington: Indiana University Press, 1991. Norman: University of Oklahoma Press, 1925. Print.

The Almond Board of California. Web. 9 June 2016. <www.almondboard.com/Growers/OrchardManagement/Pollination/Pages/Default.aspx>.

Williams, Gerald W. "References on the American Indian Use of Fire in Ecosystems." USDA Forest Service, Washington, DC, 2001. Web. 9 June 2016. <www.wildlandfire.com/docs/biblio_indianfire.htm>.

# Ruins, Places, and Photography: Toward a Cultural Aesthetics of Catastrophe

*Miles Orvell*

Anything we call a 'ruin' exists in relation to time: it is a ruin because it is 'ruined,' no longer functional in terms of its original intention or creation. As buildings age and neighborhoods change, places fall into decay, and – speaking of the United States –it is not uncommon in cities of all sizes to find what we call "urban blight" marking streets and neighborhoods in certain areas. Beyond the city, factories have been abandoned, and shopping centers have fallen into disuse; and well beyond the suburbs and exurbs, one might find forsaken mines and quarries, or derelict experimental military testing grounds. Understanding ruins is a pathway into an understanding of the immense network of industrial and technological forces that are changing the landscapes, cities, and towns of the United States.

## What is a Ruin?

In thus introducing the consideration of time into the critical discourse of space, ruins compel our attention to the historical dimension of place. In this sense, place has a past, a present, and a future, and it is always changing. Or almost always: we can think of places that are 'outside' of time (heterotopias, Foucault might call them), worlds in which time is frozen, as in a museum, and so all change is at a stand-still. So-called 'living history museums' have this status – Williamsburg, Virginia, frozen in the Colonial period (a product itself of the 1920s); or Sturbridge Village in Massachusetts, freeze-dried in the earlier Colonial period. Greenfield Village in Michigan (Henry Ford's museum of historic buildings) is different, since it is an amalgamation of buildings from different times and places, making no credible pretense to unity.

Time and change affects everything, of course, so it's worth stating that ruins are a function of human construction and the materials humans have used and that we've had ruins for as long as we've had human construction. I suppose one can by analogy speak of the ruins of an ant hill or a beaver dam or a bird's nest – these things are also built – but in our common understanding, ruins are the remains of things that have been built by human beings. We don't speak of the Grand Canyon as a 'ruin,' even though in a sense it is one, since what we see in the canyon are the remains of forces of nature that have eroded and destroyed what once was there. But the word 'ruin' has an essential honorific quality as well. We don't call something that is merely used up – a tube of tooth paste, a broken down tricycle, an abandoned car – a ruin. For something to be a ruin, it must rise to the level of the elegaic; it must contain some former greatness or glory, in contrast to its present condition. We must feel a sense of loss, a sentiment that is often transformed into a cultural fact by virtue of its representation – either literary or visual.

We all know ruins at first hand, but our more extensive knowledge is through visual representation, and especially for the past 150 years through photography. Like painting, photographic representation can change our perception of the ruined thing into something that is part of a cultural narrative. Photography has created an archive of our contemporary civilization, a paradoxical record that reveals the energy – more exactly the destructive energy – of our time, revealing the way we have come to terms with the passage of time and the transformation of space. Taking the ruin, then, as the visible marker of the intersection of time and space, I want to map three zones of inquiry, each embodying a distinct cultural narrative.

## Ruins Seen as Part of a Temporal Cycle

Seeing ruins as part of a longer cycle of change has, itself, a long history, beginning as early as the seventeenth century and cycling through to our own time. From Poussin to Piranesi, artists of the seventeenth and eighteenth centuries found ruins fascinating as embodiments of picturesque decay and as melancholy emblems of mortality. In the early nineteenth century, Shelley's traveler, in "Ozymandias," reports the discovery of a statue in the desert that has fallen into ruins. To the poet, it is a symbol of earthly pride, with the further implication that regimes of power are, like everything else, ephemeral, that fortunes rise and fall, that history is fundamentally cyclical, and that nature will triumph in the end. In the same year as Shelley's poem, 1818, artist Thomas Cole's family emigrated from England to America, and in the mid-1830s, the painter who would profoundly influence the Hudson River School, began his prolonged meditation on destruction, *The Course of Empire,* a cycle of five paintings that imagines the same landscape, seen from different angles, as the constant setting for the stages of civilization pictured. Cole posits a universal succession of history in five acts, beginning with the rude first phase of "The Savage State," in which hunters roam the earth, and moving in part two to a more pastoral "Arcadian State," in which the shepherd tends his flock while the philosopher meditates on geometrical shapes and maidens dance happily in the woods. Cole then takes a huge leap from the simple and singular Druidical temple of part two to the dense architectural landscape portrayed in part three, "The Consummation of Empire," in which we see a fully developed imperial political state, with Roman temples and a flourishing civilization. That peak is followed by the plundering and ruin of civilization pictured in part four, "Destruction," in which barbarian hordes over-run the city, leaving a massive headless statue of a warrior in the foreground. Part five is the aftermath of ruin, "Desolation," and the architectural remains in the landscape – devoid of human presence – are overgrown by vegetation as nature reclaims the scene. We are back to the savage state and the recommencement of the cycle.

Cole's work has been variously interpreted as an allegory of American civilization and more specifically as a conservative response to his fears of Jacksonian America. Though painting less than fifty years after the US Constitution was ratified, Cole delineates the fear that all would perish in a nation that exalted the common man as against the patrician and that promised a spoils system for political winners. If the United States was founded as a polity upon an idealized neo-classical vision of the Roman Republic (from Latin mottos of civic virtue to the classical columns of Federal architecture) then why not extrapolate, along lines that Gibbons had already suggested, the Decline and Fall of the Amcrican Empirc?

That Cole took his title from the famous poem of Bishop George Berkeley is one of the ironies of "The Course of Empire," for Berkeley was seeing the destiny of America (from his vantage point in Ireland) as the most promising work imaginable in the history of human progress. Berkeley's 1725 poem, "Verses on the Prospect of Planting Arts and Learning in America," sees Europe as barren, decaying and pedantic, while in the New World "nature guides and virtue rules." America is "fresh and young" and is pictured as the fifth and final act of the human drama. Berkeley's famous line, "Westward the course of empire takes its way," became a great inspiration for Americans of the mid-nineteenth century, widely quoted and serving as the title of several chromolithographs enthusiastically depicting the manifest destiny of an expanding America. Cole's take on it – pre-dating the popular chromos – was far more ominous than Berkeley's optimism and derives its inspiration instead from Lord Byron's *Childe Harold* ("'Tis but the same rehearsal of the past/ First freedom and then Glory – when that fails,/ Wealth, vice, corruption – barbarism at last") which he quoted in a newspaper advertisement for the series. In this reading, the present repeats the past, and the future is destined to replay the cycle again.

The depiction of ruins as part of the cycle of civilization carries with it an implicit sense of the larger framework of organic process, in which things die and are born and die again, and it was in this spirit, a legacy of the Romantic era, that photography began to claim ruins as one of its major subjects, beginning in the 1930s. Translated into a static image, the notion of cyclical change is often represented as an image of nature taking over or reclaiming man's work. Traveling in the South in the mid-Thirties, Walker Evans photographed several abandoned ante-bellum plantation houses, including one in Vicksburg, Mississippi, capturing the side of the house, front and back columns on either side, with tall grasses growing in the foreground up to the building line. An even more dramatic image is the *Louisiana Plantation House*, 1935, which is printed in *American Photographs* (1938) and features a giant tree, uprooted and lying prone before the house, an image of man's work as well as nature's in ruins, although the tree seems to be sprouting branches that reach into the house. Evans invites us to see in decay and ruin the history of objects that is part of their meaning to us, recognizing that objects exist in space but also in time.

Arthur Drooker's more recent photographs make this point even more graphically and explicitly. Drooker's 2007 *American Ruins* collects work from across the United States, all photographed with infrared film and filters which produce a dramatic effect of dark skies and white, glowing trees (buildings appear within the gray scale and look more or less normal). Drooker's subjects are pueblo ruins, the stone and brick ruins of plantations and bridges, abandoned castles and follies, and occasional industrial sites. The growth of vegetation around these remains stands out radiantly in Drooker's images, accentuating the strangeness of the images, which show nature encroaching upon and overtaking the remains of human construction. Drooker's stylized images (just this side of kitsch) exploit the capacity of infrared film to create, as the photographer puts it, "a spirit world of haunted beauty [...] ethereal landscapes where shadows hover like apparitions, leaves and grass glow in downy white, clouds float in their own dreamy dimension, and ruins appear as fragments of an unsolvable mystery" (Drooker 9). Christopher Woodward states most explicitly the connection between the Gothic Romantic tradition and the sensibility of the photographer when he observes that in Drooker's images "ruin is not the end of the story of a building but, rather, an episode in the cycle of the life, death, and reincarnation of great buildings" (19).

A somewhat less histrionic approach to ruins – though still deeply Romantic – can be seen in Andrew Moore's photographs of Detroit, taken in 2008 and 2009. In large format color images, Moore captures the details of Detroit's decay with a clarity that is at the other end of the aesthetic spectrum from Drooker. There is no heightened 'mystery' in Moore's images: the materiality of the object before us is pictured with a clinical precision and detail that reveal the physical process by which objects metamorphose from one state to another. Underlying the process is the slow work of reclamation, by which 'nature' takes back the earth that human civilization has attempted to control. Moore shows us a twofold, complementary process. On the one hand, materials fail: iron oxidizes and rust forms on metal surfaces; paint surfaces fray, flake, and decompose (57, 59); the tensile strength of supporting beams gives way and the structure sags (19); glass breaks, leaving gaping windows in once proud houses (95). And on the other hand, organic growth occurs: stalactites form on ceilings (14); mold seems to grow out of an office carpet, creating a new material substance (30); saplings grow densely in a school cafeteria courtyard scattered with plastic chairs (60); vegetation overtakes a book depository that has opened up to the elements (36); trees and shrubs grow wild in a junkyard littered with sofas and tires in between two collapsing houses (191); school books and supplies in a depository warehouse become coated with mold, creating shapes found in Romantic grottoes (23, 83); houses and abandoned cars become invisible, covered with a dense overgrowth of vines (96, 109).

Moore's photographs constitute a kind of phenomenology of ruin and decay, and they are overwhelming in their aesthetic effect. It would be possible to become lost in the beauty of these images, but we must call ourselves to order, remembering that outside the frame lie the causes behind the process of decay, the reasons for a city's falling into ruin, and we need to at least acknowledge that underlying causality. As Thomas Sugrue has argued, the origins of Detroit's failure go back to the early twentieth century, when racial practices governing housing and employment combined to keep African Americans segregated and held back, while the city otherwise prospered during the high days of its industrial period, the 1940s, when it was known as the 'arsenal of democracy.' Detroit was designed for production, with rail lines, along with the Detroit River, creating a network of supply and delivery routes. Consequently it never developed the self-sufficient neighborhoods that allowed some other cities, like Pittsburgh and Philadelphia, to survive the demise of their factories (Saunders). Detroit's factories were the pride of Henry Ford, and Ford's new River Rouge plant was photographed as a triumph of modern industry, capitalism – and of modernism – in the geometric photographs of Charles Sheeler, commissioned by Ford in 1927. But Detroit's single concentration on the automobile, with its subsidiary industries, left the city vulnerable and economically stranded when the car industry vacated the city, unable to compete with the global competition, from Japan especially, that came in the last decades of the twentieth century. The industry's management, staking its future on inefficient SUV's had no immediate response to a world growing more and more conscious of fuel consumption. None of this is visible in Moore's photographs. Or we could say that all of this is visible, or implicit, in the images of Detroit in ruins: the office buildings that housed the automobile industry management, the factories that supported it, the movie theaters that entertained workers, the schools the educated their children – all of this material foundation for Detroit culture is what we see crumbling in Moore's photography, as nature reclaims what Ford had built.

## The Ruin as a Singular Event

In the second category, the ruin is seen as a singular event that interrupts the linear course of time. Unlike the cyclical narrative, which implies a gradual change, this is a narrative of catastrophe, of sudden disruption, the making of chaos where previously there had been a space of everyday life and normal habitation. Placed in a temporal perspective, the ruins in the previously described category are the result of a gradual process of decay, and the reclamation of the built environment by the natural environnment can be seen as part of a cyclical evolution. In this second category, ruins result from a sudden catastrophe rather than a gradual one, where the causal agent is an event that intervenes violently into the course of history.

The first extended treatment of such an event took place in the 1860s. Photography was emerging from the daguerreotype era and moving into the wet-plate era (a process requiring a portable darkroom), when the Civil War occurred, and the war left in its wake a ruined landscape littered with corpses, put on record indelibly through the photographs of Mathew Brady, Alexander Gardner, Timothy O'Sullivan, and George Barnard. The latter, especially, who accompanied Sherman in his march through the South, pictured the shocking remains of the army's violence. These were not scenes of a battlefield, where we might expect carnage and destruction; these were scenes in which houses and public buildings were left as rubble, as a lesson to the Southern aristocrat that no one was immune to the ravages of war. Barnard's views were taken after the fires had gone out and in some of them he will place a human figure amidst the wreckage, a figure of bewilderment with whom the viewer can identify. The War was not the destruction envisioned by Cole, not part of any cyclical vision of history; instead, it was understood to be and represented as a singular event in history, an event that certainly had its foreground in conflicts between North and South that went back to the nation's founding in the 1770s but was still unique in its causation, execution, and aftermath. And it was represented by photographers as a kind of Armageddon, leaving destroyed buildings, burned cities, scorched earth, and a multitiude of corpses in its wake.

The destruction wrought by the war was most visible where there were buildings to be bombed or burned – as in Charleston and Atlanta. Such catastrophic ruin would be photographed in later events of sudden destruction – from the Great Chicago Fire of 1871, with whole areas fallen into rubble and ruin; to the Johnstown Flood of 1889, which resulted in photographs of a flattened city; to that most spectacular of ruined cities – San Francisco in 1906, the place of the famous earthquake.

Several photographers captured the aftermath of the quake, with panoramic views of the rubble and skeletal remains of buildings that anticipate images of fire-bombed Dresden. Arnold Genthe's often-reproduced view down Sacramento Street, with dozens of people standing and sitting in make-shift bleacher chairs, has a surreal edge, contrasting the spectators' calm and fascination against the smoke of the city in the background, as they seem transfixed by the spectacle before their eyes. Fires, floods, and earthquakes are surely part of a natural process, but they are still rare events – at least at the scale of these examples – and they appear even as singular events. We don't therefore think of the ruins that result as part of a natural process, and the representation of such events tends to stress the immediate catastrophe. Yet ruins produced by such events can and often are reclaimed and rebuilt through the force of civic energy and enterprise.

Urban spaces that are rebuilt following a catastrophe offer a moment of civic decision, an identity crisis that presents itself as the choice between duplicating what was destroyed, restoring the past as if nothing had ever happened; or creating some new thing in place of the old, something that represents a new identity, a defiant boast against catastrophe, a moment of opportunity to look forward. Such was the case following the most catastrophic ruin in American history, the destruction of the World Trade Center in September of 2001. Much has been written about photography and 9/11 (by myself, among others) and I won't recapitulate that story, except to place it in the present context. What is striking about the representation of 9/11 is the fact that we have photographs of the event as it was happening, including the first plane, moments before its impact; and of course we can follow the unfolding of the catastrophe thereafter through a composite of the many photographs taken – from a distance and also from up close. We have as well a dense documentation of the wreckage in the aftermath of the buildings' collapse. Taking place in full view of millions who held cameras in their hands (cell phone cameras, at least), the fall of the World Trade Center is the most completely documented catastrophe ever to be recorded. Because of that multiplicity, one can argue, as I have elsewhere, that no iconic images have emerged from the World Trade Center disaster, that what we have is a new kind of documentation, a summative representation that exists through its cumulative effect (Orvell 2006, 2011). And, ironically, it is also an event that left few if any images of human death (bodies were pulverized) – excepting the images of people falling to their death, leaping from the burning towers. Though many witnessed and recorded the destruction of the towers, the massive job of cleaning up the site itself was off-limits to photographers, with just a few exceptions; and of the images taken of the aftermath – most notably by James Nachtwey and Joel Meyerowtiz, two of the best known documentary photographers of the time – none portray the ruins as part of a cycle of natural events, none portray the reclamation by nature of the wreckage. The ruins of the twin towers are represented as a gigantic and unnatural wound inflicted on the collectivity of the United States, and the underlying attitude of the photographers has been to celebrate the heroic response to that injury.

One more example in this second category must suffice, and that is New Orleans after Hurricane Katrina in August 2005. There are very few photographs of the hurricane as it was happening, for understandable reasons: if you were close enough to photograph it, you had other things on your mind that were more imperative – namely surviving it. In this sense, Katrina's devastation was more vast than the localized catastrophe of the World Trade Center. Moreover, taking pictures of Katrina after the event was no easy matter, since it required getting into an area of wreckage that was off limits. Only as the waters receded, was it possible to get into that zone and photograph it. Dozens of photographers did gain access, and of these Robert Polidori's work is the most impressive.

Polidori employed a large format camera in his portrayal of the neighborhoods, streets, and houses of New Orleans post-Katrina, and the results have been exhibited in very large images, approximately 4 by 5 feet, allowing the viewer to examine the photographs in the greatest of detail and clarity (Polidori's printed version, is itself a giant book, but of course smaller than the prints on the exhibition wall). What we see are the ruins of houses, pictured as an astounding disarray of objects, wrenched from their customary places and turned into objects in a surrealist nightmare. Polidori frames his images with a strong structure of order, so that they can contain the unimaginable disorder of the places he is picturing. We see close-ups of books, beds, shelving, chairs, tables, framed pictures, clothing. Everything is ruined, of course, by the water and many objects, including interior rooms are (by the time the photographs were taken and given the heat and humidity) collecting mold. To see things in such disorder challenges the meaning of substance, form, and function: we see things transformed, useless, damaged, to the point where their former identity becomes part of a history of the object whose present and future we could not have imagined. Yet seeing Polidori's interiors is also, one must report, an aesthetic delight. Leaving aside for a moment the loss and suffering implied in these images, one looks at Polidori compulsively: the pictures draw us in, they challenge us by their visual wonders and fascination (the color is essential here) and they provide an aesthetic thrill. Polidori's exterior images are likewise fascinating, suggesting to us how close to surrealism we live in our daily lives, separated by the thin line of an exceptional natural (almost unnatural) force.

Polidori's work, like Nachtwey's and Meyerowitz's, has an implicit moral dimension: though Katrina was at the far end of the spectrum, in terms of hurricane force, it wreaked damage on New Orleans that was in excess of what might have occurred had the levees been better designed and constructed. And the human cost of the flood should also have been far less than it was. The aftermath of Katrina revealed, in other words, the failures of several overlapping civic and governmental agencies that were charged with public safety and emergency care; the photographs become in their extreme detail a spectacle of natural force against human habitation and also a spectacle of the moral and/or political failure of human ministration.

## Ruins: The Apocalytic Narrative

The two preceding ways of imagining and representing ruins – either as part of a *repeating* cycle of history or as *singular* catastrophic events that interrupt the line of progress – are obviously opposed. There is yet a third perspective on ruins that is implicit in the imagination of the late twentieth century and the twenty-first, in which the ruin is seen as an irreversible condition that casts doubt and confusion on the future of the planet itself.

This third category of ruin photography – the apocalyptic – encompasses imagery that portrays the land in relation to man-made structures or in relation to manufacturing processes, picturing the destruction of the earth during the last half century or more, and portraying that destruction as quite probably an irretrievable process. Ruins here are not part of a cyclical view; nor are they presented as an anomalous intervention in linear time. Instead, these images suggest a future which is uncertain, as if we are at the end of time. Of course, eschatological visions have been characteristic of religious thought and imagery for centuries; the difference now is that we are confronting the end of the world in graphic pictorial imagery that is global in nature and that is presented entirely without any theological framework, redemptive or otherwise. But the apocalyptic mode is not uncomplicated and offers itself in the nature of an aporia, presenting us with contradictory representations that cause confusion in the viewer, as we try to figure out the paradoxical representation of beauty and destruction that is embodied in the image.

Though the central subject of apocalyptic photography is the land, we are not talking about landscape photography, in which representing a view of the land (see the literal meaning of landscape) is the motive. Rather it is the land in relation to human construction, alteration, or intervention that is the focus. We can go back again to Walker Evans' 1938 *American Photographs* to find one of the early images staking out this terrain for photography, especially *Joe's Auto Graveyard, Pennsylvania, 1936*, which reveals a band of junked cars stretching horizontally across an otherwise pastoral scene of farmlands. At a moment when extravagant car advertisements were beginning to populate the pages of mass magazines, Evans's image portrays an aesthetic of ruined objects as a counterpoint to a consumer culture that promotes novelty and invention, the superbly designed automobile, washing machine, vacuum cleaner, whatever. Evans' photographs of junked metal (also in *American Photographs*) have an elegance that reflects his own aesthetic appreciation for the object gnarled by time, the object as the embodiment of a kind of authenticity that results from its erosion. And that aesthetic valuation is likewise a characteristic of the later photographers of ruined landscapes, who find in the ravages of industry and construction a beauty that is at odds with the philosophical authority of the view.

This tension between subject and treatment is nowhere more evident than in the powerful work of contemporary Canadian photographer Edward Burtynsky. Burtynsky's work is inspired by some of the same observations of the changing landscape that had motivated the so-called New Topographical photographers of the seventies – Robert Adams, Lewis Baltz, Joe Deal, Frank Gohlke, and others who were featured in a renowned exhibition at the George Eastman House in 1975 and curated by William Jenkins. These photographers were working in the shadow of Ansel Adams, who had developed an exalted aesthetic that celebrated the beauties of the natural landscape, and they were turning in another direction entirely: instead of a high modernist aesthetic that gloried in spectacle, they were working in a deliberately undramatic mode, emphasizing vernacular scenes framed in a more basic idiom of quotidian black and white. The alterations of the landscape by man-made features – architectural and planning – were their subject. Burtynsky, in turn, went back to the high drama of Ansel Adams, but his intent was not to celebrate nature but to show how the natural world had been subjected to the violations and depredations of human industry. And in contrast to the New Topographic photographers, Burtynsky was exploiting the possibilities of late twentieth-century color photography in extravagant prints that are not only densely saturated but are in size and scale far greater than the earlier black and white photographers. Burtynski's giant prints hold the wall in museum spaces, as Albert Bierstadt's painted landscapes did for nineteenth-century audiences, and in book form they are reproduced in large format and full color that likewise accentuate the sheer size and materiality of the images. Standing before a Burtynski image, in which everything is in focus, the viewer is overwhelmed by the density of detail; using an elevated perspective, Burtynski's camera is often looking into a space in which foreground and middle ground are ambiguous; scale is also difficult to decipher, except for the occasional visibility of a human being or a truck; and the viewer can sometimes be confused as to whether space is advancing or receding (Torosian 52). These effects are all deliberately created to achieve Burtynsky's aesthetic end, which is an immersion in the image and at the same time a confusion that sustains the viewer's interest. The 2003 exhibition, *Manufactured Landscapes*, is thus well-named, pointing not only to the subject matter of Burtynsky's work but also to the careful contrivance of the view that the photographer produces. Burtynsky's motivation has come in part from his sense of awe at the industrial landscape, which he experienced as space from which the human viewer is alienated – he discovered this by chance when he came upon the coal mining region near Frackville, Pennsylvania. And it is that sense of alienation – "our thunderstruck incapacity to comprehend the total world system," as one writer puts it – that his work represents and that fulfills one of the functions of photography in the contemporary world: not to explain the world, but to present it as something immensely complex, beyond our easy comprehension (Baker 44).

This is partly what accounts for the viewer's profound unease in looking at Burtynsky. As much as we are drawn into the work aesthetically, we are left with a sense of incomprehension, overwhelmed by the sheer scale of industry and its mark on the earth. Burtynsky always seeks to photograph the largest quarry, the largest tire dump, etc. to emphasize this effect. One cannot possibly have imagined so many tires, so many densely packed automobiles, so many oil wells, the huge work of breaking apart oil tankers, the immense outpouring of nickel tailings on the landscape, and so on. The scale of global capitalism is, we begin to realize, immense when it is pictured in its concrete effects, and we sense that Burtynsky is depicting at once the glory of industry, unimaginable in its scale, and also the irreversible ravages of this process – the end of the world as we know it.

This issue of how to read Burtynsky – as formalist or as environmentalist – is at the heart of our response and at the heart of the debate about his work. And if we look to Burtynsky himself, we can see a shift from the earlier to the later. In conversation in 2003 Burtynsky placed himself in the long aesthetic tradition of ruins, which artists have represented as "a subject of contemplation, of something melancholy and monumental." And he went on to say that "a lot of what I photograph are the ruins of our society, the ruins in the landscape, the things that are left behind" (Torosion 48). But that "melancholy" sense of ruins, as noted earlier, connotes a cyclical view of things, and not the end of the world. Moreover, Burtynsky was at that time at pains to deny a merely environmentalist motivation, which he labeled as "simplistic." Rather, we are "compelled to progress," he says, we can't just stop and reverse our consumption of the world's materials. "The only thing we can do tomorrow that is different from today is to manage what we are doing in a better way. We happen to be very successful, and that may eventually be our undoing, because we are also very destructive" (Torosion 49). Lori Pauli confirms this narrative when she writes that for Burtynsky "nature itself, over time, can reclaim even the most ambitious of human incursions into the land" (33).

With the publication six years later of *Oil*, Burtynsky seems to have changed his mind as to how easy it might be to "manage what we are doing in a better way" (Torosion 50). It's true that many of his images of oil refineries and highways are representations of a world and an economy that is fully functioning. Nevertheless, with the 2009 volume, *Oil* – also based on an exhibition –, Burtynsky seems to have edged closer to an apocalyptic mode. Tracing the oil industry from extraction to refinement to consumption to a final section, "The End of Oil" – junk and ruins – Burtynsky's epic work represents the immense network of industries that compose our oil-based civilization. Some of the images in the 2006 volume were published in *Manufactured Landscapes*, but there is a detectable shift in tone as Burtynsky introduces the work, explaining its genesis, by saying, "I began to think about oil itself: as both the source of energy that makes everything possible, and as a source of dread, for its ongoing endangerment of our habitat" (9). More to the point, the essays accompanying the photographs in this volume make plain what Burtynsky, even in the twenty-first century, seems reluctant to affirm, most notably in the essay by ecologist William E. Rees who speaks of the trends and consequences of our oil-based planet and the path to self-destruction that it is leading us to, one that is based on a model of expansion and growth and that "requires unconstrained expansion and accumulation." Rees writes:

> The problem is that since the 1950s, the governing elites of the market democracies have cajoled virtually the entire world to adopt a common economic myth of uncommon destructive power. All major governments now share a vision of glabal development and poverty reduction based on continuous material growth fed by globalizatoin, specialization and trade. (195)

Calling Burtynsky a "forensic photographer," Rees affirms the extraordinary beauty and ambiguity of his work at the same time that his images document "in meticulous detail humanity's futile efforts to thwart the second law." Rees refers of couse to the second law of thermodynamics, which suggests, as he puts it, that "degradation/dissipation is the dominant process in our part of the universe. We should not be surprised that useless and often toxic detritus is the major product of human economic activity" (198).

This extreme a statement of the case would not seem to be authorized by Burtynsky's usually more equivocal stance. But since the essay is in the book – what are we to think? Is Burtynsky using Rees to make a statement he doesn't want to make himself? Or is the commentator taking the reins of the argument – and the visual evidence – and going where he feels he must go? Or is it sufficient to say that in generating this question, in raising the issues of the future of our planet, Burtynsky's work has done its job, and that we can't look to photographic images to answer our questions, but to raise them, in the most decidedly unavoidable ways.

For the generations after World War II, it is not only the fact that we are living with the possibility of ultimate and final destruction, it is the sense that our natural landscape and our built environment are profoundly vulnerable to a variety of forces that seem beyond control, primarily economic and technological forces. If we don't die in a universal cataclysm brought about by nuclear warfare, we may simply survive as witnesses to the gradual destruction of our natural habitat as a result of human forces. But change on a gradual scale is difficult to see, especially when it takes place away from the usual paths of human intercourse and habitation. And this is, of course, one of the greatest obstacles to social change: the invisibility and incremental nature of changes that may be irreversible. The function of photography in our time has been, accordingly, to illuminate these gradual changes, to picture our contemporary landscape in a way that forces us to pay attention. In constructing a response, photographers have at the same time constructed a new aesthetic that depicts the horror and also, disturbingly, the strange beauty of this process.

## Works Cited

Baker, Kenneth. "Form versus Portent: Edward Burynsky's Endangered Landscapes." Pauli 40-55. Print.

Berkeley, George. "On the Prospect of Planting Arts and Learning in America." *Poems of Places: An Anthology in 31 Volumes.* America: Vols. XXV–XXIX, 1876-79. Ed. Henry Wadsworth Longfellow. Web. 9 June 2016. <http://www.bartleby.com/270/13/15.html>.

Burtynsky, Edward. *Edward Burtynsky: Oil.* Göttingen: Steidl, 2009. Print.

Byron, Lord. *Childe Harold's Pilgrimage.* [1812]. Project Gutenberg. Web. 9 June 2016. <http://www.gutenberg.org/files/5131/5131-h/5131-h.htm>.

Drooker, Arthur. *American Ruins.* London and New York: Merrell, 2007. Print.

Evans, Walker. *American Photographs.* 1938. Reprint. New York: The Museum of Modern Art, 2012. Print.

Gibbon, Edward. *The Decline and Fall of the Roman Empire.* Vol. 1-6. [1776-1789]. London: Everyman's Library, 2010. Print.

Moore, Andrew. *Detroit Disassembled.* Akron and Bologna: Akron Art Museum and Damiani editore, 2010 / London: Everyman's Library, 2010. Print.

Orvell, Miles. "Against Iconicity: Photography and 9/11, a Response to Rob Kroes." (Roundtable feature). *Journal of American Studies* 45 (2011): 11-15. Print.

---. "After 9/11: Photography, the Destructive Sublime, and the Postmodern Archive." *Michigan Quarterly Review* (Spring 2006): 239-56. Print.

Pauli, Lori. *Manufactured Landscapes: The Photographs of Edward Burtynsky*. Ottawa: National Gallery of Canada and New Haven: Yale University Press, 2003. Print.

---. "Seeing the Big Picture." Pauli 10-33. Print.

Polidori, Robert. *After the Flood*. Göttingen: Steidl, 2006. Print.

Rees, William E. "Degradation and the Arrow of Time." Burtynsky 195-200. Print.

Saunders, Pete. "Nine Reasons Why Detroit Failed." *The Urbanophile* 21 February 2012. Web. 9 June 2016. <www.urbanophile.com/2012/02/21/the-reasons-behind-detroits-decline-by-pete-saunders/>.

Shelley, Percy Bysshe. "Ozymandias." *The Literature Network*. Web. 9 June 2016. <http://www.online-literature.com/shelley_percy/672/>.

Sugrue, Thomas. *The Origins of the Urban Crisis: Race and Inequality in Postwar Detroit*. Princeton: Princeton University Press, 1996, 2005. Print.

Torosian, Michael. "The Essential Element: An Interview with Edward Burtynsky." Pauli 46-55. Print.

Wilson, Eric G. *Everyone Loves a Good Train Wreck: Why We Can't Look Away* New York: Sarah Crichton Books, 2012. Print.

Woodward, Christopher. "Arthur Drooker's *American Ruins*." *American Ruins*. Ed. Arthur Drooker. London and New York: Merrell, 2007. 10-19. Print.

# Critical Regionalism and US Borders

*Claudia Sadowski-Smith*

In the last few decades, the field of US-American studies has moved beyond its original focus on the US nation state into hemispheric and transnational perspectives, to which the Mexico-US border has been central.[1] Attention to the nation-state has been replaced by an emphasis on various transnational cultural zones, including the Mexico-US border area, that are conceived as sites for the movements of people, ideas, and goods, and function outside of the framework of the nation-state.

As it describes the relationship among localities inside nations, regionalism has had no role in this move toward the internationalization of US-American studies. In fact, in regionalist approaches transnational localities like US borders have occupied a problematic position. In US studies, borders are often treated as *part of* the Southwest or the West, both of which have functioned as representations of the whole nation. In Canada, the Canada-US border has figured as a symbol for state-sponsored cultural nationalism that defines Canada's autonomy from the economically and politically stronger United States. This view of the border has elevated the Canadian South, the country's most prosperous area with urban centers of power like Vancouver and Toronto, to a metonym for Canada. Mexican studies also show increasing interest in the literature, history, and economics of the northern border area. Approaches to *la frontera mexicana y estadounidense* highlight this region's geographical and cultural proximity to the United States, and illustrate centrist misgivings about the Mexico-US relationship and the threat of Americanization.

In contrast to the marginal position regionalism occupies in US literary studies today, in cultural geography, sociology, and international relations interest in regionalism re-emerged in the 1960s and particularly the 1980s. Scholars in these fields do not simply regard regionalism as opposed to nationalism; instead, they are interested in examining how the local and regional is impacted by global and translocal forces. Geographer Kenneth Frampton, for example, has famously employed the term 'critical regionalism' to theorize how universal modernism can be inflected with elements derived from local cultures (such as scenary, light, historical references) to create a place-oriented culture that can resist the consumption-driven universal megalopolis. Some literary scholars, such as Fredric Jameson and Cheryl Temple Herr, have linked critical regionalism to literary and cultural studies in order to understand the cultural productions of particular regions

[1] On the importance of scholarship about the US-Mexico border for transnational and hemispheric perspectives in US-American studies, see Kaplan and Pease, Porter, Wald, Jay, and Rowe.

in the United States. In a review essay, José Limón has also called for infusing studies of the Mexico-US border with the lens of critical regionalism, which, as he argues, can connect various localized identities to each other, especially those that stand in relationship with globalization (1998: 167).

Limón here comes close to calling for a shift in attention from regions within nations, such as the US West or the Mexico-US border, toward the comparative study of regions or region-formation *across* nations. Such a perspective would recognize that globalization reinforces distinctions among regions within individual nation-states and, simultaneously, also formalizes the emergence of transnational regions that increasingly relate to one other. Scholars in other fields have made this point more clearly. Philosopher Thorsten Botz-Bornstein, for example, employs the term critical regionalism to highlight how various hybridized regionalisms are currently multiplying in such a way as to question any understanding of regionalism as a self-enclosed movement and regions as only related to individual nations (14-15). For him, critical regionalism describes something akin to what others have called 'glocalization,' namely the interactions between the global and regional/local that produce hybridized cultures. For Gayatry Spivak critical regionalism denotes associations among nation-states in Asia or South Asia that are based on common economic or political ties and that signal shifts in the global balance of power. To her, these regional "cross-hatchings" produce something other than nation-statism that keeps in "check the post-cold war Europe-US's perennial dream of universalism" (90-91).

This understanding of critical regionalism as a *comparative* approach to several subnational or supranational regions highlights the need to focus on questions of space, which figure less prominently in or are entirely absent from the current emphasis on diasporic cultural zones.[2] In an approach that also includes attention to space, the notion of critical regionalism could be employed to rethink US borders from metaphors for hemispheric nations or diasporic cultural zones into *transnational* regions with comparative dimensions to similar areas. Such a refocusing would not only move beyond the traditional regionalist emphasis on an individual nation, but also enable *comparative* accounts of transnational regions, such as border zones.

## Literary Studies of the Hemisphere and the Question of Region

At their origins, regionalist literary studies in Canada, the United States, and Mexico (or Latin America more generally) actively participated in and were formed by nationalist projects. The three fields contributed to the emergence of

2 In his article in *American Literary History*, José Limón criticizes the work of José David Saldívar and others, which initiated the view of the Mexico-US border as a cultural zone of globalization, for a lack of focus on the regional, the local, and place.

national canons that subordinate regions to nation. As Raymond Williams has argued in his book *Keywords*, the etymological roots of 'region' imply both notions of autonomy, where the region is seen as a cohesive entity in its own right, and subordination, where the region is seen as part of a larger entity like the nation-state. Even though regionalist discourses have taken different forms in each of the three fields, they have equally treated regions in ways that draw on William's definition. On the one hand, certain places are conceived as distinct from the rest of the nation and simultaneously as representative of the nation's uniqueness. In this usage, regions are both autonomous from and representative of the nation in ways that neutralize their distinctiveness. On the other hand, discourses of literary regionalism that acknowledge a region's autonomy do so to contain the threat of its secession. This form of regionalism describes writing from ostensibly peripheral areas in ways that conflate aesthetic concerns with subject matter, text with place.

Because Canada is a country with a relatively short and self-critical tradition of nationalism, the constructed nature of its national myth-making has perhaps been more obvious than in other nations. Regions became essential to the process of fashioning 'Canadianness' in order to address Canada's dependence upon other countries. In the 1920s and 1930s, Canada gained political independence from England, as formalized in the 1931 Statute of Westminster, but also entered into less formal dependence on the ascending United States. This period was marked by an emphasis on the natural environment of the north in the landscape paintings of the Group of Seven, which came to be emblematic of the national Canadian spirit. Driven by a great sense of nationalism, the artists' focus on solitary trees, rocks, and serene icebergs attempted to capture a distinctively Canadian spirit by characterizing this region as representative of the nation's distinctiveness.

While an attention to the north still marks narratives of Canadian nationhood, throughout the nineteenth century, the Canadian West also became elevated to a region. Its distinctive nature came to be contained in accounts that described the West as representative of the whole country, characterized by the clash between human settlement and the vast terrain of the inhospitable continent. The 1950s and 1960s were marked by developments that also drew on notions of region. Cultural nationalism became elevated to state-sponsored status amidst intensified fears of Americanization and in the general context of rising anti-Americanism fuelled by the Vietnam War. These efforts, which were especially strong in the realm of literary studies, often relied on the metaphorical use of the border with the United States to define 'Canadianness' in explicit opposition to the United States.

Since the 1980s, Canadian identity has been understood as 'post-national' in ways that acknowledge the country's internal regional and cultural distinctions within paradigms of multiculturalism and regionalism. Regionalism emphasizes differences among areas like the Prairies, the Maritimes (Atlantic Canada), the North, Québec, Ontario, and the 'New West.'[3] While this spatially-oriented lens

3 For regionalist approaches to Canadian writing, see, for example, Riegel and Wyle.

has not revisited existing approaches to the Canada-US borderlands, it resulted in the construction of various regionalist traditions of literature, particularly that of Prairie and Atlantic/Maritime writing, placing the study of Québec on an equal footing with other regions helped to contain the political threat of this area's secessionist difference. The ways in which Québec's particularity became neutralized in regionalist approaches resembles how the multicultural paradigm, originally developed to conceptualize the divide between English Canada and Québec, was extended to other racial and ethnic groups in Canada. These approaches to Québec ultimately served to reinforce the notion of a distinctly Canadian national identity that sets the country apart from the United States, a nation that has not affirmed equally strong forms of multiculturalism and regionalism.[4]

In Latin America and Mexico, regional perspectives have also emerged in direct opposition to the United States' dominant role in the hemisphere. Particularly during the 1920s and 1930s, Latin America had a richer tradition of regionalism than Canada or the United States (Jordan 3-4). Emphasizing the lack of national coherence and national mythologies at the time, *realismo*, the prose fiction movement which commenced concomitantly with *modernismo* and lasted well into the 1930s, spawned notions of regionalism. Doris Sommer has characterized one such form, *costumbrismo*, as a response to modernity that required the construction of cultural differences between nations in order to make sense of increasing economic and military competition. Forging values and customs specific to the nation was intended to support patriotism at the same time that producers and consumers developed a universalizing taste for global goods. *Costumbrismo* fostered interclass alliances, where the ascending middle class offered local color (associated with a particular class background) to a modernizing elite that could thus identify with the people. But local elites were eventually pried away from their internal alliances, and *costumbrism* lost its consolidating force. "Local color" subsequently became ascribed to internal groups that supposedly refused to be homogenized (Sommers 2).

With regard to Mexico more specifically, an awareness of the differences between the center and its northern border in terms of regional distinctions emerged in the 1980s. But like other regional perspectives, this recognition attempted to subordinate the region to the larger nation. Constructed in the aftermath of the Mexican Revolution and in the context of increasing US dominance, Mexican national identity neutralized important internal regional differences among the borderlands and the center. Associated with the work of Minister of Education José Vasconcelos, the left-leaning and anti-imperialist version of *mexicanidad* that became elevated to state-sponsored identity in the 1920s and 1930s is grounded in a deep, albeit highly constructed sense of a shared historical experience. This concept highlights the nation's common racial origin in

4 On this point, see Mackey.

the New World encounter between Europeans and indigenous people in the concept of *mestizaje*. Set in explicit opposition to notions of US nationhood that have largely dismissed or romanticized the influence of indigenous people, *mestizaje* describes Mexican identity as a mixture of European and pre-Columbian cultures, symbolized in the union of Spanish conqueror Hernán Cortés and the indigenous woman Malitzin or La Malinche. Vasconcelos's focus on the strong dualism between the Anglo-Saxon and the Ibero-American world was undoubtedly influenced by his upbringing and later exile along the Texas-Chihuahua boundary, while his emphasis on indigeneity as the main element of nationhood is grounded in notions more prevalent in central and southern Mexico than at the border. Vasconcelos also drew on the association of the borderland with revolutionary activity as political figures like Francisco Madero, Francisco Pancho Villa, and Venustiano Carranza lead movements of national importance there. In addition, the anti-imperialist potential of *mexicanidad* as a representative of a larger Latin American union in opposition to the United States was shaped by his life in Latin American expatriate communities in France, Argentina, and Brazil.

As it gained state-sponsored status, Vasconcelos's version of *mexicanidad* became squarely rooted in Mexico City, in the process transforming the northern borderlands into a marginalized location onto which continuing anxieties about the dominance of the United States in the hemisphere could be projected. Such fears also shaped the emergence of 1960s cultural nationalism, cultural imperialism, and dependency theories that address changes in the relationship between the United States and Latin America.[5] Characterized by its historical association with Indian fighters and revolutionaries, in the contemporary context the northern borderlands continue to function a as location onto which anxieties about the dominance of the United States are projected. When the northern borderlands became the fastest growing and most prosperous region of Mexico in the context of 1980s border industrialization, centrist discourses started to emphasize the region's uniqueness, its proximity to the United States, and its greater exposure to this country's influence. As Debra Castillo and María Socorro Tabuenca Córdoba have shown, in anticipation of NAFTA's legislative approval, in the 1980s then president Miguel de la Madrid even created cultural border programs to counteract national anxieties about appropriation by the United States and to include border populations into centrist narratives of the Mexican nation. Coupled with border industrialization, the establishment of these federal programs provided the context for heightened cultural activity that signaled the emergence of an internal awareness of the border region's distinctive nature and the connections among individual portions of the borderlands with each other.

5 Octavio Paz's *El laberinto de la soledad* (1950), the best-known of a series of state-sponsored works that appeared between the 1940s and 1960s, elaborates on Vasconcelos' notion of mestizaje by foregrounding how male identity is linked to anxieties about the raped indigenous woman and by declaring Mexican and US national identities to be two distinct versions of Western civilization.

Regional approaches in US literary studies were also subsumed under US national mythmaking, which transformed regions into an integral part of rather than a threat to national unity. In the United States, forms of regionalism emerged simultaneously with attempts at defining US nationhood as independent from colonial Britain. The founding of the United States prompted calls for the creation of a national literature that would capture and express distinctively 'American' characteristics. Frederick Turner has shown that the idea of US-American literature emerged when US writers started producing work that reflected a certain 'spirit of place,' which was characteristically US-American rather than British.[6] Such narratives of US nationhood highlighted the distinctiveness of the land and sometimes of its indigenous inhabitants. While some early literature portrayed the landscape as empty, other representations claimed fictive kinship with indigenous peoples but never went as far as Mexican claims to *mestizaje* by acknowledging racial intermixture. Throughout the nineteenth century, the ascendance of the United States to global power enabled a shift from an emphasis on the native characteristics of nationalism to a focus on racial and cultural continuities with Europe *against* the new land and its inhabitants (Murphy 110-11). Just as 'Americanness' was initially said to be rooted in the distinct landscape of the Northeast, with westward expansion the West became another symbol of US-American identity, figuring metaphorically for the whole nation and its distinctive identity as well as its expansionist policies.

While regionalism served to neutralize the specificity of locales like the Northeast and the West by using them as symbols for the entire nation, other regions became more directly subordinated to the nation. Nineteenth-century local color fiction and the Agrarian movement of the twentieth century ultimately worked to contain the threat of regional secession during the US Civil War. Similar to Mexico's Revolution, the aftermath of the US Civil War promoted the rise of national identity in ways that united distinctive regions, each with their own geographical and climatic particularities, residents, histories, and cultures. This sentiment prompted renewed calls for a national literature to which much of the post-war cultural productions responded. The fiction that most explicitly answered calls to nationalism was regionalist writing. Richard Brodhead has argued that, despite its seemingly sectionalist impulse, regionalist literature supported the reunification of the Unites States after the Civil War. He posits that through its presence – and, later, its absence – local fiction contributed to the narrative of unified nationhood that late nineteenth-century United States sought to construct. In this account, regionalism emerged in direct relationship to nationalism as an assemblage of various regional particularities converged to describe the uniqueness of the entire nation.

[6] Frederick Turner analyzes the works of Henry David Thoreau, Mark Twain, Willa Cather, William Faulkner, John Steinbeck, and William Carlos Williams.

It is no coincidence that, from 1920 to 1940, when the US literary canon was created to serve nation-building goals, regionalism also became a popular field of study. As Lothar Hönninghausen argues, regionalism manifested the desire to discover 'true' US-American values during the Depression, which seemed to have signaled the end of boundless economic expansion (Hönnighausen 355). The Fugitive/Agrarian movement with its explicitly regionalist political focus on the US South and its difference from the hegemonic North gained national attention at the time. Between the 1920s and the 1930s, the movement attempted to establish "Southerness" as a cornerstone for the creation of a southern literary canon as well as a critical apparatus to interpret this literature. New Criticism emerged as a critical method and a mythical and dehistoricized South as the embodiment of metaphysical unity amidst the chaos of modernity as its subject (Brinkmeyer 206). But today, the legacy of the Agrarian movement is not so much its establishment of a distinctly regionalist lens as the creation of a formalist agenda that came to dominate literary studies for decades to come.

## Cultural 'Regions' in US Hemispheric Studies

Interest in regionalism declined after the Second World War with the United States's surge to superpower status, which led to the further unification of the country through a common economy and an increasingly ubiquitous popular culture. National defense demands during the Cold War also had a strongly integrative effect, reinforcing the sense of national community, national interests, and the need for national unity in the face of external enemies and threats. After the civil rights struggles in the United States and the diversification of US-American literature as a discipline, regionalism as a critical lens further declined, even as fields like history re-articulated narratives of regionalism particularly by theorizing developments in the US West.

In contrast to the emphasis on internal regional distinctions in the contemporary Canadian nation, regionalism has also not been employed to critique the US myth of internal coherence. Instead, several transnational models like the Americas, the Circum-Atlantic, the Trans-Pacific, and the Black Atlantic developed in the last few decades.[7] Each theoretical lens has grown out of a particular US ethnic studies fields and thus privileges specific historical processes, geographical spaces, regions, and languages. The trans-Pacific foregrounds links between Asian America and various Asian countries, usually in terms of historical and contemporary movements of trade and immigration. Paul Gilroy's notion of the Black Atlantic as a historically interrelated network of influence spanning Britain, Africa, and the United States has initiated a trans-Atlantic perspective, which focuses on the social, cultural, and historical legacies of the slave trade. Joseph

[7] For examples of inter-American work, see Brickhouse, Gruez, and Saldívar.

Roach's work on the Circum-Atlantic, in turn, stresses links between New Orleans, the Antilles, West Africa, and London, and is one of the founding concepts of New World studies. Whereas Black Atlantic scholars tend to focus on Anglophone sources, New World studies also pays attention to other languages, such as French, Spanish, and Portuguese.[8]

While they remap US concerns onto the transnational level, these internationalized models are not grounded in theories of region or regionalism. But two of these paradigms – New World and border studies – essentially expand the focus on areas in the United States that are still viewed as regions. These zones remain removed from the centers of national power and cultural production on both coasts.[9] New World studies focus on the US South and the African diaspora by stressing intersections between African American and Caribbean cultures. This approach has fused various fields with longstanding links, including Black Atlantic, African American, and Caribbean studies. Border studies foreground the Southwest (often understood to be identical to the Mexico-US borderlands) and its ties with Latin America through a focus on Latin-Chicana/o populations.[10] The field has brought into dialogue fields like Chicana/o, Latina/o, Latin American, and US-American studies.

While early regionalism identified the South with 'white' southerners and their opposition to the North in terms of Confederate history, New World studies replace

8 For examples of the New World studies perspective see the work of Cohn, Handley, and Cox. Other theorists have described New World studies simply as a synonym for inter-American studies.

9 Despite the ways in which both the US West and US Southwest have traditionally been marginalized, in comparison to the significant body of writing about southern literature and the attention this geography has received since the 1920s (Brinkmeyer 206), much less scholarship on the Southwest exist. With regards to the South, Richard Gray has asserted that its understanding as a region begins with a consciousness of its own marginality and its position on the edge as result of historical events. This understanding has created a specific southern tradition of writing (2000). Gray writes that "the acceptance of the writing of the American South as distinctively regional [...] distinguishes many writers from the southern states themselves as they struggle with the sense of being different, writing somewhere of and from the periphery" (2002: xvv). David King Dunaway has similarly described the marginality of Southwestern writers, positing that "they are frequently told their work is not of national interest; [that] they are too regional in their concerns, [that] their characters, often non-Anglos, are too exotic or don't fit the proper stereotypes, and [that] their settings, whether urban or rural are seen as being too distant and removed from the experiences of what the publishing industry considers its general book-buying public" (14).

10 José Limón argues for an analysis of the role of the South within the geopolitical relationship between the United States and Mexico to more closely align New World studies and border studies. As he posits, both regions' socioeconomic systems were predicated on similar structures – the plantation and the hacienda – whose presence involved parallel race, class, and economic issues. The needs of the Southern political economy also had an active role in bringing about the US-Mexico War and in determining the course of development of Greater Mexico as a racially stratified economy following 1848 (1998: 8-9). The marginalized US South was thus party to the imposition of US federal authority on parts of marginalized Mexico as well as to the maintenance of slavery in other parts of the world.

this focus on the oppositional relationship between the US North and South with an emphasis on the legacy of race slavery and its association with the plantation economy. Shifting the perspective of the South further southward, New World studies emphasize the region's experience of defeat, occupation, and reconstruction, particularly in its broadened sense to include the African American experience of defeat under slavery, as a point of intersection with other parts of the Americas. The factors that make the South exceptional within the context of the United States thus also create similarities to other areas in a larger global context. Covering an extended zone, including the Caribbean, northern Brazil, and the United States, New World plantation colonialism was closely linked to the emergence of the modern capitalist world-system (Smith and Cohn 2). While New World studies do not employ this terminology, the field thus redefines the South from a sub-region within the United States to part of a larger, transnational 'region' characterized by similar histories, economies, and cultures.

But the South has never been treated as representative of the US nation. Instead, as in the case of Québec, notions of literary regionalism have come to contain the threat of Southern secession. As opposed to the South whose 'uniqueness' is grounded in the secessionist impulses of the Civil War and in its plantation history, a larger variety of features, including climate, landscape, alignment with several nation-states, and clashes among diverse cultural groups, have also been used to construct accounts of the distinctiveness of the Southwest. But neither its history, literature, or geographical outlines have been fully articulated.[11] Writer J. Dobie's description of the Southwest is fairly representative of this fact. He has proffered his own tongue-in-cheek definition of the Southwest as including "Arizona, New Mexico, most of Texas, some of Oklahoma and anything else north, south, east or west that anybody wants to bring in" (14).

The Southwest has been largely subordinated to the idea of the West, whose settler history and expansionism came to represent the whole nation during the nineteenth and early twentieth century. The initial understanding of the West as a distinct region is indebted to historian Frederick Jackson Turner's frontier thesis, which defined 'the West' as the historical progression of spaces where the 'civilizing' activities of European settlers encountered the 'wilderness' of the landscape and entered into limited interactions with indigenous inhabitants to create a distinctly 'American' population. Denoting conceptually and geographically shifting spaces rather than a distinct region, however, his frontier actually encompassed a wide variety of places that are now accorded their own regional status, including the Midwest, the Pacific Northwest, the Southwest, and California. As it represented US national myths and expansionist policies in the image of the frontier of Anglo conquest, this view of the West became extremely

[11] Attempts at forging a canon of US Southwestern literature by theorists like David King Dunaway are less well-known. He discusses Mary Austin, John C. Van Dyke, Helen Hunt Jackson, Zane Grey, Willa Cather, Frank Waters, Joseph Wood Krutch, Edward Abbey, John Nichols, N. Scott Momaday, Tony Hillerman, Barbara Kingsolver, and Linda Hogan.

influential in US-American studies, a field that attempted to forge a distinctly 'American' sense of identity. This approach to the West as the frontier also became very much detached from the geographies from which it originally emerged.[12] While the New Western history transformed the West into a multicultural region, this perspective remained limited to the borders of the United States and did not view the West as a transnational region or as a territory for comparative analyses by, for example, invoking the differential construction of Canadian westward settlement within that country's nationalist narrative.

Another view of the Southwest highlights its links to its Mexican American population, which was created as a result of the establishment of the Mexico-US border in 1848. The 1950s-1970s activist struggles in California, Texas, and New Mexico around issues of labor, education, and land rights further cemented the connection between Chicana/os and the US Southwest. Active in California, César Chávez's United Farm Workers' Union (UFW) introduced most of the symbols of Chicanismo and the idea of collective land ownership, which it borrowed from the Mexican Revolution. Reies López Tijerina's *Alianza Federal de Mercedes* (Federal Alliance of Grants) in New Mexico highlighted violations of the 1848 Treaty of Guadalupe Hidalgo, which secured community land grants provided in the seventeenth century to Mexican farmers and villagers by Spanish kings and the Mexican government. José Angel Gutiérez's Mexican American Youth Organization (MAYO) in Texas emphasized community control of institutions and resistance to educational segregation, organizing school boycotts or 'blowouts' in California, Colorado, New Mexico, and Texas.

The shift to cultural nationalism and the subsequent creation of Chicano studies synthesized the symbolisms and goals of these three regionalized activist struggles by connecting *Chicanismo* to the larger area of the 'Southwest.' Even if it did not use the term regionalism, *Chicanismo* defined itself in explicit relationship to the Southwest to envision the creation of a Chicano nation on territory originally inhabited by Aztecs and later ceded to the United States after the Mexico-US War. *Chicanismo*'s founding document, "El Plan Espiritual" called for the recreation of the lost Aztec/Chicana/o homeland in the US Southwest. By diverging from historical reconstructions of Aztlán that locate its origin somewhere close to Mexico, "El Plan" associated this mythological concept with the entire Southwestern territory ceded by Mexico to the United States in 1848 as the place "from whence came our forefathers" (1). The manifesto claimed indigenous status for Chicanos in the Southwest by establishing them as descendants of the Aztecs and defined Chicana/o cultural identity though the rediscovery of their devalued

[12] That mythmaking about a particular geography may become completely detached from the space in relation to which it was first conceptualized can be seen in the example of the Southwest. As David Teague has shown in his ecoliterary study of the US Southwest in representation, for example, the painter Thomas Moran combined different angles on the Grand Canyon into a view that only exists on canvas, thus reproducing shapes that already pre-existed in the imaginations of the larger culture.

*mestizo* and indigenous roots. Aztlán thus embodied the need to anchor utopian cultural nationalist narratives in a particular region that is overlaid with interrelated notions of national and ethnic origins.

Because it idealizes pre-colonialism and calls to ancestry as the basis for Chicano/a unity, Aztlán was replaced with the notion of borderlands in the 1980s and 1990s. This shift also drew renewed attention to the work of early borderland scholars, such as Eugene Bolton and Américo Paredes. Bolton coined the term "borderlands" in the 1920s to argue for a hemispheric view of history that transcends US borders. In the 1950s Américo Paredes conceptualized the Mexico-US border region as "Greater Mexico," encompassing Mexico and the Mexican diaspora. José Limón has taken up this idea to describe historical and contemporary connections between Mexico and the US Southwest. But the catalyst for the transformation of Chicano studies in the 1980s was Gloria Anzaldúa's first book-length artistic treatment of the border, *Borderlands/La Frontera* (1983). While the opening chapters of her book display her sense of *placed-ness* in the Southwest (especially in the border region between Texas and Chihuahua), however, the book ultimately foregrounds her *displacement* from the pre-Columbian indigenous Southwest and from Mexico, which is symbolized in her use of the border as a metaphor for her own identity, made up of indigenous, Mexican, and Anglo elements. As she foregrounds questions of Chicana identity vis-a-via the US nation and the Chicano community, Anzaldúa initiated the metaphorical use of the Mexico-US border that separates it from an analysis of space and geography. What Anzaldúa calls an "unnatural boundary" (3) is disidentified from the actual site where two nation-states meet to signify her own divided *cultural* identity as a Chicana, which mirrors the division between Mexico and the United States. She describes the border fence as "running down the length of my body,/staking rods in my flesh,/splits me splits me/*me raja me raja*/This is my home/this thin edge of barbwire" (2-3). To theorize a place in which these divisions can be overcome, Anzaldúa forges the notion of a mestiza borderlands consciousness that is signified in the concept of a "third country" (3).

The notion of *la frontera* became the guiding notion of Chicana/o studies and promoted the widespread use of the borderland as a metaphor for bicultural experiences. In the framework of the more inclusive Latina/o studies, Chicana/os are regarded as members of a modern diaspora that, even though somewhat characterized by visions of return to a place of origin (symbolized in the notion of Aztlán), is mainly constituted through dispersal from Mexico.[13] In this sense, the notion of *la frontera* continues Aztlán's focus on ethnic unity, allegorizing the boundary between the United States and Mexico so that it coincides with the

13. The equation of 'borders' with analyses of a particular racialized group has not been limited to US-American and cultural studies. In their overview of disciplinary work on international borders, Donnan and Wilson have argued that studies of the US-Mexican border in anthropology, history, sociology, and political geography focus most prominently on Mexican and Mexican American life (14).

concept of an ethnically constructed identity. As Mexicanists like María Socorro Tabuenca Córdoba and Robert McKee Irwin have argued, however, *la frontera* has largely excluded Mexican representations about or from the northern Mexican part of *la frontera mexicana y estadounidense.*

## Transnational Critical Regionalism and Transregional Borders

Drawing on the notion of critical regionalism as a comparative approach to supranational regions, I want to end by proposing a different understanding of US borders, not as symbols for regions that represent nations or as metaphors for diasporic zones, but as transnational regional entities that exhibit distinctly regional and transnational features. Such an emphasis is indebted to geography, which has since the 1960s focused on notions of space to address the overemphasis on time in Western thought. The most important contribution of the so-called 'new geography' has been its critique of the geographical determinism that underlies traditional notions of space as objective units marked by unique geographical, historical, cultural, or economic features, which subsequently shape human activity. Regions were similarly viewed as internally homogeneous "imagined communities" (Wyile 146). In contrast, cultural geography emphasizes the function of space (and regions) as active agents of change, as geographies to which people and communities forge allegiances, and locations in which important transformations take place. Individual localities embody and are transformed by social, political, economic, and topographic conditions that enable, shape, and sustain certain forms of social organization as well as cultural production. In geographer Henry Lefebvre's definition, places constitute both "products to be used" and also "means of production" (83).

Border areas are spaces where regionalist and transnational forces interact perhaps more visibly than in other geographies. What seemingly makes the Mexico-US border zone so unique within the US context also provides for similarities with other border regions in the Americas and the world. These similarities enable new understandings of US borders as interlinked regional zones with transnational connections that allow new theories of boundary-making in the Americas. Even a comparative view of the two US land borders with Mexico and Canada, for example, questions the focus on the uniqueness of the Mexico-US border for both theories of the US nation and the Latina/o transnation. Both border zones have exhibited considerable similarities in terms of their transnational and regional features, and their relationship to national and hemispheric forces from the time that they were established in conflicts among colonial empires in the Americas and US imperial expansion.

The two land borders have also been characterized by multi-faceted histories of racialization. The making of reservations and reserves in Canada and the United States created a number of additional international boundaries, and attempts at confining native people to individual nation-states further reinforced US borders. In the nineteenth century, both borders became similarly enforced as a result of the US exclusion of Chinese (and later other Asian) immigrants. The 1882 Chinese Exclusion Act banned virtually all ethnically Chinese immigrants from entering the United States, created the Chinese Division inside the Immigration Service, and implemented a requirement that immigrants possess certificates of return, residency, or identity to document their exception from exclusion. While many immigrants subsequently entered at official US ports with fraudulent documents, others employed national differences in immigration laws between the United States and neighboring countries to enter the United States via its land borders (Lee 196-97). After Congress passed the 1920s Quota Acts, the number of Europeans who crossed US borders without the required visa or who arrived on easily obtainable tourist visas and overstayed them far surpassed that of Chinese immigrants.

Contemporary border enforcement has also affected a variety of groups. The Mexico-US border was first *systematically* re-enforced with 10-foot-high chain-link fence in the context of an economic downturn and energy crises in the United States that shifted attention to issues of immigration (Dunn 38). By 2005, the Secure Fence Act also provided for *virtual* fencing along *both* US boundaries, which consists of networked cameras, sensors, radar, heat and motion detectors, and communications gear technology. Enforcement, new border-cossings policing controls, and surprise checkpoints on buses and trains have lead to an increase in detentions of border crossers. They have also drawn renewed attention to the treatment of indigenous peoples, especially tribes like the Iroquois Confederacy, the Blackfoot/Blackfeet, and the Tohono O'odham whose ancestral or reservation lands straddle the border.

Tribal members are increasingly forced to carry government-issued identification documents rather than identification cards issued by their own tribal governments to be able to move freely within aboriginal territories. In response, the Blackfoot Confederacy whose members live on reservations in Alberta and Montana have repeatedly called for the establishment of separate border crossings. The Mohawk have had to face incursions of US authorities onto tribal land in pursuit of undocumented immigrants despite agreements that prohibits police from patrolling tribal territory (Gibbins 160). Similarly, the Tohono O'odham nation in Arizona has faced increases in the crossings of people and drugs ever since US federal enforcement efforts to stop trafficking in other areas of the border funneled these movements to the Sonoran Desert with predictable spillover effects to local people (Luna-Firebaugh 349). Crossing through informal crossing gates and holes for access to health services, friends and relatives, and religious ceremonies on reservation land is now viewed as a violation of US federal law, and the Border Patrol often stops and searches tribal members and in some cases returns them to Mexico (Taliman 12).

In their struggles to maintain their sovereignty and border-crossing rights, indigenous people have become the most avid comparative critical regionalists. The Tohono O'odham of Arizona have several times attempted to sponsor legislation that would expand legal rights to free passage granted to native people on either side of the Canada-US boundary under the 1794 Jay Treaty to indigenous peoples on the southern border. The bill was supported by several border tribes unified in the Indigenous Alliance Without Borders, whose annual regional summits have included the Tohono O'odham and other border tribes like the Kickapoo, the Cocopah, the Kumeyaay, as well as the Gila River and Yavapai Apache and Yaqui who have a distinct identity both as an ethnic group and a tribal nation. But so far, these bills have not been passed into law.

Given the sovereignty of Indian nations, they have tended to proceed independently in their attempts at resolving border-crossing issues and restoring their rights as sovereign nations (Luna-Firebaugh 362). But as native people are realizing the similarities in their exposure to enforcement in US border zones, they have also tried to establish joint initiatives whose transnationality constitutes real potential for success if it is further expanded to include both border sides. The 1999 "Declaration of Kinship and Cooperation among the Indigenous Peoples and Nations of North America," that identified the maintenance of border-crossing rights and the full recognition of indigenous cultures as concerns common to native people in the United States and Canada.[14] In the 2006 Border Summit of the Americas, native peoples assembled to protest the Secure Fence Act arguing that enforcement divides the ancestral lands of many indigenous tribes at the Mexico-US border.

At this time, a critical transnational regionalism that pays comparative attention to the spatial nature of both US boundaries can perhaps gain the most political traction in indigenous struggles for sovereignty and border-crossing rights. But any emphasis on national and transnational developments also needs to take into account populations in various transnational border regions rather than remain focused on how nation-bound regionalism or diasporic populations have imagined the space of the national border. This perspective can recognize interaction between transnational and regional developments in border zones rather than subordinate them to a focus on the nation or a particular ethnic transnation.

[14] The declaration states that indigenous peoples in the Americas are "bound by common origin and history, aspiration and experience" and that "arbitrary lines [between Canada and the United States] have not severed, and never will, the ties of kinship among our peoples."

## Works Cited

Anzaldúa, Gloria. *Borderlands/La Frontera: The New Mestiza.* San Francisco, CA: Aunt Lute Books, 1987. Print.

Assembly of First Nations. "Declaration of Kinship and Cooperation among the Indigenous Peoples and Nations of North America." Web. 9 June 2016. <http://www.afn.ca/en/about-afn/national-congress-of-american-indians>.

Bolton, Herbert Eugene. "The Epic of Greater America." *Do the Americas Have a Common History?* Ed. Lewis Hanke. New York: Knopf, 1964. 67-100. Print.

Botz-Bornstein, Thorsten. "Is Critical Regionalist Philosophy Possible?" *Comparative and Continental Philosophy* 21 (2010): 11-25. Print.

Brickhouse, Anna. *Transamerican Literary Relations and the Nineteenth-Century Public Sphere.* Cambridge: Cambridge University Press, 2004. Print.

Brinkmeyer, Robert H., Jr. "Inventing Southern Literature: A Review Essay." *The Southern Quarterly* 38.3 (2000): 206-12. Print.

Brodhead, Richard. *Cultures of Letters: Scenes of Reading and Writing in Nineteenth-Century America.* Chicago: University of Chicago Press, 1993. Print.

Castillo, Debra, and María Socorro Tabuenca Córdoba. *Border Women: Writing from La Frontera.* Minneapolis: University of Minnesota Press, 2002. Print.

Cohn, Deborah H. *History and Memory in the Two Souths: Recent Southern and Spanish American Fiction.* Nashville: Vanderbilt University Press, 1999. Print.

Córdoba, María Socorro Tabuenca. "Viewing the Border: Perspectives from 'The Open Wound.'" *Discourse* 18.1-2 (1995-96): 146-68. Print.

Cox, Timothy J. *Postmodern Tales of Slavery in the Americas: From Alejo Carpentier to Charles Johnson.* New York: Garland, 2001. Print.

Dobie, Frank J. *Guide to Life and Literature of the Southwest.* Dallas: SMU Press, 1952. Print.

Donnan, Hastings, and Thomas M. Wilson. *Borders: Frontiers of Identity, Nation and State.* Oxford: Berg, 1999. Print.

Dunaway, David King. *Writing the Southwest.* New York: Plume, 1995. Print.

Dunn, Timothy J. *The Militarization of the U.S.-Mexico Border, 1978-1992: Low-Intensity Conflict Doctrine Comes Home.* Austin: CMAS Books, 1996. Print.

"El Plan Espiritual de Aztlán." *Aztlán: Essays on the Chicano Homeland.* Ed. Rudolfo A. Anaya and Francisco A. Lomelí. Albuquerque: Academia/El Norte Publications, 1989. 1-5. Print.

Frampton, Kenneth. "Toward a Critical Regionalism: Six Points for an Architecture of Resistance." *The Anti-Aesthetic: Essays on Postmodern Culture.* Ed. Hal Foster. New York: The New Press, 2002. 16-30. Print.

Gibbins, Roger. "Meaning and Significance of the Canadian-American Border." *Borders and Border Politics in a Globalizing World.* Ed. Paul Ganster and David E. Lorey. Lanham: SR Books, 2005. 151-67. Print.

Gilroy, Paul. *The Black Atlantic: Modernity and Double Consciousness.* Cambridge: Harvard University Press, 1993. Print.

Gray, Richard. "Foreword: Inventing Communities, Imagining Places: Some Thoughts on Southern Self-Fashioning." *South to a New Place: Region, Literature, Culture.* Ed. Suzanne W. Jones and Sharon Monteith. Baton Rouge: Louisiana State University, 2002. xiii-xxiii. Print.

---. *Southern Aberrations: Writers of the American South and the Problems of Regionalism.* Baton Rouge: Louisiana State University, 2000. Print.

Gruez, Kirsten Silva. *Ambassadors of Culture: The Transamerican Origins of Latino Writing.* Princeton: Princeton University Press, 2002. Print.

Handley, George B. *Postslavery Literatures in the Americas.* Charlottesville: University of Virginia Press, 2000. Print.

Herr, Cheryl Temple. *Critical Regionalism and Cultural Studies: From Ireland to the American Midwest.* Gainesville: University of Florida Press, 1996. Print.

Hönnighausen, Lothar. "Region, Nation and the Definition of American Identity in the Early Twentieth Century." *Negotiations of America's National Identity.* Ed. Marietta Messmer. Tübingen: Stauffenburg, 2000. 348-61. Print.

Irwin, Robert McKee. *Bandits, Captives, Heroines, and Saints: Cultural Icons of Mexico's Northwest Borderlands.* Minneapolis: University of Minnesota Press, 2007. Print.

---. "Toward a Border Gnosis of the Borderlands: Joaquín Murrieta and Nineteenth-Century U.S.-Mexico Border Culture." *Nepantla* 2.3 (2001): 509-37. Print.

Jameson, Fredric. *The Seeds of Time.* New York: Columbia University Press, 1994. Print.

Jay, Paul. "The Myth of 'America' and the Politics of Location: Modernity, Border Studies, and the Literature of the Americas." *Arizona Quarterly* 54.2 (1998): 165-92. Print.

Jordan, David. *New World Regionalism: Literature in the Americas.* Toronto: University of Toronto Press, 1994. Print.

Kaplan, Amy, and Donald Pease. *Cultures of United States Imperialism.* Durham: Duke University Press, 1993. Print.

Lefebvre, Henry. *The Production of Space.* Transl. Donald Nicholson-Smith. Oxford: Blackwell, 1991. Print.

Lee, Erika. *At America's Gates: Chinese Immigration During the Exclusion Era, 1882-1943.* Chapel Hill: University of North Carolina Press: 2003. Print.

Limón, José E. "Border Literary Histories, Globalization, and Critical Regionalism." *American Literary History* 20.1-2 (2008): 183-86. Print.

---. *American Encounters: Greater Mexico, the United States, and the Erotics of Culture.* Boston: Beacon, 1998. Print.

Luna-Firebaugh, Eileen. "At Hascu Am O I-oi – What Direction Should We Take: The Desert People's Approach to the Militarization of the Border." *Washington University Journal of Law & Policy* 339 (2005): 339-63. Print.

Mackey, Eva. *The House of Difference: Cultural Politics and National Identity in Canada*. London: Routledge, 1999. Print.

Murphy, Gretchen. *Hemispheric Imaginings: The Monroe Doctrine and Narratives of U.S. Empire*. Durham: Duke University Press, 2005. Print.

Paredes, Américo. *George Washington Gómez: A Mexicotexan Novel*. Houston: Arte Público Press, 1990. Print.

---. *"With His Pistol in His Hand": A Border Ballad and Its Hero*. Austin: University of Texas Press, 1958. Print.

Paz, Octavio. *The Labyrinth of Solitude: Life and Thought in Mexico*. Trans. Lysander Kemp. New York: Grove Press, 1961. Print.

Porter, Carolyn. "'What We Know that We Don't Know': Remapping American Literary Studies." *American Literary History* 6.3 (1994): 467-526. Print.

Riegel, Christian, and Herb Wyle (eds.). *A Sense of Place*. Edmonton, Alberta: University of Alberta Press, 1997. Print.

Roach, Joseph. *Cities of the Dead: Circum-Atlantic Performance*. New York: Columbia University Press, 1996. Print.

Rowe, John Carlos (ed.). *Post-Nationalist American Studies*. Berkeley: University of California Press, 2000. Print.

Saldívar, José David. *Border Matters: Remapping American Cultural Studies*. Berkeley: University of California Press, 1997. Print.

---. *The Dialectics of Our America: Genealogy, Cultural Critique, and Literary History*. Durham: Duke University Press, 1991. Print.

Smith, Jon, and Deborah Cohn. *Look Away!: The U.S. South in New World Studies*. Durham, Duke University Press, 2004. Print.

Sommer, Doris. "The Places of History: Regionalism Revisited in Latin America." *The Places of History: Regionalism Revisited in Latin America*. Ed. Doris Sommer. Durham: Duke University Press, 1999. 1-10. Print.

Spivak, Gayatri, and Judith Butler. *Who Sings the Nation-State?: Language, Politics, Belonging*. London: Seagull Books, 2007. Print.

Taliman, Valerie. "Borders and Native Peoples: Divided, but not Conquered." *Native Americas* 18.1 (31 March 2001): 10-16. Print.

Teague, David W. *The Southwest in American Literature and Art: The Rise of a Desert Aesthetic*. Tucson: University of Arizona Press, 1997. Print.

Turner, Frederick. *Spirit of Place: The Making of an American Literary Landscape*. San Franscico: Sierra Club, 1989. Print.

Vasconcelos, José. *The Cosmic Race/La Raza Cósmica*. Los Angeles: Centro de Publicaciones, 1979. Print.

Wald, Priscilla. "Minefields and Meeting Grounds: Transnational Analyses and American Studies." *ALH* 10.1 (1998): 199-218. Print.

Williams, Raymond. *Keywords: A Vocabulary of Culture and Society*. New York: Oxford University Press, 1976. Print.

Wyile, Herb. "Regionalism, Postcolonialism, and (Canadian) Writing: A Comparative Approach for Postnational Times." *Essays on Canadian Writing* 63 (1998): 139-61. Print.

# The In*Sur*gent Imagination of Tijuana: Transculturation, Ironic Disciplines, and TransBorder Studies

*Silvia Spitta*

> [Borders make us ask] not for generic affiliations but for a dialogue, not for one language but for many languages at odds with one another, not for unity of style but for heteroglossia, not for monologic but for dialogic imagination. A cultural space that cares little about formal classifications but much more about vitality and connection, for culture itself perishes in purity and isolation. (Fuentes 27)

> [I]f one tells us or subsequent generations that culture ought to incorporate the foreign and do justice to transcultural components, then we will set about this task, and then corresponding feats of integration will belong to the real structure of our culture. The 'reality' of culture is, in this sense, always a consequence too of our conceptions of culture. (Welsch 200)

The US-Mexico border has been called all sorts of names, most not worth repeating, but in the last decades there is one that has gathered traction. Perhaps because of the proliferation of assembly plants or maquiladoras, critics and writers have increasingly come to see the border as a – if not the – *laboratory* of the future.[1] That is, a space (anything but sterile as the term would imply) where a myriad realities rub up against one another in messy, ambiguous, ironic, creative, and often deadly ways, anticipating the complexity of the everyday negotiations that only promise to become second nature for us as the world becomes ever more interconnected. Like Fuentes in the epigraph, border writer Eduardo Arellano observes that to live on and fully understand the border, indeed, to be a border writer, you have to be able to conjugate "not one but multiple secretly and dynamically interconnected realities" (130). The multiple realities that crash up against the border, make Tijuana a highly complex and contradictory space, a space where the heightened impact of mass migration and multiple languages and cultures is felt sooner than in regions further from the border. The multilayered transcultural processes, which shape and fully traverse every aspect of life and territory make Tijuana extremely "symptomatic" – a thermometer of sorts – invaluable in predicting the changes that will inevitably come in to view elsewhere. It is no easy task, then, to write Tijuana much less to come to terms with the intricacies of transborder dynamics.

1 See Bowden; and deBuys.

Arellano does not analyze the cultural monofocality we have inherited from the nineteenth century's construction of the nation as everything but heterogeneous and inclusive, but a critique of this provincialism, also echoed in Fuentes's and Welsche's observations, is of course implicit. This constricting frame is especially difficult to overcome, not only because it has become a new normal to us, but also because its effect is amplified throughout our educational system underlying the disciplines as they are traditionally understood. Cultural "monofocality" as I would call it, thus doubly shapes our (mis)understanding of the world and renders us culturally illiterate in many contexts. Taught to see cultures as homogeneous despite the fact that they have always been shaped by transcultural processes, then, how do we bring into focus the myriad cultural others, that is, the foreignness that increasingly inhabits the very heart of nations once dreamt as pure? How do we imagine, then, much less create, multifocal disciplines and foster generous, open ways of understanding the difference at the heart of our culture(s)? That is the task at hand, the aim of this essay, and the challenge that border writers present to us.

While it is easy to argue for multifocality, it is less clear how one learns – and much less teaches – this kind of transcultural approach, not to mention the correspondingly complex narratives that arise as a consequence of living amid ever proliferating borders. The attempt to nudge the disciplines across to the other side, as is evident in the creation in the last decades of inter and trans disciplinary programs in the US academy, seems to be slowly loosing steam in the face of the difficulty academics have in thinking beyond the nation and thus bi- and even tri-nationally. In contrast to what one could see as an institutional failure of the imagination, I am placing the border savvy that arises at the US-Mexico border as an example of routes that could be taken. I will end with the transborder work of architect Teddy Cruz who studies the complex urban transcultural processes that occur across the US-Mexico border which are shaping the lived space of both Tijuana and San Diego. In his own praxis he then uses the immensely creative – urgent – imagination of Tijuana as a model of how to shape future cities.

Early attempts to think beyond the nation and in shaping interdisciplinary studies, were immensely fruitful thanks to Fernando Ortiz's creation of the neologism transculturation to discuss the counterpoint between sugar and tobacco production in the emergence of modern Cuba. The term was then applied to twentieth century regionalist-inflected Latin American literature by Angel Rama, and I in turn mobilized it across the hemisphere to theorize the work of US Latino writers in the United States.[2] However, since then, much like "deconstruction," the term has become a household name devoid of substance across the English-speaking world. Even worse, "transculturation" has reverted back to earlier, more essentialist and even regressive notions such as those of mestizaje and hybridity.

Nevertheless, there have been examples that have proven immensely productive at what we could call disciplinary border crossing, at imagining

2 See Ortiz; Rama; and Spitta 2005.

ourselves as not identical to ourselves.[3] They have led to a profound questioning of notions of identity and have developed into an exemplary praxis, but they are few and far between because transculturality entails a "deep," embodied knowledge of at least two languages and cultures and their accompanying intricacies. That tends to be a norm across Europe, and it is perhaps because of this lived experience that the term "transculturality" was invoked there in the 1990s by Welsch to claim the continent's history of migratory flows and posit the continent's globalized, internationalized ways of crossing cultures as a model for understanding culture so brilliantly historicized by Saskia Sassen. I am here returning the term transculturation as a series of complex processes and negotiations to its roots in colonial Latin America where it is understood as the outcome of the series of complex and creative negotiations between cultures and languages. Within this historical context, transculturality emerges as a form of being not identical to one's self in response to profound social inequality. Transculturation, then, can illuminate the dynamics that arise at the US-Mexico border, which is one of the most unequal and violent borders in the world – perhaps only matched by the creation of "fortress Europe" and the deadly role the Mediterranean is playing today as a "border" between Europe, Asia, and Africa. Indeed, transculturation, as it plays out along the US-Mexico border, entails much more than a familiarity between Mexico and the United States similar to that which occurs almost 'naturally' across cultures in Europe. At the border it is shot through (often quite literally) with an inequality that challenges any form of idealization of border crossing. Indeed, inequities are so great as to elicit a contempt of sorts, an irreverence in any case, which allows for creative forms of irony and profound (often comic) playfulness to intervene.[4] Transculturality, then, involves the endless play along what Linda Hutcheon famously called "irony's double edge." In this case, however, the "edge" is literally the border wall and therefore both real and imaginary, creative and deadly. A distinctive ambiguity results. It does not stem from the failure to make a choice between cultures but rather the outright *refusal* to "make a choice between alternatives."[5] Border writers, artists, and popular icons therefore create a transculturated artistic landscape that is oftentimes rendered doubly hard to read because it is permeated with ambiguity and irony.

As will become clear below, the border crossing disciplinary praxis and theory that I am beginning to develop here, presupposes an equally active, urgent, and even an "insurgent" imagination. Given the conditions of profound inequality

3 One important study triangulating US, Mexican, and tribal cultures' interactions in the creation of a racial geography across the colonial spectrum is María José Saldaña-Portillo's *Indian Given*.

4 This play and oftentimes biting ironic stance can be seen in the interventions of artists across Europe who reflect upon their minoritized, oftentimes immigrant and second class status.

5 The Spanish *Oxford Dictionary* defines "ambiguity" as a "lack of decisiveness or commitment resulting from a failure to make a choice between alternatives." See <https://www.google.com/search?q=oxford+spanish+dictioary&ie=utf-8&oe=utf-8#q=ambiguity> (accessed 10 March 2015).

prevailing at the border, border writers and artists understand culture as bi- and multi-focal, bi- and multi-directional. A transcultural disciplinary lens therefore has to match how border artists and writers see themselves through the eyes of the other(s); that is, how they make culture strange to themselves. However, while this bidirectionality and multifocality lets artists and writers gain the perspective necessary to translate/explain their culture (and oftentimes themselves) for and to an other, they have to do so through a thicket of age-old stereotypes.

The double move I am implying here is best symbolized by the border installation "Toy an-Horse" as it was designed by the Tijuana born artist ERRE Marcos Ramírez (fig. 1). Transculturating two important symbols that underlie western civilization, the Greek myth of the Trojan Horse and the Roman god of new beginnings, Janus, who faces in two directions at once, Toy an-Horse was a 10-meter high two headed wooden horse which faced North *and* South.[6] Unlike the Trojan horse, it had slats in the belly that allowed the viewer to see through it. ERRE's horse was incongruously (mis)placed *exactly* on the border line marked at the San Ysidro/Tijuana check point as a performance for inSite 1997. Born in Tijuana but constantly crossing the border between his two studios in San Diego and Tijuana, ERRE could not have created a more apt symbol of the complex nature of the negotiations involved in living on the border (either on the US or the Mexican side). The horse's two heads literally represents the flow of traffic North and South that takes place at the border as millions of people cross back and forth often on a daily basis. While the traffic (in people, goods, and ideologies) across the border goes both ways, it is not equal, thus, the effect of the bidirectional flow across the border affects both countries deep into their heartlands but in different ways. Given traditional flow patterns it is typically assumed that migrants cross North while capital crosses South.[7] The parental warning to look both ways before you cross a road (with its dire implication) is however recovered by ERRE's Toy an-Horse as a healthy injunction to think and imagine looking simultaneously North *and* South. Indeed, Toy an-Horse allowed the people stuck sometimes for hours in their cars, to reflect on what is being trafficked across the border. What does Mexico "get" and what the United States? Does the horse carry a hidden

6 As Ila Sheren reports, "[c]onstructed entirely of wood and positioned so that each head looked towards a different country, the horse was seen by the more than 136,000 people each day who pass through the crossing either on foot or by car. The artwork had appeared overnight at the border crossing, seemingly a 'gift' from each nation to the other and recreating the scene from Greek mythology."

7 This easy equation remains understudied despite being put into question by ever larger numbers of US citizens looking south of the border in search of affordable health and retirement options. Baja California for example, has largely become a US retiree enclave. And Tijuana and Ciudad Juárez are becoming medical hubs for US citizens seeking affordable medical and dental care as well as cheaper prescription drugs. This reverse movement south is being promoted by American health insurance companies, which even provide reduced airfares, and have made Medicare and Medicaid valid south of the Rio Grande (see Romero 267).

cargo despite the slats that allow people to see through its belly where once Greek soldiers had hidden? One could argue that the implied cargo of the horse is actually not deadly, but a "gift" which entails the development of a bifocal and bidirectional capacity; the imagination to see yourself and your culture through the eyes of the other. True bi-national understanding, ERRE's horse could be implying, will only then emerge and with it also a livable future. Reminding us of the notion of the laboratory with which I began, Toy an-Horse is a performance that creates an instantaneous sense of being in a workshop, in a laboratory of future possibilities.

As a bi-headed monster of sorts, standing out incongruously in the midst of the perpetual border traffic jam, the horse's two heads faces in different directions, North and South. But do they actually *see* the North or the South? Given the long tradition of hurling abuse at the border from within both the United States and Mexico, what Mexicans first see is a negative reflection of themselves. For US citizens, however, Mexican stereotypes of "gringos" are easily dismissed given their privileged position. What makes matters worse, is that Mexican border dwellers also have to deal with Mexican negative representations about the border, which stem from the country's center. They therefore find themselves in a doubly negative space. Despite this, their engagement is with the United States and to date no border writer has tackled the center's negativity vis-à-vis the border. In both cases, then, the United States and Mexico, the border wall acts as a "double-sided screen, receiving the images projected upon it by San Diego and Tijuana, the two cities it divides" (Cruz 74). Within this context, Toy an-Horse can only be seen as an ironic and highly ambiguous transcultural symbol. It is ironic because the border mise en abîme (of people imagining what others are thinking of them across the border) results in people saying one thing but actually meaning to say what they think the other across the border would say. But this linguistic folding in upon itself results in a sort of duplicity (saying one thing and meaning another) which serves to further exacerbate the ambiguity which tends to arise at the border. It is no accident then, as I will go on to show below, that an ironic stance characterizes the work not only of artists like ERRE but also that of most, if not all, border writers, artists, and filmmakers. It is also at the heart of the architectural praxis of Guatemalan born Teddy Cruz, who, like many border dwellers, moves between his studio in San Diego and the shantytowns of Tijuana, applying what he learns there to his praxis everywhere. It is my hope here, that interdisciplinary studies or TransBorder studies as I am beginning to outline them here, have much to learn from Tijuana.

But to begin at the beginning: How do we "fit" the border into current disciplinary frames? How do we delimit a disciplinary border? When attempting to grapple with these questions one is inevitably first confronted with and immediately confounded by the elusiveness of the border. For, what is the space of the border? Which the border of the border? As Borges so beautifully illustrated in his parable "On Exactitude in Science," the map can never truly account for the territory. Abstraction lies at the root of the disciplines. In order to truly account for the US-Mexico border, geography would *literally* have to encompass the entire border region. Borges seems to imply that a literal discipline is utterly useless, a dead end, an impossibility. Simultaneously, the parable opens the door to the possibility of disciplines being ironic, which is the unsettling notion that I am playing with here. That is, if applied to the border, Borges's parable would imply that a TransBorder discipline would have to be bifocal like Toy an-Horse, that is, simultaneously look North *and* South and vice versa. That is, both sides would have to learn to see themselves through the other's eyes. This double move results in a profound translational praxis. Given power differentials, however, US stereotypes aimed at the border are felt much more strongly on the Mexican side than Mexican stereotypes aimed at the United States. The Mexican influence is nevertheless felt in the United States but in a different, often less immediately obvious, but equally powerful way. As the work of Teddy Cruz shows, Mexican and Central American immigrants who settle across communities in the United States change the lived environment oftentimes in quite radical ways. They retrofit US suburbs and transform them into multiuse, multigenerational spaces and thus anything but sterile landscapes. And let us not forget that US culture today is unthinkable without tacos, burritos, and margaritas. Not to speak of the seeming omnipresence of the Virgin of Guadalupe as miracle, religious icon, and/or fashion statement.[8]

Everything but literal, then, TransBorder studies would have to be multifocal in order to account for the ripple effect that the border has deep into Mexico and the United States, especially today as it increasingly becomes the gateway for migratory flows from South America and as far afield as countries in Africa and Asia. Given this scenario, it is not surprising that the question of the *location* of the border has become especially urgent today and raised calls for increased militarization. And it is also not surprising that seemingly everything, even the most random encounters, are being metaphorized (and by this I mean, trivialized) in terms of the border. The metaphorical borderization of the world that is at work in the academy, the media, the publishing world, and the national imaginaries of both Mexico and the United States are all symptoms of our inability to fully take into account the nomadisms that increasingly characterize our world and which were named almost prophetically a number of years ago by performance artist Guillermo Gómez Peña when he apodictically declared that in today's world, every encounter between two people constitutes a border experience. Acting almost like a boomerang, the metaphoric proliferation of "borders" renders the border elusive and unknowable. It doubly fuels the border's abstraction that I have been outlining. To give a literary example: in the United States, Latino or Hispanic writers are so misunderstood that they are misplaced and considered "border writers" even

8 See Spitta 2009.

though they might hail from Chicago or New York.[9] Paradoxically, from the vantage point of Mexico City, the very same US Chicano or Hispanic writers are viewed as "border" writers. Regardless of how many generations a writer's family might have been in the United States, then, and even if they were in the United States long before 1848 and long before the constitution of this country as a nation, as if by a sleight of hand, the exoticism attached to the border is attached to border dwellers as well on *both sides of the border*! This is in part due to market demands and the premium carried by exoticism that invariably tends to "sell" in the United States. But surprisingly, the exoticism of the border also increasingly sells in Mexico pointing to the fact that both countries, since the inception of the official national border and already well before its creation, wove a black legend around the border. This black legend has been slowly transformed over time. In the United States, the nostalgia for a once quaint South has given way to border noir. Likewise, in Mexico City, publishing houses today feed the market for exotic narco and even snuff border noir fictions.

The distorting lens with which border writers are seen, has led border writers to repeatedly bemoan the fact that most conferences and anthologies that claim to be about the border actually tend to include Chicano writers and exclude actual border writers. This sleight of hand makes border writers repeatedly vanish by utterly disregarding the specificity of place that makes a border writer a **border** writer. Worse yet, it uproots the word **border** from its actual geographical and cultural specificity and renders it practically meaningless. The fact that border writers are made invisible may perhaps help explain border narratives' obsession with specters. From the point of view of both the US and the Mexican national literary scene border writing therefore occupies a non-space, as many argue. And much as roads disappear in the desert's mirages, the border tends to disappear in the disciplines and border dwellers are made to inhabit an indeterminate space between life and death. In disciplinary terms, these misplacements of the border would help explain why the border or border studies continue to occupy a precarious position on the borders of Hispanic and/or Latin American as well as American studies and even within Latino Studies. That is, the border as a *region* disappears despite the seminal contributions of historians such as Eugene Bolton, Americo Paredes, David J. Weber, and others, as well as the myriad paeans to the borderlands spawned by Gloria Anzaldúa's publication of *Borderlands/la frontera: The New Mestiza Writes* in 1987.

[9] The border in this case is simply used interchangeably to either denote someone who is Hispanic or who has a Hispanic origin and therefore is implicitly tainted as 'undocumented' (or an 'illegal alien' – in the phobic language deployed in this current right wind political climate). This is so much so that billionaire Donald Trump considers it a good idea to launch his bid for the presidency of the United States proclaiming in the media that those who cross the border are Mexican rapists and drug smugglers. Despite huge criticism, two weeks later he only reaffirmed his position (see "Donald Trump").

If the border exists at all, then, it does so as a purely imaginary construct exclusively defined by negativity and crossing/movement. Despite seeing, in Mexico, the largest population and economic growth, the border is seldom understood as the home that it is for millions.[10] For both the United States and Mexico, and ever since its creation, the border has been an interminable noir, the untamed, outer limit of the nation, the border of the border, and always already the embodiment of the wild zone of both countries' national imaginaries. It is therefore not surprising that the newest generation of border writers argue that a literature of the North of Mexico exists but they immediately have to ask: "but where is the North?" These types of questions are playful, of course, but also symptomatic of the spectral geography I am outlining here. For Heriberto Yépez, for example: "The North of Mexico has always been fantasmatic.[11] It was invented in 1848 when the separation from the United States was traced in the new political drawing. Something which is now the North was, at some point, part of the center. History re-situates us […]."[12] For Yepez as for ERRE, then, the border is the highly complex, ironic space inhabited by millions of border dwellers who look North and South and who inhabit an indeterminate space that is both North *and* South and yet neither. I write "space" here instead of "region" since regions tend to be more coherent entities and thus more readily integrated into academic disciplines. Indeed, different varieties of regionalisms emerged historically as moments, parenthesis of sorts, within nations. Other than some exceptions, such as Peruvian writer and ethnographer José María Arguedas's attempt to straddle two nations (one within the other) and two languages (Quechua and Spanish), there are few regions that straddle a borderline as militarized and fraught as the US-Mexico border. In the end, regionalisms tend to vanish as nations consolidate; persisting as literary movements.

Tired of this continuously vanishing, spectral, border I recently, somewhat quixotically it turns out, began reading countless border authors in search of the "real" border – that is, in search of the ways border writers describe the space they inhabit in their narratives. It quickly became evident that even on the border no one really knows where the border really is, nor who is or is not a border writer, and much less to which discipline the border belongs. This lack of definition, or spectral geography, perhaps helps explain why the literary boom currently underway begins with the works of a writer born in Leon, Guanajuato, that is, close to the center of Mexico but who became a border writer after living and working in

10 Colectivo Nortec, whose music blends techno with the corrido, plays with border death and irony in their videos, especially "Bar Infierno" <https://www.youtube.com/watch?v=e5zEIj L4SR0>.

11 "Fantasmatic" in Lacanian psychoanalysis refers not to what is merely imagined or made up so much as the narrative (fantasmatic) frames through which we make sense of the world.

12 He continues, reminding us of Gloria Anzaldúa's early formulation of the border as a wound: "The 'North' is the dismembered body of a nation […] it is what we have repressed so as not to memorize, that is, remember, the wound. The North in itself is a silence. Border writers enjoy and abuse of this mirage" [gozan y abusan esa condición de espejismos] (Yépez 2003).

Monterrey which is 200 km south of the border but considers itself a border city. From this distance, Eduardo Antonio Parra inaugurates the literary boom describing the confusing border geography and creating a series of images that have become paradigmatic of border literature. Winner of the prestigious Juan Rulfo prize in 2000, he is the author of numerous collections of stories and novels such as *The Borders of the Night*/Los límites de la noche (1996), *No One's Land*/Tierra de nadie (1999), *No One Saw Them Leave*/Nadie los vio salir (2001), *Parables of Silence*/Parábolas del silencio (2006), and the novel *Nostalgia for the Shadow*/Nostalgia de la sombra (2002). As his titles make evident, the border for Parra is spectral, a mirage where characters seamlessly transition between the abject and the sublime. In *No One Saw Them Leave* the impressive novella that made him famous, a young American couple dance, drink, and make love completely engrossed in one another utterly oblivious to the filth and stench of the border dive. Their unearthly beauty draws the surreptitious attention of the bar's regulars but, despite their attention, the couple vanishes at the precise moment when one of the oldest prostitutes on her death-bed on the floor above draws her last breath. The tension between love and death, filth and beauty, as well as the fact that the couple is so out of place, yet in place, have made this image paradigmatic of one type of "spectral" border writing.

Border writers first have to confront the spectralization of the border as well as the barrage of negativity stemming simultaneously from both the center of the United States and the heart of Mexico's despair about its most Americanized region.[13] No longer surprising us, in the collection of essays *Tijuana la horrible/Tijuana the horrible* which echoes the title of one of the most polemical Latin American anti-colonial manifestos, writer Humberto Félix Berumen, like many border writers, first begins by working through all the negative stereotypes associated to Tijuana emerging from the United States where Tijuana has always seemingly been seen as morally suspect if not outright evil. Let us remember that already in the 1920s Tijuana was invented as 'the' city of vice when pornographic

[13] But the border also becomes spectral in the United States where since 1848 the Mexican presence has been erased from the national imaginary and historiography. I don't have time to dwell on this here and have already written about this elsewhere, so will let a few examples suffice. In Texas, where most of the textbooks for US schools are published, conservative groups have been intent on censoring the inclusion of information about the Hispanic colonial legacy of the country. In Arizona an attempt was recently made to ban ethnic studies courses and universities censored 7 books that questioned the official historiography, which has its origins with the Mayflower. The state of Georgia has gone even further and banned undocumented students from attending the state's universities. In response, my colleagues founded Freedom University in 2011. These extreme forms of discrimination are mere examples of the centuries old transformation of all Hispanics regardless of origin into "wetbacks" willfully overlooking the fact that many stem from families that were in the United States before 1848 and thus before the United States became the United States. This type of spectralization makes millions of people disappear and forces them to live in the shadows both real and symbolical. The Dreamers of course, are contesting this vanishing and have become key political players under the sign "To emerge from the shadows."

comics with a sadomasochistic bent began to circulate underground in the United States. They were known as 'Tijuana Bibles'[14]. It is not known who or how many people wrote them but it was generally held that they originated in Tijuana because already then for the United States, everything that was perverse and morally filthy originated in TJ. This negative image gained full force in the 1930s during prohibition when early Hollywood films represented Tijuana as a brothel full of bandidos, an image that persisted until the late 1950s when the famous film *A Touch of Evil* by Orson Welles brilliantly closed the early noir cycle. But this notion of a border associated to death and somehow sick was not created by the United States alone. In Mexico, too, the border is despised despite being the space of greatest economic and urban growth in the country. Indeed, for Mexico, the border serves as the safety valve for those people the country is incapable of taking care of as well as the thousands that are fleeing from the violence in Central America. And now, complicating the border even further, increasingly migrants from all over the world are taken there by human traffickers. Given the wave of femicides at the border and the hundreds of women who have been thrown on garbage dumps along it, raped and dismembered, it is hard not to associate the border and migration with death also. Further reinforcing this association of the border with death, is the current unregulated chemical dumping that is occurring along the border due to the lack of enforcement of environmental laws which seem to evaporate in the hot sand. This lack of environmental regulation has contributed to transforming the negative images of the border yet again only now the border is viewed as depraved but increasingly also as "toxic" and "sick."[15] The wall itself reflects this change having become a memorial site where white crosses mark the death of the nameless (sin nombre or no identificado) who have disappeared while crossing and purple crosses mark the femicides.

More recently, the younger generation of border writers playing the edge between life and death in a different way, reject, critique, and ironize the bi-national reflections and the negative stereotypes that are imposed on the border. Their split tongued narratives re-reproduce the presuppositions that underlie stereotypes, but more importantly, they also self-ironize themselves and their reality and put its ontological status and that of border dwellers in general into question. These multiply reflective gestures make the boundaries of the border even more elusive and spectral, but at the same time they are shot through with humor and the ironic distance that emerges when the North looks at itself with the

[14] Yépez 2005: 41. For some examples of these erotic and sadomasochistic comics see <https://www.google.com/search?q=Tijuana+Bibles&tbm=isch&tbo=u&source=univ&sa=X&ved=0ahUKEwjpj_ao0KTJAhUE1CYKHZaqDn8QsAQIIw&biw=1324&bih=644>)

[15] The United States has attempted time and again to 'store' the country's nuclear waste at the border. Given this utter disregard for the border environment, in addition to being morally suspect, the border has now become 'toxic' – an environmental disaster zone along both banks of the Rio Grande (see Dan).

eyes of the South and vice versa, a bifocality that in fact is highly unfocused given that of necessity, it has to include, as I have been showing, all the misperceptions that inevitably creep in when we try to engage with how we think others see us.

While the border is made to incorporate ideological and toxic material garbage of all sorts, then, border writers respond by absorbing and recycling all the trash images that have been associated with it and particularly border cities such as Tijuana. While spectralization was a first response as in the work of Parra, the newer generation of writers and artists is profoundly irreverent, playful, and ironical. They tend to carnivalize and cannibalize the stereotypes heaped upon the border. Mexicali-based writer Eduardo Arellano, whom I discussed in terms of the border, therefore celebrates Tijuana as **the** space par excellence of "saturation" arguing that the city "continually admits and incorporates everything, however strange, because it seems that for Tijuana nothing is strange" (133). For this writer and many others like him, Tijuana emerges triumphantly as an omnivorous monster happily gobbling up differences of all sorts. It thus serves as the model for hybridization in the world today. Like the maquila industry that is its economic motor, Tijuana becomes a great assembler of vast differences, be these cultural, human, technological, musical, or linguistic. It is therefore also seen as a space of radical acceptance, "everyone's house," la casa de toda la gente in Nestor Garcia Canclini and Patricia Safa's happy formulation.

Ensenada-Tijuana born Gerardo Yépiz, known as Acamonchi, a slang term for piggyback riding in northern Mexico, started out doing mail order stencils under the influence of the Mail Art movement and Fluxus, changing how street artists work in SD/Tijuana. His chosen artist's name symbolizes a refusal of imposed geographical borders, that is, in the terms of this essay, an embrace of ambiguity thanks to the refusal to make a choice between them. Yépiz decided to make art by freezing ephemera, making the impermanent permanent and the intangible graspable. Interested in mass produced waste, he sees a plastic bag as a parachute, a piece of paper as an airplane, a water bottle as something that can float, and "discarded material […] something that can be used."[16] His designs of CD covers for the music industry, particularly Collective Nortec, for cyclists, skateboarders, the fashion industry, as well as his work as a web designer, are often humorous making people wonder whether his art is serious or a joke. His artistic praxis as well as the ambiguous reading it forces, is "healing" in the words of the artist and representative of a contemporary identity of what it means to be Mexican because it involves "projecting a daring vision of self and the internal struggle, breaking the mold and creating a brave new example for future generations."[17]

[16] See ArtPulse Look-in interview directed by Saulo Cisneros <https://www.youtube.com/watch?v=pFeW5Dz3Y0w>. Accessed 8/7/2015.

[17] <http://www.google.de/imgres?imgurl=http%3A%2F%2Fgraffiti.org%2Facamonchi%2Facamonchi.cop.jpg&imgrefurl=http%3A%2F%2Fgraffiti.org%2Facamonchi%2F&h=480&w=640&tbnid=aA24UdQhYDFlTM%3A&zoom=1&docid=HjxXkSyod0QTQM&ei=ztQnVbSeDc

Less ambiguous, but equally ironic Heriberto Yépez's work celebrates Tijuana as a city where a combinatory alchemy produces a space different from all others, because just like the maquiladora industry (assembly plants hiring mostly women) that has made it famous, Tijuana assembles not only technological products but also differences.[18] Tragically, however, as I pointed out earlier, the emergence of the maquiladora industry along the border was overshadowed by the gruesome murders and dismemberment of young women marked by purple crosses set up right on the border wall oftentimes alongside the white *sin nombre* ones. The emerging image of the city as one of assembly was therefore indissociably linked to that of disassembly, and this is perhaps where Yépez best fits. An intensively-lived space where two countries most intimately touch one another, the border devolves into a form of mutual cannibalism in Yépez's formulation, which combines the image of TJ as a devourer of differences with the famous Brazilian Cannibalist Manifesto, underlying early theorizations of transculturation. But Yépez complicates the figure arguing that as both sides cannibalize each other they also ironize one another. The result of this double move is not hybridity understood as a somewhat essentialist celebratory union or conjoining of two equals but also the fission and violence that accompanies relations of deep inequality. This double move explains why "whatever is considered typically Tijuana is frequently an ironic cannibalization produced from the United States; but simultaneously this ironization makes Mexicans in Mexico become other than themselves" (2005: 17). Because of these multiple reflective and incorporating dynamics, border culture is a

> form of swallowing ourselves as if we were the other; of swallowing the other to make it a part of us. Not a mixing pure or impure but something far more radical than that: a grotesque banquet where all the artifacts, all the signs and images of the other "the Gringo, the Mexico City native, the Chicano, the Black, the Indian" – [lo Gringo, lo Chilango, lo Chicano, lo Negro, lo Indio] are retracted, overcodified, parodied to make visible the fact that the so called union of these two worlds is not peaceful but freaky, comic, kitschy. (ibid.)

The Toy an-Horse's stomach may be see-through but it is not empty.

These ideas come from Yépez experiences working on Avenida Revolución a street full of zonkeys, which are the symbolic counterpart to the Toy an-Horse. Indeed, Yépez understood the full import of this funny hybrid invention. The *zonkey*, a donkey painted as a zebra, was created because Americans – in the words of one of the entertainers on the street who used it to attract US tourists to his bar –

uRsAHc04Jg&tbm=isch&iact=rc&uact=3&dur=481&page=1&start=0&ndsp=17&ved=0CCEQrQMwAA>. See his website: <http://www.acamonchi-art.com/.

18 An important precursor of this type of association (the border as the space of assembly and disassembly) was poetically rendered by Ursula Biemann's documentary *Performing the Border* (1999), one of the first to document and grapple with the femicides.

do not want to leave the United States while being in Mexico (fig. 2). That is why the guy trying to attract people, the *enganchador* as he is known in Spanish, transforms Tijuana into the theme park he thinks Americans desire and pulls the tourists in, speaking "to them in Spanglish or overcodified Spanish using words such as 'señoritas' or 'Tequila,' etcétera." He transforms himself into an autosimulated Mexican that both fits and plays with the expectations of the North American tourists. Or perhaps even better, he plays with the expectations that he thinks the North Americans have.[19] What Yépez is describing in effect are all the strategies whereby Mexican border culture turns itself into a simulacrum, and plays with the stereotypes and projections of the other, but at the same time incorporates these expectations and stereotypes and regurgitates them mimetized and parodied. It is a performance-for-the-other of a simulated identity ["el performance-para-el-otro de una identidad simulada"] (32). Any notions of an identity identical to itself fly out the window leaving traces in the language Yépez deploys. It is neither Spanish nor English but a multiply ironized language. While he allegedly writes in Spanish, it is a Spanish that turns the stomachs of traditional Hispanists. It comes on the heels of a series of international congresses that have celebrated the triumphant incursion of Spanish into the United States in response to which Harvard University created a Cervantes Institute, which highlights the 233% growth of Spanish in the United States since 1980 on its website. Glaringly absent is the fact that 70% of all new words that enter Spanish come from Latin America – not to speak of border neologisms such as those deployed by Yépez and others: "shockarte," "joliwúdico," "las beibis," "tripeando," "simón," "creizi." Today there are entire sentences written in Spanish sounding like English that imply a bilingual, bicultural reader

> "Cuando me canso, entro a un bar, me echo unas cervezas y ya estuvo, laik brand niu." (18)
> "Guasumara, beibi, du yu fil laik ay du?"(14)
> "El uno para el otro, meid for ich óder, ¿no crees?" (15)
> "juar juar, de yoks on dem." (15)
> "Ser, ¿yu guana taxi?" (25)
> "Guats in a neim?" (41)
> "El spánich and ay guont spik enithing els." (41)

An emphasis on Latin America – and therefore by implication border studies – puts one's academic career in serious jeopardy in Germany according to a publication of the Iberoamerican Institute in Berlin where I largely wrote this essay. While I read that news to my great dismay but not surprise, I wonder at the continued

[19] An Anglo American friend of mine from San Diego recalls crossing the border and posing on the zonkeys and thinking they were 'cute.' She only began to reflect on her unexamined position after editing this essay underlining what I argued above regarding the power differential in the effect stereotypes have on the border.

nearsightedness of disciplinary boundaries that never dare cross and thus have no capacity, or tools, of learning anything from the border. This is important, I think not only because the border is a "laboratory of the future" in Charles Bowden's now famous formulation,[20] and as such it is there that symptoms of what will become dominant worldwide first appear as we are seeing in the spread of femicides world wide as well as a generalized lawlessness and impunity. Indeed, the zonkeys invented on Av. Revolución long ago do become real.[21]

If what happens on the border anticipates what will happen in the culture at large and is therefore important to study, how do we describe and/or theorize what is taking place on the border? In today's world territories are no longer continuous nor internally coherent but full of borders, as I have been showing. The gap between the map and the territory, which assumed a coherent, continuous space, has become even wider than in Borges's time. For, even when situated far away from the actual border, we are increasingly experiencing that the territories we traverse daily are shot through with spaces constructed by myriad cultures and that every encounter between two people can indeed constitute a border experience. This of course makes us wonder, to which discipline do the multiply ironized objects, languages, and ways of knowing which are emerging in spaces such as Tijuana belong? And more importantly perhaps, can an ironized discipline really exist? And what exactly would an ironized discipline entail?[22]

One example that has been both inspiring and illuminating of the type of work and intellectual praxis that I am calling for here can be seen in the theorizations that arise from the transborder praxis of Teddy Cruz's studio in San Diego. A Guatemalan architect, Teddy Cruz has mobilized his fluency in Spanish and English, his profound understanding of Hispanic and US-America, and focused his work on the complex dynamic interconnecting flux which takes place across the border, and which is never unidirectional, as so many studies tacitly assume, and as Toy an-Horse challenges.[23] While Cruz works trying to improve the urban and

20 See Bowden.

21 The nineteenth century, the Zonkey first became really famous when one was accidentally sired in Colchester Zoo in the 1970s, and they have since continued to exhibit Zonkeys as a popular tourist attraction, <http://a-z-animals.com/animals/zonkey/>.

22 My call for the emergence of ever more 'ironic' disciplines is a tall order for, while the great humanists of the eighteenth and nineteenth century made the whole of Europe their home and made it a point of honor to get to know as many lands and languages as possible, in today's world, paradoxically, as borders proliferate we are nevertheless moving away from the time commitment this type of expansive knowledge horizon entailed. Most people think that knowing English and being fluent in computer-speak are enough and we are even hearing louder and louder calls for shortening Ph.D. programs which were the only spaces left where a student could hone the expansive knowledge horizon that a creative transculturality presupposes.

23 As his website lays out, Teddy Cruz is recognized internationally for his urban research of the Tijuana-San Diego border, advancing border immigrant neighborhoods as sites of cultural production, from which to rethink urban policy, affordable housing and civic infrastructure. His investigation of this "geography of conflict" has inspired a practice and pedagogy that

lived environment of Tijuana's slums, he also shows how the everyday forms of creative interventions that arise out of necessity extend deep into both the United States and Mexico. Like Toy an-Horse, the transborder lens that shapes his interventions allows him to see what is happening on the Mexican side from the vantage point of the United States and in the United States from that of Mexico.

Thus, for example, he shows how what is considered trash in California such as the so-called "Levittown" houses that spread with endless and deadly monotony in bland suburbs are being dismantled and replaced by bigger, modern houses. This creates a flow south of garage doors (fig. 3) and sometimes even entire houses on flatbed trucks make quite a sight at the border crossing. In Tijuana, where there is such a need for housing, everything is recycled, adopted and adapted. Garage doors serve as walls to build fragile shelters sited typically on the arid hillsides overlooking the city and which tend to wash away with heavy rains (fig. 4). The Levittown houses are put on top of sturdier housing to create a new form of architecture (fig. 5). And the mountains of discarded tires are cut up and filled with cement to create retaining walls (figs. 6 and 7). Learning from this "urgent imagination," Teddy Cruz gets maquiladoras to donate steel ladders and other such materials so that his studio can "retrofit" the temporary shelters making the housing more resistant to rain and mudslides (fig. 8).

Studying the flow in the opposite direction, he finds that the lack of zoning in Tijuana, coupled to the constant influx of immigrants who make it their home, makes for a visually highly-pixelated and chaotic city. In contrast, San Diego recedes away from the border, leaving an empty, highly militarized zone at the border, as it retreats into homogenous, non-pixelated, gated communities. But this is beginning to change under the impact of Tijuana, since migrants bring with them their "urgent imagination" and in turn "retrofit" the McMansions built in the 80s boom and which now few can afford, thus creating Tijuana-style multifamily, multigenerational, and multiuse spaces (fig. 9; for more graphics and videos on the Teddy Cruz architectural praxis see <http://estudioteddycruz.com/>). From the illuminations gained by his transborder praxis Teddy Cruz reflects that "the best ideas for the future of cities will not come from enclaves of economic abundance but from within sectors of conflict and scarcity from which an urgent imagination can inspire us to rethink urban growth today."

It is this urgent imagination, this TransBorder focus on movement, crossings, vectorial processes, migrations – and therefore also ironizations of all sorts – that I would argue is what we should reclaim as transborder, transcultural critics in the

emerges from the particularities of this bicultural territory and the integration of theoretical research, pedagogy and design production. His practice and research convene knowledges from across the fields of architecture and urbanism, environmental and social practice, political theory and urban policy, visual arts and public culture, and mediate the interface between top down institutions (governments, universities, foundations) and bottom-up socio-economic, cultural, and environmental intelligence embedded in communities, <http://visarts.ucsd.edu/faculty/teddy-cruz>.

hopes of creating a truly imaginative and useful epistemology. Indeed, if the border allows us to chart developments that await us in the future in far flung parts of the world, it is as I have been arguing a key place to understand and study. It needs to be treated as a bi- (if not tri- and multi-) national region, if you take into account tribal stakes on both sides of the border.[24] Moreover, the urgent imagination of the border needs to be reclaimed in its full potential and as the basis for reinventing regionalism.

Indeed, I largely wrote this essay in Cusco, Peru, a city that has gone from 50,000 to over 500,000 in less than five decades. It was once a stronghold of a relatively stable Andean and regional culture. As I looked out my window, I could see myriad examples of the "urgent imagination" that Cruz prizes. Like in Tijuana, in Cusco, ramshackle houses increasingly rise up the mountain sides overlooking the city. What once was a backwater with a strong regional culture and sense of identity (when viewed from the centralized national scene) has become multicultural, multiethnic, and multilingual. Today, Cusco is continually adapting to the forces that impinge upon it as it has become the "archeological capital of America" attracting over 3 million tourists annually. Much like on the US-Mexico border, where English and Spanish intermix, in Cusco Quechua and Spanish increasingly intermingle in everyday speech and ironizations of all sorts can be seen almost everywhere: from the fake, unsavory "Inka" that stands in front of the famous stone monolith of the twelve angles, to the invention of "traditions" that are only accelerating as dynamic processes overtake what this once tranquil indigenous enclave. While tourism is the engine of growth in Cusco, the unprecedented mass migratory flows that we are seeing worldwide promise to establish the border dynamic evident at the US-Mexico border elsewhere in the world as the new normal.

[24] I recently had the pleasure of reviewing María Josefina Saldaña Portillo's forthcoming study *Indian Given: Racial Geographies across Mexico and the* United States. In this exemplary work she triangulates three main groups on the border: Indian tribes (invariably overlooked in border studies despite their centrality) and the US and Mexican national claims on the space as they have evolved historically through conquest and colonization – and more recently 'free' trade agreements. In this, she follows in the footsteps of scholars of the borderlands who have creatively grappled with the border as a region, yet whose studies have invariably been relegated to oblivion because of the discomfort their scholarship produces by their center staging of the border as a paradigm not only of the future but of future possibilities and disciplines.

## Illustrations

**Fig. 1:** Marcos Ramírez “ERRE.” Toy an-Horse installation on the US-Mexico border line for inSite1997. Courtesy of the artist.

**Fig. 2:** “Zonkey” on Avenida Revolución, Tijuana.[25]

[25] For more images of zonkeys on Avenida Revolución taken by tourists and other visitors to Tijuana see <https://www.google.com/search?q=donkeys+on+avenida+revolucion&biw=1324&bih=644&tbm=isch&tbo=u&source=univ&sa=X&ved=0ahUKEwjOqpqW0aTJAhXMRyY

**Fig. 3:** Garage doors from dismantled Levittown houses in the suburbs of San Diego heading south where they are used to build shelters in the hills of Tijuana. Photo by Teddy Cruz.

**Fig. 4:** Fragile housing in Tijuana's hills built out of garage doors from San Diego. Photo by Teddy Cruz.

KHZhiCzcQsAQIHg>. All from ERRE Toy an-Horse Marcos Ramírez website. See <http://marcosramirezerre.com/toy-an-horse/>.

**Fig. 5:** Levittown houses from San Diego transported across the border and put on top of other housing in Tijuana to create a new "urgent" architectural style. Photo by Teddy Cruz.

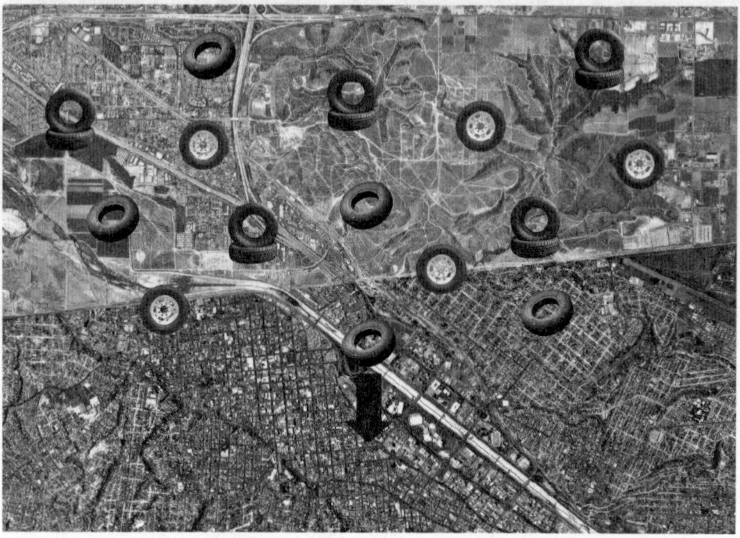

**Fig. 6:** Thousands of discarded tires flow south across the border. Photo by Teddy Cruz.

**Fig. 7:** Retaining walls to prevent mudslides. Photo by Teddy Cruz.

**Fig. 8:** Steel donated by the maquiladoras used by Teddy Cruz and his studio to "retrofit" Tijuana housing. Photo by Teddy Cruz.

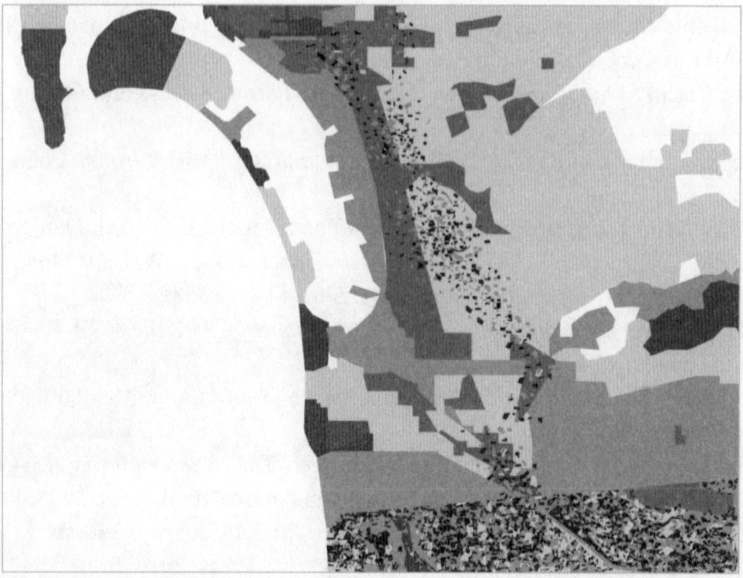

**Fig. 9:** The non-conforming uses of space and the increased pixelation of San Diego. The highly urbanized region south of the border is represented as full of confetti and stands in sharp contrast to the relatively empty spaces of San Diego. Yet the confetti like sprinkling in San Diego shows the impact of immigrants from the south as they in turn retrofit the suburbs. Photo by Teddy Cruz.

## Works Cited


Arellano, Eduardo. *Estado de Sitio: Ensayos (y Otros Asaltos) Sobre Literatura y Arte*. México: Plaza y Valdés Editores, 2003. Print.

deBuys, William. *A Great Aridness: Climate Change and the Future of the American Southwest*. New York: Oxford University Press, 2011. Print.

Bowden Charles (ed.). *Juárez: The Laboratory of Our Future*. Preface by Noam Chomsky; afterword by Eduardo Galeano; photographs by Javier Aguilar. New York: Aperture, 1998. Print.

Canclini, Néstor García, and Patricia Safa. *Tijuana: La Casa de Toda la Gente*. INAH-ENAH, Programa Cultural de las Fronteras, 1989. Print.

Cruz, Teddy. "Two-Way Journeys: Border Walls, Border Cities, and the Two-Headed Trojan Horse of Tijuana." *Thresholds* 20 (2000): 72-77. Print.

"Donald Trump Comes out Fighting on Prime Time: Tycoon Says His Controversial Comments on Mexican 'Rapists' Were 'Totally Accurate' and Univision Had no Right to Cancel Miss USA Broadcast." *Daily Mail* 1 July 2015. Web. 9 June 2016. <http://www.dailymail.co.uk/news/article-3145436/Donald-Trump-comes-fighting-prime-time-Tycoon-says-controversial-

comments-Mexicans-rapists-totally-accurate-Univision-no-right-cancel-Miss-USA.html#ixzz3efDMVq2p>.

Fuentes, Carlos. *Myself and Others*. New York: Farrar, Strauss and Giroux, 1988. Print.

Hutcheon, Linda. *Irony's Edge: The Theory and Politics of Irony*. London and New York: Routledge, 1994. Print.

Oko, Dan. "The Toxic Border: Researchers Ponder Increasing Birth Defects in the Valley." *The Austin Chronicle* 9 November 2001. Web. 9 June 2016. <http://www.austinchronicle.com/news/2001-11-09/83589>.

Ortiz, Fernando. *Contrapunteo Cubano del Tabaco y el Azúcar*. 1940. Madrid: Edito CubaEspaña, 1999. Print.

Rama, Angel. *Transculturación Narrativa en América Latina*. Mexico City: siglo xxi editors, 1982. Print.

Romero, Fernando, and LAR. *Hyper-Border: The Contemporary US-Mexico Border and Its Future*. New York: Princeton Architectural Press, 2008. Print.

Saldaña-Portillo, María Josefina. *Indian Given: Racial Geographies across Mexico and the United States*. Durham: Duke University Press, 2016. Print.

Sheren, Ila. "From the Trojan Horse to the Human Cannonball: InSite at the US-Mexico Border, 1997-2005." *Academia*. Web. 9 June 2016. <http://www.academia.edu/1659868/From_the_Trojan_Horse_to_the_Human_Cannonball_InSite_at_the_U.S.-Mexico_Border_1997-2005>.

Spitta, Silvia. *Misplaced Objects: Collections and Recollections in Europe and the Americas*. Houston: Texas University Press, 2009. Print.

---. *Between Two Waters: Narratives of Transculturation in Latin America*. 1995. College Station: Texas A&M Press, 2005. Print.

Welsch, Wolfgang. "Transculturality: The Puzzling Form of Cultures Today." *Spaces of Culture: City, Nation, World*. Ed. Mike Featherstone and Scott Lash. London: Sage 1999. 194-213. Print.

Yépez, Heriberto. *Made in Tijuana*. Mexicali: Instituto de Cultura de Baja California, 2005. Print.

---. "El Mito del Escritor Fronterizo." 27 September 2003. Online Blog. 9 June 2016. <http://horstmatthaiquelle.blogspot.de/2006/05/el-mito-del-escritor-fronterizo.html>.

# “Branches of the Same Tree”: Chicano/a Vietnam Solidarity and the Making of Aztlán

*Carmen Brosig*

“¡Raza sí, guerra no!”[1] was a widely known and often invoked slogan during the Chicano anti-Vietnam War movement which concisely sums up its two central aims. “¡Raza sí!” seized on the growing affirmation of race rather than the refusal of Chicanos/as to accept their partly indigenous and mestizo/a heritage, while “¡Guerra no!” called for the end of the war in Southeast Asia. The two phrases combined refer to a close connection between Chicano/a attempts to secede from the US and the Vietnamese struggle for liberation: both were the reactions against decades of suppression and thus revealed broader patterns of colonization that became manifest locally but at the same time fostered or produced counter-hegemonic positions, both local and global.

Nevertheless, in terms of sequentialization, one must bear in mind that Vietnamese decolonization processes, as well as other liberation movements throughout the world, preceded what in the United States is now periodized as the “sixties.” Fredric Jameson stresses that it was the sixties of the “third world” that marked the beginning of protest and liberation movements around the world. He argues that the “first world 60s” clearly followed on the heels of decolonization movements in “British and French Africa” (180). Emphasizing that the black liberation movement in the United States can be considered the “one significant exception,” he follows African American leaders, intellectuals, writers, and artists in calling the African American movement “also a movement of decolonization,” (ibid.) and in pointing towards the considerable influence the various movements had on each other. With regard to the Chicano Movement that emerged in the last years of the sixties, and hence several years after the first sit-ins in Greensboro, influences from both third world liberation movements as well as from the Civil Rights Movement can be identified.

In the following, I will deploy Douglas Reichert Powell’s critical regionalism as “methodological umbrella” (5) in order to identify the links between these two seemingly unrelated incidents against the backdrop of underlying patterns of

[1] “*¡Raza sí! ¡Guerra no!*” is also the title of one of the rare books historically reviewing Chicanos’/as’ relationship with and protest against the Vietnam War. Oropeza traces back the conditions under which the protest movement could surge. Arguing that the sixties and the war had a significant influence on the way Chicanos/as perceived their racial background, she suggests that the “tripod of American citizenship” rests on three pillars: whiteness, military service, and manhood. She argues that “[j]ust as movement activists no longer considered themselves ‘white,’ they likewise contested the other two traditional parameters of belonging” (102-03).

politics, culture, economy, and history. Subsequently, it will be shown that the Vietnamese struggle for liberation had a substantial impact on the Chicano Movement and helped to legitimize and shape claims to national independence from the Unites States. In order to culturally underpin these nationalist claims, Chicanos/as often referred to Aztlán – both the designation of the ancient Aztec empire as well as the presumed mythic place of origin of the Chicano/a ancestors. Analyzing Aztlán as a mythic conception, my analysis will retrace, in a geographical and a metaphorical sense, how Aztlán has been adopted and adapted by the Chicano Movement to legitimate the founding of a Chicano/a nation during the Vietnam War era. My thesis is that Chicanos/as appropriated the (North) Vietnamese struggle for liberation in order to legitimate culturally nationalist claims to the Southwest of the United States based on a mythical understanding. I argue that Chicano/a liberation efforts and the Vietnamese resistance to the US invasion reveal a "strange" (Reichert Powell 137) connection that becomes manifest in the Chicano/a anti-Vietnam-War movement. Moreover, it is important to stress that both these local/regional manifestations of liberation agendas produce counterhegemonic discourses on the basis of appropriations of indigeneity in order to deconstruct Western racist and imperialist discourses and to disrupt Western power. However, the ways in which the movement missed opportunities of liberatory change due to the (perhaps inadvertent) reproduction of hegemonic discourses, especially sexism, as well as racial essentialism and the reinforcement of patriarchal structures within the movement will also be pointed out.

Within that context, one needs a closer examination of how global patterns engender, facilitate, or obstruct local liberation movements and how these local movements can be understood in light of a broader context. Further, it is necessary to bear in mind that local histories or myths always already refer to larger structures. At the same time, however, they potentially resist such embeddedness and thus might challenge unjust and unequal power structures.

In order to address these questions on a more abstract level, I would like to initiate an Inter-American(ist) dialogue between Douglas Reichert Powell's *Critical Regionalism* (2007) and Walter Mignolo's *Local Histories/Global Designs* (2012). Not only do the two books emphasize the necessity to continually renegotiate the relationship between the local and the global and the implications of power herein implied, they also challenge traditional notions of the relation between the local and the global as a dichotomous one. Both point towards the discursive intertwinement of the local and the global as well as the transformative potential local histories or regional incidents might have on underlying economic, cultural, and political patterns and conditions.

While it is common knowledge that the United States's anti-Vietnam movement gathered people of all ethnic backgrounds, ages, classes, genders, as well as political ideologies; and while it is widely known that there is no single or homogeneous anti-war movement, but rather several fractions with different motives and aims, it is little known that one of the largest anti-war demonstrations in the United States was organized and held by Chicanos/as. The so-called Chicano Moratorium,[2] part of a series of Chicano/a anti-war demonstrations, took place on 29 August 1970 in East Los Angeles and attracted between 20,000 and 30,000 protestors walking over Whittier Boulevard and eventually encountering the police.[3] Although the police claimed to have been called due to reports of plundering, other reports and newspapers state that the police had already been on site to ensure that the protestors did not deviate from their planned route (Oropeza 161-65). In the aftermath of the march, four people died due to police violence; among them Rubén Salazar, a reporter at the *L.A. Times*.[4] The outbreak of violence between Chicanos/as and the police was symptomatic for the situation in the *barrios* and thus, the Chicano Moratorium was not only a protest against the war. Rather, it was also a protest against police brutality as one of the many forms of racial discrimination Chicanos/as at home had to face on a daily basis in their *barrios* and overseas in the military in Vietnam. This experience of violence and racism certainly did not only parallel the atrocities and imperialism in Vietnam; however, from a Chicano/a perspective, both had to be seen as comparable manifestations of the military industrial complex in which both the racism within the United States as well as the war against the North Vietnamese had its roots.

Like African Americans a few years earlier, Chicanos/as engaged in a liberationist discourse that often produced a counterhegemonic stance and, in a cultural nationalist vein, aimed at the establishment of a Chicano/a nation-state in the Southwest. Although the idea of the nation-state had been widely accepted among radical currents of the movement early on, the concept became popularized within the broader Chicano/a community by means of its (re-)introduction and distribution during the National Chicano Youth Liberation Conference in 1969 as "El Plan Espiritual de Aztlán."[5] It called for the founding of a Chicano/a nation-state on the exact territory Mexico had been forced to cede in the peace treaty of Guadelupe Hidalgo in 1848. The plan's preamble, which originally had been a poem by Chicano poet and activist Alurista, was read at the opening of the conference:

2 The Chicano/a marches against the war as well the organizational committee were called "Chicano Moratorium" because they called for Chicanos/as to let their normal activities rest in favor of protesting the war (Alaniz and Cornish 186).

3 There are different sources. Oropeza gives the *L.A. Times* as an example that published the lower figure of 20,000 protestors based on police information as well as Chicano/a newspapers such as *El Gallo* and *Regeneración* that insisted on 30,000 participants (228).

4 Before his death, Salazar had published regularly about the Chicano Movement in Los Angeles. He expressed suspicions that the Chicano Moratorium had been infiltrated by the Los Angeles Police Department. He was killed in a liquor store where he hid from the police. The police claimed to have killed him and Gustav Montag, a supporter of the movement, in self-defense, while Lynn Ward, who died of her injuries in September, and José Díaz were shot accidentally. Apart from that, about 150 demonstrators were arrested (Oropeza 173-74).

5 For the earliest printed versions of "El Plan Espiritual de Aztlán" that were widely distributed, see Gonzales and Urista.

> In the spirit of a new people that is conscious not only of its proud historical heritage but also of the brutal gringo invasion of our territories, we, the Chicano inhabitants and civilizers of the northern land of Aztlán from whence came our forefathers reclaiming the land of their birth and consecrating the determination of our people of the sun, declare that the call of our blood is our power, our responsibility, and our inevitable destiny. (Gonzáles and Urista 5)

The text refers to Aztlán as an ancient founding myth of the Aztec people seizing on both the paradise-like region where the Aztecs were said to have come from and the designation of the Aztec empire. Somewhat surprisingly perhaps, the location of Aztlán shifted several times as it was adapted to specific discursive configurations. Throughout its history, the location has been moved from Tenochtitlán (now Mexico City) up north as well as to Mexico's west coast.[6] Due to the oral character of the myth and the precarious status of the texts about it in times of colonization, it is hardly possible to trace back or to exactly locate this "northern land of Aztlán" or "the land of [the Aztecs'] birth."

According to Reichert Powell's *Critical Regionalism*, "the emphasis is not on what regions are but why they are that way, on what they do as much as what has been done to them" (5). Thus, the discourse formulated in the sixties about where to locate Aztlán is more relevant than the location itself. Along the same lines, Cooper Alarcón deals with the difficulties of identifying and filtering competing notions and descriptions of Aztlán and the implications of asymmetrical power structures in terms of textuality and orality. He anticipates critical regionalist methodology when he provides an alternative approach to the problem of competing (hi-)stories and their respective truth claims: he rejects both the Chicano/a nationalist tendency to romanticize the past as well as the 'other' extreme, practiced in the West since the Enlightenment, to ignore and reject mythic narratives altogether and to regard them as irrelevant. Introducing the palimpsest as a suitable metaphor for Aztlán as a multilayered and ambiguous construction, he argues that myths and histories are complex "site[s] where texts have been superimposed onto others in order to displace earlier or competing histories; [...] the submerged texts are often visible, returning to haunt and complicate the dominant text" (34). With regard to such competing notions about a particular region within the framework of critical regionalism, Reichert Powell hopes to "create that kind of critical intersection where these coexisting and overlapping revisions of regionalism can find common ground" (5).

Reichert Powell argues that the region can never be conceived as an "isolated space, withdrawn from larger cultural forces and processes" (4-5), no matter how much regions or the people defining them emphasize their stability and uniformity

[6] Several scholars have tried to figure out where to locate Aztlán; see J. Chávez, who presents a rather romanticized image of the use of Aztlán, or Price, who provides a broader picture of how different currents have placed Aztlán on the map.

over time. Thus, regions and their narratives are always intertwined in one way or another with global patterns of politics, culture, and history and with alternative narrations. If considering the Southwest as a region, it is notable that its definition has been in a constant state of flux over the decades and centuries, depending on who defined it and what kind of claims were laid to it. Aztlán has always been connected with larger cultural formations; be it as the legendary place of origin of the Aztec people; be it as a mythical "golden north" presented to the Spanish *conquistadores*; be it as a kind of promised land where the colonized indigenous people could find shelter; or be it as the vision of a Chicano/a nation-state independent from the United States, arising in the sixties against the backdrop of the Civil Rights Movement and the protests against the Vietnam War.

Reichert Powell suggests critical regionalism as a methodology to study exactly those links that in an unexpected, yet completely logical way connect these seemingly unrelated social movements. He defines critical regionalism as a strategy for cultural critique that can

> link individual moments of cultural struggle to larger patterns of history, politics, and culture, by understanding how they are linked not only in time and in the nebulous networks of discourse but also in space, through relationships of power that can be material and cultural. (20-21)

Referring to the Chicano Movement, I suggest that it is significantly important to link it with contemporary liberation struggles and decolonization movements around the world since the discursive strategies, the rhetoric, and the aims – no matter where the liberation or decolonization took place – were more or less the same. Just like the Civil Rights Movement, the Chicano Movement struggled for social equality, civil rights, decent housing, healthcare and proper job opportunities, and fought against racism. Drawing not only on the experiences of African Americans but also on Third World Movements, Chicanos/as argued that they formed part of an internal colony[7] and thus referred to a (global) colonialist framework that facilitated the economic and capitalist exploitation of people of color by the military industrial complex. Manuel Gómez, the first Chicano to publicly refuse the draft and to fight in Vietnam, argued:

> The sweat of my people watered the fields and their aching bones harvested your food. Today we continue to do the sweat-work for you, with our hands

7 The idea of the Chicano/a community as an internal colony was adopted from African American thinkers who attempted to provide a model that would better explain the situation of black people in the United States than the assimilation model. The model was further developed and adapted to the Chicano/a situation by Barrera and Muñoz. The idea of the internal colony can be traced back to its indigenous roots in the Andean region as well as to its use by African Americans in the sixties (Gutiérrez).

> and backs. Though you occupy the land you have not conquered us. I am a free man. I choose my own battles. My fight is here. (7)

This text, which was published in *La Raza*, a Chicano/a nationalist newspaper, shows that the annexation of the former Mexican territory by the United States had left deep wounds in the Chicano/a collective memory and that the experience of living under occupation had constantly been kept alive by the ensuing exploitation of labor and resources. Moreover, reading the quote with a critical regionalist approach, one could argue that Gómez establishes a link between Chicanos/as within the United States living under this economic exploitation and racial oppression on the one hand, and the struggle of the Vietnamese people on the other. By refusing the draft, he chooses his "own battle" at home, not in Vietnam. He challenges power structures with a very small and local act: refusing the draft is thus a strong political act of uncovering, subverting, and resisting existing power structures. Hence, not only does the draft refusal challenge the practice of racism und subjugation at home, it also offers a critique of US imperialism in Vietnam.

However, one needs to take a closer look at what Reichert Powell understands as "patterns" of meanings. He uses "patterns" synonymously to "contexts," "broader cultural conflicts" (14), "broader configurations" (18), "broader cultural, political, historical, and geographical connections," "broader forces" (19), "broader networks of cause-and-effect" (120), "larger contexts of the world" (137). This lack of semantic specificity leaves room for interpretation. In order to provide more clarity about what his term "broader patterns" means and what kind of implications with regard to power asymmetries are inherent, I will complement Reichert Powell's concepts with Mignolo's thinking. Mignolo starts one step earlier in detecting that "patterns" are not just there locally, but are "global designs," the product of another local history. Although I acknowledge that Mignolo's "global designs" are not the same as Reichert Powell's "broader patterns," I believe that Mignolo's view might add some substantial insights. Mignolo defines global designs as the complement of universalism in the making of the modern colonial world. He argues that "[u]niversal histories in the past five hundred years have been embedded in global designs" which "have been the hegemonic project for managing the planet" (21). Thus, although these global designs are fostered by hegemonic discourses and specific narratives, they are also supported, maintained, and driven forward by hard structures – which would be analogous to Reichert Powell's "patterns." Mignolo's central argument is the following:

> What have been seen as 'contradictions,' are indeed the two faces of the same coin – 'modernity/coloniality.' Global designs also hide the local history from which they themselves emanate and are presented, as if they were a natural unfolding of history. There is no contradiction here either, between local histories and global designs: global designs respond to the logic of coloniality,

> but they are described and promoted in the image of progress and development for the local histories whose actors and institutions benefit from global designs. (xvi)

What is specific to Mignolo's line of argument, in contrast to Reichert Powell's, is that both those "broader patterns" and "global designs" respond to the logic of coloniality and continue to reproduce that binary logic since there are certain actors and institutions which benefit from them and which are interested in not only maintaining them, but also in extending and consolidating them. At this point, one has to acknowledge that global designs are the result of the universalization of the particular and local (model of) history of the 'West.' As a consequence, this dominant narrative of progress and modernity overwrites local histories. While some actors benefit from those global designs, others, whose local histories are overwritten, do not and instead suffer from the elimination of their identity-constituting local histories. In a benevolent understanding, local histories are not completely erased, but rather embedded and inscribed in and adapted to global designs. While some actors benefit from that 'progress,' others suffer from coloniality by economic exploitation, cultural imperialism, and racial subjugation. That is why Mignolo refers to "modernity/coloniality" as the "two faces of the same coin."

In terms of the relation between the Chicano/a protest movement and the Vietnamese fight against US imperialism, one can follow Mignolo in asserting that the global design at work hiding those local histories is that of modernity/coloniality. Both Chicanos/as and Vietnamese argued that the 'progress' towards modernity proclaimed by the United States when occupying their territory was part of colonization, imperialism, and capitalism. Therefore, the resistance against this colonial logic can be considered a decolonial project, and, in Mignolo's sense, this interconnection between the two seemingly separate incidents involves the potential of what he calls "border thinking" (xxii).

In this context, Mignolo introduces his central term "colonial difference." For him, "[t]he colonial difference is the space where local histories inventing and implementing global designs meet local histories, the space in which global designs have to be adapted, adopted, rejected, integrated or ignored" (xxv). Thus, local histories have always held the potential to challenge broader patterns and global designs. Reichert Powell warns against the destabilizing consequences of displacing and ignoring those narratives and underscores the importance of local histories:

> [T]his accommodation [with prevailing power realities] involves subsuming and isolating local histories from broader national or global narratives, [...] hierarchically positioning the local below or outside the realm of vital cultural conflict and public debate, and thus mystifying the actions and decisions of

> small groups of citizens and broad patterns of economic, social, and political change. (120)

Hence, if we regard worldwide decolonization as such a broad pattern of economic, social, and political change, it is important to see the local anti-war protests as an attempt to conceive of local history and subalternized forms of knowledge in Mignolo's sense with the mythic construction of Aztlán as one strategy of local resistance. Implicitly, local histories always carry the potential to resist being overwritten by universalized narratives and thus to refuse to co-exist with superimposed hegemonic narratives of the region.

In this vein, it is necessary to analyze how Aztlán is conceived in the Chicano/a imaginary. Luis Leal stresses that Aztlán as a symbol has two meanings; it represents the Southwest of the United States and designates a spiritual home, "something that is carried within the heart, no matter where they [Chicanos/as] may live or where they may find themselves" (8). Drawing on that imaginary of Aztlán as a "mythical geography" (ibid.), I suggest reading Aztlán as a regional and spiritual concept at the same time, which according to modern Western reasoning are two different things. In many other traditions, the regional (or spatial) and the spiritual (or mythical) can never be disentangled since one constitutes the other.

In order to better understand that Aztlán as an identity-shaping concept has undergone constant transformation and is constantly being (re-)constructed, Cooper Alarcón suggests a palimpsestic reading of Aztlán. He points out the risk of both the nationalist tendency to romanticize the myth as well as its omission as "esoteric trivia" (34). He proposes that Aztlán should be read not as just one narrative, but as a multi-layered text where "the submerged texts are often visible, returning to […] complicate the dominant text" (ibid.) – that is, the text(s) of those in a position of power. There are other authors that propose similar approaches, i.e. to read not only what is spiritual, discursive, or mythical about Aztlán as a palimpsest, but also what is 'spatial' or 'regional.' Pérez-Torres asserts that

> land in its representation and significance within Chicano culture is a type of palimpsest, a text overwritten by numerous forms: It serves as the material condition underlying the alienated labor performed by farm workers, as the object of colonization under the regime of Manifest Destiny, as a connection between a mestizo present and an indigenous past, as a territory marked off by national boundaries that confound and complicate notions of Chicano and Chicana identities. (152)

Suggesting a palimpsestic reading, Pérez-Torres shows how the meaning of the land (Aztlán) has been transformed over time, depending on the form of colonial rule and resistance to that rule. These meanings attached to the land are to some extent competing, and at times even incompatible: they are claims made by some groups that compete and interfere with a meaning other groups have ascribed to that land; such as the Southwest as the homeland for many Native American tribes or the Southwest as bound to a narrative of expansion and exploration for white settlers. Nevertheless, it is important to note that most Chicanos/as in the sixties believed to be the rightful owners of the land as they felt tied to it in a unique way: through their hard labor. Aztlán is identity-shaping inasmuch as its mythical notions – along with labor conditions – create and re-affirm the spiritual rooting in the land. This element is a common one in both indigenous and (cultural) nationalist ideologies and has been used to exclude other groups from 'ownership' and entitlement. Writer and activist Enriqueta Longeau y Vásquez[8] puts it quite trenchantly:

> *During Mexico's struggle, during its weak moments, we see upon its land French troops, Spanish troops and the troops of the U.S. of A.* […] With this, which is part of the history of our very Southwest, we see Vietnam having in its history with the very same people trying to defeat another nation. Someone else is always there to rule them and attempt to colonize them. *They, too, have had French, English, Spanish and U.S. troops on their soil.* (Espinoza and Oropeza 198; original emphasis)

Chicanos/as critiqued the invasion(s) of other people into what was once considered indigenous, and then Mexican, territory and drew parallels to the colonial occupations of Vietnam. What is problematic about the position that she claims is that the land belonged to those who first inhabited it which is indicated by the phrases "our very Southwest" and "their soil." Even if it was traceable who first inhabited the Southwest, the argument is clearly devoid of any cosmological thinking, such as the indigenous notion that human beings are considered part of the world they live in and cannot be 'owners' of the land.

Price's argument mirrors the palimpsestic reading of the land. She discusses the settlers' conception of the Southwest as a "blank page" that needed to gain meaning through narratives of expansion and she describes the Southwest as a deliberate discursive construction of a vast and empty space whose alleged emptiness metaphorized as the "virgin land" served to legitimate its appropriation. In general, she argues, "[t]he polar, desert, jungle, and ocean regions were erased

8 Longeau y Vásquez was a writer with the widely distributed journal *El Grito del Norte*. The journal addressed both Chicano and Chicana issues. However, mostly women were responsible for its strong feminist agenda. There, Longeau y Vásquez was in close contact with the editor of the journal, Elizabeth Martínez, whose research will be addressed later on. In her position, Martínez went to Vietnam to not only report from the war, but also to meet with female Vietnamese activists. That way, Martínez and Longeau y Vásquez could exchange what they would call feminist positions on the war and the role of the Chicana within Aztlán and the Chicano/a community.

in the collective imperial geoimagery, so that they could be overwritten with a narrative of expansion, civilization and extraction" (41).

Chicanos/as reproached the US government for the economic and capitalist exploitation both in the Southwest and in Vietnam. The destruction of nature, the concurrent capitalization of land, and the industrialization of those areas entailed the erosion of traditional ways of life. Chicanos/as argued that the United States projected its narrative of modernization onto the Southwest, and "brought" modernity while at the same time enslaving Chicanos/as for their purpose – the growth of the American economy (Anonymous 1969: 7). The *topos* of the destruction of nature recurred repeatedly; it also served to proclaim solidarity, or brotherhood, with the Vietnamese people based on the killing of thousands of people as well as the exploitation of their land:

> The [Mexican-American] war did not end. It has continued in the minds and hearts of the people of the Southwest. Strife and bloodshed has never stopped between us. This society with its Texas Rangers and Green Berets has never allowed our people to live in peace. The blood is still moist on the land. Too many of my brothers have been killed fighting for a lie called 'American freedom,' both in our streets and in foreign lands. (Gómez 1973: 141)[9]

At this point, I suggest coloniality as the overall frame of domination and decolonization as (local) forms of resistance. It is therefore necessary to ask how Chicanos/as perceived themselves as being subject to colonial structures; how their local histories have the potential to oppose racism and imperialism both at home and abroad; how affinities between different local histories can be identified and how, through their interrelatedness, these histories point toward different designs and patterns, or, in the words of Reichert Powell: "local texts, images, and discourses must be interpreted in the light of their relationship to texts from elsewhere" (29).

In Mignolo's work, the terms *coloniality* and *decolonization* are not exclusively used for territorial or spatial configurations. However, according to the 'Western' notion of the colony, the term is bound to geographical space and thus leaves aside potential structural characteristics – such as racism, oppression, violence, and discrimination – of an internal colony. Mignolo argues that "[b]order thinking from a territorial perspective becomes a machine of appropriation of the colonial differe/a/nces" (45) and, hence, he suggests to engage in border thinking from a subaltern perspective. Nonetheless, he himself repeatedly falls back on analyzing

[9] This text was firstly published as a contribution in *La Raza* in 1969 by Manuel Gómez, the first (known) Chicano to refuse the draft. In a letter addressing his fellow activists, he criticizes the destruction of nature and the systematic but arbitrary killings of Vietnamese people. The notion of Chicanos/as and Vietnamese as being branches of the same tree has been selected as a title for this paper since it takes up on what Reichert Powell understands as or would analyze as critical regionalism.

modernity/coloniality from a territorial perspective; especially when he speaks of internal and external borders, which he qualifies as conflicts between empires and conflicts between cosmologies (11, 37). In the discussion of his examples, he exclusively binds the internal and external borders to the territorial borders of the nation; he does not clarify why conflicts between England and Spain arose from internal, whereas conflicts between the Islamic world and Spain from exterior bordering. The same holds true for the encounter of the Spanish empire with the Aztec or Incan empire: would the Aztec subjugation of other peoples in Mesoamerica be considered a conflict of empires or of cosmologies? Since many such conflicts could be qualified as involving both, border(line)s between the internal and the external are usually blurred. The contradiction in Mignolo's argument lies thus in the possibility to define borders as both internal and external at the same time.

Still, I believe his idea of the external and internal borders is promising when combined with the idea of the Chicano/a community as an internal colony. Whereas Mignolo would probably categorize the Vietnam War as another manifestation of imperial politics due to an external border, it is rather difficult to classify the relation of Chicano/a communities with the white military industrial complex (n)either as a conflict of cosmologies (n)or as a conflict of empires. Thus, it seems impossible to locate the encounter of the Chicano/a community with white American power structures either on an internal or on an external border. Although there is a confrontation of cosmologies, Mignolo's definition of the external border takes up the geographical, economic, and sociopolitical dimensions in their entanglement, whereas for the geographical dimension of the internal border, he does not take into account the idea that there might be 'borders' in a social, economic, or other dimension within society itself.

Squarely, in order to fill the gap where borders of colonial difference exist but neither fall under the definition of an internal nor external border, I would like to seize again on the idea of the internal colony.[10] The concept of the internal colony was presented as a model that explained African Americans' – as well as Chicanos'/as' – living conditions and offered the ground for political agency:

> By studying national liberation struggles Blacks and Chicanos began to imagine themselves as oppressed nations that soon would be liberated through overt revolutionary struggle as part of the larger worldwide decolonization movements. Urban ghettos and Chicano barrios had the structure of domestic

[10] Gutiérrez traces back the concept of "internal colonialism" from a Chicano/a perspective. He stresses that early variations of the concept already existed during the nation-building phase in Latin America, when "[f]orms of 'domestic' or 'internal' colonialism that existed within states emerged as concepts in the dependency literature primarily as a way to critique the then dominant view that Latin American economies were dualistic, composed of modern and backward sectors. Instead, the theorists asserted, internal colonies were of composed the mass of Latin America's poor population providing wealth to the metropolises" (286).

> colonies. Like the wretched of the earth elsewhere [t]hey wanted independence. (Gutiérrez 284)

It is possible to argue that the *barrio* opened a space where global designs of modernity/coloniality were forcefully implemented in a similar way as in Vietnam. Chicanos/as realized that it was not the supposed lack of commitment to assimilation or their alleged inferiority which was the main reason for their precarious state, but the colonial patterns imposed by hegemonic discourses and practices. Barrera and Muñoz transfer the African American conception of the ghetto as an internal colony to the Chicano/a context. They compare several parameters of the 'traditional' colony with the characteristics of the *barrio* and conclude that the *barrio* was the outcome of a colonial logic. Since the Southwest had been a site of actual invasion for Chicanos/as, the analogy was adopted deliberately. In a speech given at a Chicano/a symposium in 1969, Lozada concisely connects the situation in the *barrio*, impregnated by racism and cultural and economic imperialism, to the conflict in Vietnam:

> And we look at the barrio too, not as something confined by arbitrary city limits determined by corrupt politicians who want to think in no broader terms than your own barrio, so that you won't bother to think of the people of the Third World as brothers elsewhere. We look at our barrio as one not restricted or confined to the city limits arbitrarily determined by some corrupt politicians. Our barrio goes beyond these fictitious city limits and extends into the Plaza de las Tres Culturas in Mexico City, our barrio is projected onto the favelas of Brazil. Our barrio extends into the jungles of Bolivia and the jungles of Vietnam. And that's what our barrio is! Our barrio, in fact, is the whole world, wherever the oppressed might be. (15)

By attempting to think beyond locations and borders, the speaker stresses the connectedness of region and larger power configurations to which Reichert Powell and Mignolo refer as well. The local struggles in the *barrios* can no longer be seen as something unique and isolated, but share a complex and interconnected space with what happened in Vietnam. By thus both undermining geographic and spatial projections of coloniality and by connecting the *barrio* with Vietnam, Chicanos/as suggested that there were broader patterns of domination that needed to be addressed and transformed rather than to focus on 'localized' issues of discrimination and violence.

In this context, ethnic minorities in general claimed that the war had come home; a statement written on cardboards at many Chicano/a demonstrations stated: "Our fight is in the barrio, not in Vietnam," which was meant literally and not metaphorically. After the protest and the violent confrontation with the police on 29 August 1970, the Moratorium Committee decided to address issues of police brutality and put them on their agenda, since "[a]nyone who participated that day

[...] is now clear on the fact that our war is here" (E. Chávez 72). Juxtaposing US aggression in Vietnam with police brutality against ethnic minorities in the United States, Longeau y Vásquez and Martínez assert: "The war had come home. In the months after bloody August 29, the police rioted again and again" (297). In radically nationalist circles, there were comparisons between riots at home and the drafting of Chicanos to go to Vietnam. Since Chicanos served and died in disproportionate numbers overseas,[11] some radical newspapers and activists problematically suggested "genocide" as a comparative term to describe both a selective draft system and the violence Chicanos encountered in Vietnam. The MEChA[12] newsletter for instance accused the "system" of using Chicanos as "cannon fodder" (Aguayo) by sending them to Southeast Asia; polemically and in an exaggerated way, a contribution in *El Grito del Norte* asserted that "the cattle cars are waiting, Auschwitz style" (Arellano 9), implying that the war in Vietnam was comparable to a concentration camp. Chicanos/as argued that genocidal aims were not only pursued overseas, "but [also] when the police repress us on the streets of our own barrio [with] [s]ome cops inspir[ing] more fear and hatred than the Viet-Cong" (del Olmo qtd. in E. Chávez 2002: 64).

One of the more popular examples of such comparisons to genocide was Rosalío Muñoz's speech in front of the L.A. induction center in 1969. He protested against the war by calling on Chicanos to refuse the draft and at the same time, he invigorated the claim for self-determination by declaring his independence from the Selective Service System on the day of the anniversary of the declaration of Mexican independence from Spain:

> Today, the sixteenth of September, the day of independence for all Mexican peoples, I declare my independence of the Selective Service System. I accuse the government of the United States of America of genocide against the Mexican people. Specifically, I accuse the draft, the entire social, political, and economic system of the United States of America of creating a funnel which shoots Mexican youth into Viet Nam to be killed and to kill innocent men, women and children. (217)

Picking up on the idea of decolonizing the internal colony, one could argue that if "[i]n political terms, the situation of internal colonialism is manifested as a lack of control over the institutions that affect the barrio" (Barrera and Muñoz 286), then,

[11] It is hardly possible to trace back how many Chicanos served in the military during the Vietnam War since Chicanos/as in US census data were listed as "Caucasian" (Mariscal 3). However, Chicano scholar Ralph Guzmán conducted research on Chicano casualties in Vietnam on the basis of the number of the Spanish surnames of the war dead in local newspapers in the Southwest between 1961 and 1967. He showed that about 19.4% of the war dead listed had Spanish surnames, whereas only 11.8% with Spanish surnames lived throughout the Southwest in 1960. Chicanos had even a higher risk of being drafted towards combat units such as the Marines than whites.

[12] Movimiento Estudiantil Chicano de Aztlán.

for Rosalío Muñoz, declaring independence from colonial institutions, was a form of political agency to overcome coloniality. The use of the term "genocide" indicates that Rosalío Muñoz suggested that the US government had set the annihilation of all Chicanos/as as an objective. Although Rosalío Muñoz does not accuse 'whites' or Anglo-Americans of genocide in general – but rather speaks against systemic patterns and governmental actions – he contributes to a reproduction of counterhegemonic discourses with logics of inclusion (of Chicanos/as) and exclusion (of all others). Therefore, he himself gets caught up in nationalist binaries.

These performative actions, including for instance the public reading of the names of the Chicano casualties, *Reconquista* marches throughout the Southwest,[13] and the large L.A. demonstrations, were organized and communicated by Southwest-based Chicano/a journals and newspapers, but most importantly via posters in the streets. Not only did these posters call upon Chicanos/as to protest against the Vietnam War and to demonstrate for civil rights by presenting iconographies reminiscent of revolution and protest (such as the clenched fist as a reference to the Mexican Revolution) prior to the demonstrations; but also in retrospect, when calling for subsequent demonstrations, they processed what had occurred during previous events where Chicanos/as and the police had clashed and thus contributed to inscribing these often violent incidents into Chicano/a collective memory.

Most notable were the repercussions of the death of Rubén Salazar during the anti-Vietnam demonstration in L.A. in 1970; his image was displayed on posters and silkscreens advertising gallery expositions as well as theater plays that dealt with the relationship of Chicano/a nationalism and Vietnam. These plays narrated the story of Salazar's violent death during the anti-war demonstration in 1970 from a Chicano/a point of view (Lipsitz 75). Lipsitz stresses that Chicano/a poster artists got their inspiration from the representations of liberation movements in various parts of the world. As a consequence, they frequently cited those local and regional movements and showed their interconnectedness:

> Poster images reinforced organic solidarity within the Chicano Movement, but […] also helped create connecting ideologies to link *chicanismo* with anticolonial nationalist struggles around the world [and] inspired by the affinities between antiracist campaigns in the U.S. and anticolonial movements overseas. (78; original emphasis)

This ideological connex appeared in various forms of cultural production; poetry, theater, narratives, performances, and music linked the struggle for equality at

[13] E. Chávez asserts that this *Marcha de la Reconquista* was organized by the Chicano Moratorium that had previously organized the Chicano/a anti-war protests and then "had abandoned its single-issue focus on police brutality in favor of a wide range of vague goals" (77), as for example the 'retaking' of the Southwest as a response to Anglo invasion.

home with the Vietnamese struggle for liberation. Various forms of visual art – primarily posters and murals – were influenced both by the Cuban *talleres* established in the aftermath of the Cuban Revolution and by Mexican modern artists.

**Fig.** 1: Malaquías Montoya, "Vietnam Aztlán: Chicano Vietnam Project." Berkeley, 1973.

One of the most cited artworks on the solidarity between Chicanos/as and the Vietnamese is Malaquías Montoya's poster "Vietnam Aztlán" distributed in the San Francisco Bay Area. Vertically, it is divided into three sections; horizontally, in two mirroring halves – one representing the Chicano/a side, the other the Vietnamese one. The middle part shows a peasant on the left-hand side, who can be identified as Vietnamese by way of his conical hat *Nón lá* and his yellow-toned skin color. The right-hand side shows a Chicano *campesino*, who, in turn, can be recognized via the *cholo* headband and 'bronze'[14] skin color. By using peasant symbolism for representing the Vietnamese people and the Chicanos/as, the artist refers to the similarities both peoples presumably share. Not only is the *cholo* headband an identity marker for Chicanas/os; but it also, just like the Vietnamese hat, points towards the exhausting work on the fields and the need for a protective

[14] Apart from *brown*, *bronze* was often used by Chicanos/as to describe their skin color. Referring not only to the color but also to the alloy made of several metals, the term is used metaphorically to indicate the mix of various ethnic and cultural roots.

shield against the sun, rain, dust, and sweat. Reading this juxtaposition of headgear with critical regionalist methodology as a sign of common colonial oppression, one could argue that putting these two symbols side by side uncovers "the broader cultural, political, historical, and geographical connections" (Reichert Powell 19), namely the liberation discourses of two peoples of color both colonized under the label of 'modernity.'

Romo, dealing with Chicano/a poster production in the sixties, maintains that the clenched fists are "a cultural icon [that] signified power and revolution as it shifted between art form and human form to challenge the incompleteness of democracy" (95). In addition, the peasant symbolism integrates the clenched fists seamlessly into the iconographic representations of class struggles and the international workers' solidarity. They might signify the hands that work and cultivate the land that, both in a Marxist and in an indigenous perspective, oppose the alienation from work and land and resist colonial domination. Therefore, in order to draw the line from Aztlán territory to the lands of Vietnam, the representation of hands as clenched fists equals a critique of capitalism and of economic exploitation of people of color. Thereby, the artist refers to broader patterns of economic exploitation and to global designs of the capitalist logic that colonizes people around the world and promotes imperialist agendas. This view is based on anti-modern, perhaps even pastoral discourses, which condemn and oppose industrialization and technologization per se. This position is reinforced by the use of natural and earthy colors, presenting both Chicanos/as and Vietnamese as peoples living in accord with their environment.

The style in which the peasants' faces are depicted on the poster cites the well-known work on Che Guevara, whose picture has also been used by the Viet Cong in propaganda artworks. Noting that Guevara is not only a paragon of liberation for Chicanos/as, but also for peasants of the Latin American subcontinent, this intermediality underpins the importance of the *campesino/a* within the Chicano/a imaginary. In one of the many stagings of the Chicano/a theaters, Che Guevara and Rubén Salazar are juxtaposed while the following words are being put in Che Guevara's mouth:

> As to the war, hermanos… we will no longer be cannon fodder for the materialist capitalists who are getting rich off the blood of Aztlán. Yes, we are a brave people, but we'll melt the medals we have won to throw back at them, hermanos. (de León qtd. in Mariscal 189)

This quote indicates that the meaning Che Guevara, his achievements and his 'martyrdom' have for Latin America's left, is tantamount to what Rubén Salazar and his engagement against the war signify for Chicanos/as. Once again, the Unites States, as "materialist capitalists," are accused of genocidal intentions towards Chicanos/as. It is assumed that Che Guevara, had he still been alive, would have proclaimed brotherly solidarity with *La Raza (Latinoamericana)*. The act of "throwing back" the medals is envisioned as a political one, symbolizing a refusal to further assimilate into society through material incentives and rather wage war on "material capitalism."

The reception of street posters differs significantly from that of literature or other art forms such as poetry, photographs, films, which mostly (although certainly not always) need to be bought; the reader of a book or the visitor of a gallery must actively decide to take in such forms of art. In contrast, due to its public location, street art, which does not need to be bought, grabs the viewers' attention despite their potential indifference or ignorance regarding the concerns addressed and thus potentially raises consciousness about structural forms of racism, among both oppressed minorities and those groups in positions of power.

Conspicuously, the words are written in both Spanish and Vietnamese. Thus, one could assume that the deliberate use of these languages served to exclude monolingual Anglo-Americans as the dominant group. In spite of that, I argue that this mechanism is dialectical: it oscillates between inclusion and exclusion of white, anglophone Americans as a generalized group (and, in addition, more or less unintentionally, other groups, such as African Americans and Native Americans). Although most Anglo-Americans might not have been familiar with Aztlán as a shorthand for cultural nationalist ideologies, the simple linguistic codes, along with the distinctive peasant and protest iconography, attempt to ensure that the message is understood nonetheless: Chicanos/as, in solidarity with the Vietnamese people, claim freedom for themselves and the Vietnamese.

Although the meaning of the Vietnamese signs might have been guessed by Spanish-speaking people in the United States, their use is not only an appropriation of Vietnamese signs and language, but is furthermore the takeover of slogans that have been appropriated and often been used before by mainly white peace movements and Marxist groups (*solidarity* as a mere translation of "đoàn kết" does not exist in the Vietnamese language). Even the English-speaking viewer can possibly grasp the seemingly obvious meaning of the Vietnamese signs. On the one hand, the division of the poster suggests that both sections mirror each other and that the words are translations or at least correspondences of each other. On the other hand, invocations like "đoàn kết" were often used as slogans by other (Anglophone) peace movements. Nevertheless, the use of 'foreign' languages must have had and alienating and hence excluding effect on Anglo-American viewers in the first place. Not only does this show that English is not the exclusive language in the Unites States, but it also suggests that eventually, whites (as a generalized group) are not supposed to be part of Aztlán and/or the Southwest and would thus be excluded from the Chicano/a nation-state.

The equal levelling of the headings "Vietnam" and "Aztlán" suggests that Aztlán should be conceived as a nation-state and that the United States had invaded the Southwest illegally and needed to get *fuera de* (that is "out of") Aztlán. The 'enemy' of both Chicanos/as and (North) Vietnam, the United States, is omitted in linguistic as well as graphic representation, but is still present as the aggressor to whom the two figures turn. The representation of both oppressed peoples (of '*bronce*' and 'yellow' skin color) as farmworkers covering each other's back, so to speak, suggests 'brotherhood' and is supposed to evoke a sense of solidarity between the Chicano/a community and the Vietnamese people in their resistance against oppression.

Soon after the Vietnam War had ended in 1975, the activities of the Chicano Movement gradually discontinued since the movement "developed a broad range of agendas that were not primarily rooted in an ethnic-based, grassroots perspective [...]. Rather, they had become a complex amalgam of interests, backgrounds, and goals" (Gómez-Quiñones and Vásquez xx). However, I would like to argue that this amalgam of interests, background and goals had ever existed and that simply the unwillingness of some leading figures to keep the movement open to diversity had led to the fracturing of the movement. Chabram and Fregoso, for instance, criticize the constructivist nature of the myth as well as its normative character which is inevitably accompanied by mechanisms of inclusion and exclusion: "[i]n its most extreme cases, Aztlán was said to be located in the deepest layers of consciousness of every Chicano, an identification which thereby posited an essential Chicano subject for cultural identity" (204). Thus, Chicano/a cultural identity was built upon an essentialist understanding of *chicanismo*, further distancing marginalized Chicanas/os such as gays, women, Chicanos/as with African Americans roots, or exclusively anglophone Chicanos/as from the movement instead of unifying them under one roof. Although a grassroots movement, the movement's radical organizers as well as its intellectuals simply ignored the diversity of their constituency and thus squandered the opportunity to seek a dialogue with both subgroups and external groups.

As proclaimed in the program of "El Plan Espiritual de Aztlán," nationalism was considered "the key [that] transcends all religious, political, class, and economic factions or boundaries [and as] the common denominator that all members of La Raza can agree upon" (National Chicano Youth Conference). This notion of nationalism as an ideology shared by all Chicanos/as is questionable in at least two points. Firstly, by explicitly incorporating only Chicanos/as into Aztlán, the idea of the eventual nation-state reinforces racial boundaries and excludes all non-Chicanos/as. Thus, the idea deliberately set aside that Native Americans, African Americans, Anglo-Americans, and other groups called the Southwest their home and that likewise they tied their identity closely to that region. Secondly, the Plan assumed that (cultural) nationalism is shared by all Chicanos/as. Since the leaders of the Chicano Movement further reproduced patterns of white heteronormative and racist discourse in 'bronze,' there were large (intersecting) groups of Chicanas, gays, moderates, or Chicanos/as with white, black, or other origins that did not find themselves apprehended and therefore felt alienated from Aztlán and excluded from the Chicano/a community. In terms of critical regionalism, Reichert Powell argues that regions, albeit often constructed otherwise, are not a stable, boundaried, and autonomous place. Rather, they are the result of "the cumulative, generative effects of the interplay among various competing definitions of that region" (5). Thus, the movement – like many other movements based on essential qualities – fractured since it left aside conflicts about competing definitions of Aztlán and tried to bring all Chicanos/as into line.

Once again, taking up the idea of Aztlán as a palimpsest, one needs to emphasize that Chicanos/as failed to recognize that they too had added layers to the myth by circulating, modifying, and deploying it for their own purposes. Padilla criticizes the invention of a myth of a golden past and the potential misunderstanding of or blindness toward history. He notes that Chicanos/as worshipped their imperialist ancestors – the Aztecs – who built their empire "on the toil and blood of those thousands of native compatriots they forced into slavery, and whose history and literature they also attempted to destroy" (124) and who, in their society, were as oppressive as their current enemy (ibid.).

That way, Chicanos/as legitimized the idea of Aztlán as a future nation-state, based on their admiration of the Aztec civilization, and at the same time argued that they shared the fate of Anglo invasion with the Vietnamese people. However legitimate and comprehensible the latter is, was, or might be, large parts of the Chicano Movement did not recognize that they adopted Aztec cosmology uncritically by drawing on elements that seemed usable and by leaving out others that would undermine their claims. Rather than building on a diverse base and the commonalities and experiences people shared, the idea of Aztlán was dichotomously constructed in relation to the 'enemy.' Thereby, it referred to what it should *not* be like, rather than seizing on ideals Chicanos/as shared with other groups and which could have had the potential to bring forth alternative logics differing from the structures of white hegemonic discourses such as coloniality/modernity. By establishing a counterhegemonic discourse and in the process reproducing the racist and also sexist structures the movement originally wanted to overcome, Chicanos/as partially shed their credibility and integrity.

Especially Chicanas found themselves marginalized by the intersection of race and gender.[15] The conviction that sexism preceded racism provided the underlying framework for the revolutionist currents of the Chicana Movement. In contrast to reformist Chicanas, the revolutionist Chicanas argued that there could not be racial equality unless there was gender equality. The reformist Chicanas, on the other hand, believed that their radical Chicana 'sisters' would weaken the movement and keep it from achieving its aims. They argued that gender equality would be less of a problem once racial equality was established (Pesquera and Segura 79, 85).[16]

[15] On the intersectionalities of race and gender within and outside social movements in the Unites States, see Dietze. She investigates the power relations between African American women and white men and how, as a consequence, images of the 'black man' are constructed. The basic tenor thereof can be transferred to Chicano/a studies. In the end she raises the question of what was first: racism or sexism (357-58).

[16] Regarding the different approaches between Chicana radical feminists and loyalist Chicanas, Pesquera and Segura provide a useful overview on Chicana discourses.

The Chicano Moratorium was organized mainly by men. The most popular argument to keep Chicanas out of anti-war politics was the transfer of *machismo* from the realm of war(fare) in Vietnam to the fight in the 'war at home': women did not serve in the military and therefore did not know what it was like to fight in a war on Vietnam or on the streets at home. Hence, women were kept from engaging in anti-war or anti-draft actions and thus did not hold leading positions in the movement. For instance, even feminist writers blundered into that trap of calling especially on soldiers to fight against the war: "[a]nd our Soldado Raso knows his Machismo belongs to his people, to be used for his people not against them, to be used right here in the heartland of mi Raza, in Aztlán" (Longeau y Vásquez 199).[17] By linking *machismo* (the pun here being that *macho* in Spanish both means 'male' and 'brave') with the soldier in Vietnam, Longeau y Vásquez assumes that Chicanas cannot use their commitment for the advancement of civil rights. Although occasionally mentioned, women in this text appear rather as men's 'sidekicks' and are not called on to stand in against the war or nationalist claims.

Ironically, the notion of *machismo* and masculinity is not questioned but reversed and invigorated in a new form: not the soldier who goes to war is perceived particularly masculine and patriotic anymore; it is the man who stays at home to fight the war and exerts his abilities for his people and for *la patria*. Whereas Rodolfo "Corky" Gonzáles, leader of the Denver-based organization Crusade for Justice, considers the "rejected military service as a testing ground for Mexican American manhood" (Oropeza 75), his Californian counterpart César Chávez appropriates and crosses the Christian idea of the 'sacrifice,' both predominant among both Chicano/as and Mexicans, with his (and many Chicanos'/as') idea of manliness stemming from the Mexican Revolution and the images of the revolutionaries: "I am convinced that the truest act of courage, the strongest act of manliness is to sacrifice ourselves for others in a totally non-violent struggle for justice. To be a man is to suffer for others. God help us to be men!" (qtd. in Mariscal 205). Thus, he either does not consider women as potential addressees in a speech about courage or he implies that women are not capable nor desired to engage in anti-war politics.

The subsuming of Chicanas in the political project and the overwriting of Chicanas' histories, thus, excluded them from substantial decisions over the political agenda and orientation. Reichert Powell once again refers to a kind of layering – i.e. a kind of palimpsest – when he speaks of the experiences and interpretations that are tied around a specific location. Metaphorically speaking, he

[17] In a footnote, Longeau y Vásquez explains the meaning of the Soldado Raso as follows: "The song 'El Soldado Raso' became popular among Mexican Americans during the Second World War. It spoke of a plain foot soldier, a 'soldado raso' from the verb 'rasar' meaning to level, saying goodbye to his mother and his sweetheart. In the original articles the phrase was spelled 'soldado razo' perhaps an unintentional allusion to 'la raza' although in Spanish the 's' and the 'z' sound alike" (Espinoza and Oropeza 197).

argues that "the layers have been bent, folded, broken, and melted into each other" (35). Thus, Chicanas had their own specific experiences of both the Vietnam War and their interpretations of Aztlán. These differed significantly from those of Chicanos. The competing, and sometimes incompatible, interpretations laid bare structural problems within the organization of the movement and challenged the idea of what independence actually meant.

While Chicanas were implicitly included in Aztlán, other groups, such as Native Americans, Chicanos/as with African American roots, or Chicanos/as departing from a tacit heteronormativity, were rejected. The Chicanos/as understood themselves as an indigenous people who inhabited the Southwest before anybody else and who rejected their European and *mestizo/a* heritage; the notion that the community had potential connections with other groups did not register to any larger extent. Although even radical parts of the movement cooperated frequently with other groups, those alliances were subordinated to the project of the nation-state. "El Plan" explicitly excluded other minorities: "Por La Raza todo. Fuera de La Raza nada" (National Chicano Youth Conference). On the other hand, one needs to bear in mind that this kind of regressive nationalism, both found in Chicano/a discourses as well as in African American discourses, hindered the movements from fruitful cooperation. It restricted their potential in building macro-narratives, which "are neither (or at least not only) revisionist narratives nor narratives that intend to tell a different truth but, rather, narratives geared toward the search of a different logic" (Mignolo 22). Manuel Gómez, the draft refuser aforementioned, responds to the colonial logic in one particular way when he puts the Chicano Movement's line of thinking in a nutshell: "Too many of my brothers have been killed fighting for a lie called 'American freedom,' both in our streets and in foreign lands" (141).

## Works Cited


Aguayo, Emilio. "La Chispa: Chicanos and the Vietnam." *MEChA Newsletter*, 1972. Print.

Alaniz, Yolanda, and Megan Cornish. *Viva la Raza: A History of Chicano Identity & Resistance*. Seattle: Red Letter Press, 2008. Print.

Anaya, Rudolfo A., and Francisco Lomelí. *Aztlán: Essays on the Chicano Homeland*. Albuquerque: Academia/El Norte Public, 1989. Print.

Anonymous. "Chicano Moratorium." *La Raza* 1.1 (1969): 5-8. Print.

Arellano, Joseph. "Victims of Machismo." *El Grito del Norte* 4.9 (1971): 4-5. Print.

Barrera, Mario Charles, and Carlos Muñoz. "The Barrio as an Internal Colony." *La Causa Política: A Chicano Politics Reader*. Ed. F. Chris Garcia. Notre Dame: University of Notre Dame Press, 1974: 281-301. Print.

Chabram, Angie, and Rosa Linda Fregoso. "Chicano/a Cultural Representations: Reframing Alternative Critical Discourses." *Cultural Studies* 4.3 (1990): 203-16. Print.

Chávez, Ernesto. *"¡Mi Raza Primero!": Nationalism, Identity, and Insurgency in the Chicano Movement in Los Angeles, 1966-1978*. Berkeley: University of California Press, 2002. Print.

Chávez, John R. *The Lost Land: The Chicano Image of the Southwest*. Albuquerque: University of New Mexico Press, 1984. Print.

Cooper Alarcón, Daniel. "The Aztec Palimpsest: Toward a New Understanding of Aztlán, Cultural Identity and History." *Aztlán* 19.2 (1988): 33-68. Print.

Dietze, Gabriele. *Weiße Frauen in Bewegung: Genealogien und Konkurrenzen von Race- und Genderpolitiken*. Bielefeld: Transcript, 2013. Print.

Espinoza, Donne, and Lorena Oropeza. *Enriqueta Vasquez and the Chicano Movement: Writings from El Grito del Norte*. Houston, TX: Arte Público Press, 2006. Print.

Gómez, Manuel. "I Am My Brother in the Same Struggle for Justice." Reprinted from *La Raza* 1.1 (1969): 7. *The Chicanos: Life and Struggles of the Mexican Minority in the United States*. Ed. Gilberto López y Rivas. New York: Monthly Review Press, 1973: 140-42. Print.

---. "Untitled." *La Raza* 1.1 (1969): 7. Print.

Gómez-Quiñones, Juan, and Irene Vásquez. *Making Aztlán: Ideology and Culture of the Chicana and Chicano Movement, 1966-1977*. Albuquerque, University of New Mexico Press: Contextos, 2014. Print.

Gonzales, Rodolfo, and Alberto Urista [Alaurista, pseud.] "El plan espiritual de Aztlan." *El Grito del Norte* 2.9 (6 July 1969): 5. Print.

Gutiérrez, Ramón A. "Internal Colonialism: An American Theory of Race." *Du Bois Review: Social Science Research on Race* 1.2 (2004): 281-95. Print.

Jameson, Fredric. "Periodizing the 60s." *Social Text* 9.10 (1984): 178-209. Print.

Leal, Luis. "In Search of Aztlán." Translated by Gladys Leal. Anaya and Lomelí 6-13. Print.

de León, Nephtalí. *Five Plays*. Denver: Totinem, 1972. Print.

Lipsitz, George. "Not Just Another Social Movement: Poster Art and the Movimiento Chicano." Noriega 72-90. Print.

Longeau y Vásquez, Enriqueta. "El Soldado Raso de Hoy." 29 August 1970. *Enriqueta Vasquez and the Chicano Movement: Writings from El Grito del Norte*. Eds. Donne Espinoza and Lorena Oropeza. Houston, TX: Arte Público Press, 2006: 197-200. Print.

Longeau y Vásquez, Enriqueta, and Elizabeth Sutherland Martínez. *Viva la Raza!: The Struggle of the Mexican American People*. Garden City, NY: Doubleday, 1974. Print.

López y Rivas, Gilberto. *The Chicanos: Life and Struggles of the Mexican Minority in the United States*. New York: Monthly Review Press, 1973. Print.

Lozada, Frobén. "What it's about." Chicano Symposium. Hayward. 13 November 1969. Ed. Roger Alvarado et al. *La Raza! Why a Chicano Party? Why Chicano Studies?: A Socialist Workers Party Pamphlet on the Chicano Movement.* 2nd Printing. New York: Pathfinder Press, 1970: 12-15. Print.

Mariscal, George. *Aztlán and Viet Nam: Chicano and Chicana Experiences of the War*. Berkeley: University of California Press, 1999. Print.

Mignolo, Walter. *Local Histories/Global Designs: Coloniality, Subaltern Knowledges, and Border Thinking*. Princeton, NJ: Princeton University Press, 2012. Print.

National Chicano Youth Conference. "El Plan Espiritual de Aztlán." Denver, 1969.

Noriega, Chon A. (ed.). *Just Another Poster?: Chicano Graphic Arts in California*. Santa Barbara: University of California Press, 2001. Print.

del Olmo, Frank. "Moratorium Unit Blames Violence on 'Repression.'" *Los Angeles Times* 29 January 1971: 6. Print.

Oropeza, Lorena. *¡Raza Sí! ¡Guerra No! Chicano Protest and Patriotism During the Viet Nam War Era*. Berkeley: University of California Press, 2005. Print.

Padilla, Genaro M. "Myth and Comparative Cultural Nationalism: The Ideological Uses of Aztlán." Anaya and Lomelí 111-34. Print.

Pérez-Torres, Rafael. "Remapping Chicano Expressive Culture." Noriega 151-70. Print.

Pesquera, Beatriz M., and Denise A. Segura. "Beyond Indifference and Antipathy: The Chicano Movement and Chicano Feminist Discourse." *Aztlán* 19.2 (1988-1990): 69-92. Print.

Price, Patricia L. *Dry Place: Landscapes of Belonging and Exclusion*. Minneapolis: University of Minnesota Press, 2004. Print.

Reichert Powell, Douglas. *Critical Regionalism: Connecting Politics and Culture in the American Landscape*. Chapel Hill: University of North Carolina Press, 2007. Print.

Romo, Tere. "Points of Convergence: The Iconography of the Chicano Poster." Noriega 91-115. Print.

# From Grafenwoehr to 'Graf': A Transnational American Region in Bavaria

*Birgit M. Bauridl*

## Introduction

On June 30, 2010, American soldiers stationed in Grafenwoehr, a military training area in the Upper Palatinate, Bavaria, Germany, gathered together with invited German soldiers and with the German local and the American civilian communities of Grafenwoehr. They witnessed the reenactment of the first shot fired at the Grafenwoehr Training Area (GTA). This shot was not fired by the US Army after World War II during the times of the occupation, but by the Bavarian Army's 21-year-old cannoneer Michael Kugler in 1910 from Gruenhund Hill, now the area of the 7$^{th}$ US Army's Joint Multinational Training Command's Shooting Range 114. After the German Brigadier General Johann Berger, the Deputy Commanding General for Defense District Command IV, and German soldiers clad in historic Bavarian army uniforms had executed the reenactment with a historic howitzer, the Commanding General of the 7$^{th}$ US Army's Joint Multinational Training Command (JMTC), Steven L. Salazar, set off a US 1$^{st}$ Battalion, 84$^{th}$ Field Artillery's M109A6 Paladin howitzer, "the most technically advanced howitzer in the US Army today," as the corresponding US Army news article claims (Beaton). Salazar commented on the symbolic ringing-in of the GTA's second century: "We at the JMTC aspire to be the most impressive, respected training facility in the US Army. We are working with the Bundeswehr, our many multinational partners, and the city of Grafenwoehr to move this installation forward into the 21$^{st}$ century. It is tremendously gratifying to me" (Beaton).

The commemorative event of 1910/2010 celebrating German-American cooperation in Bavaria illustrates paradigmatically how the Grafenwoehr Training Area and its cultural phenomena fuse diverse levels of spatio-cultural discourses ranging from local to regional to national, from domestic to foreign, from communally defined to transnational. It reveals that the area surrounding the GTA is by no means a closed-up entity but a culturally complex space open to and defined by diverse past and present appropriations and constructions. As a 'region,' the Grafenwoehr area does not constitute a clearly defined geographical, politically-organized, and mono-cultural static space. It rather is a palimpsestic dynamic and processural construct, ever-evolving from diverse and at times even clashing cultural, communal, and political discourses, ideologies, definitions, and memories. In his book *Critical Regionalism*, Douglas Reichert Powell notes:

> And, of course, no definition of region – whether it is offered by a scholar, a government commission, a novelist, a Hollywood film – exists in a vacuum. At any site on the landscape, multiple definitions of place are continually in play and at work, sometimes convivially and sometimes antagonistically. Ideas of property, of homeland, of natural resource, of infrastructure; of city, county, school district, economic development zone, environmental hazard; of shit-hole, unspoiled paradise, dullsville; of wildness and weirdness and domestication and discipline – all swirl and interconnect and contend and contest in any given space. (5)

Reichert Powell identifies the practice of critical regionalism as "scholarship on regional culture that approaches the idea of region as a rich, complicated, and dynamic cultural construct rather than a static, stable geophysical entity" (5). "[A] region," Reichert Powell claims, "is not a thing so much as a cultural history, an ongoing rhetorical and poetic construction" (5). In consequence, the critical study of a region may not classify or categorize a space according to presumed particularities that may render that region unique or authentic. On the contrary, it needs to be interested in the dynamics and negotiations of the diverse constructions and appropriations of a region and in the actors and objects, the interests and impacts of such definitions. "In short," Reichert Powell concludes, "the emphasis is not on what regions are but why they are that way, on what they do as much as what has been done to them" (7). 'Region' itself is not a factually demarcating but a conceptually working denomination that symbolizes and points to a "matrix of inquiry" (22). In her programmatic essay "Critical Regionalism and Post-Exceptionalist American Studies," Heike Paul makes a point for a critical regionalism that engages perspectives of transnational American studies. She "argue[s] that the framework of 'critical regionalism' is useful for conceiving of American studies not in narrowly confined national and exceptionalist models and that it allows us to address matters of space, place, and occasionally, 'placelessness' […] in terms of interconnections and comparisons moving beyond and across the nation state" (397). Paul's seminal assessment of the state of critical regionalism and of transnational perspectives within critical regionalism – explorations of the hemispheric (American) South, of the (American) "West in local and global dimensions" (406), of connections between the Midwest and Ireland, or of transnational diasporic formations such as the Black Atlantic – as well as her own discussion of the role of Frederick Jackson Turner and his version of the American frontier in German discourse, not only stress the "discursive 'production'" of regions (398). With the innovative appropriation of Elisabeth Bronfen's "concept of 'crossmapping'" (399) in order to "explore the function of regional formations" and their involvement in "local-local" or "local-global trajectories" (420), Paul emphasizes a critical regionalism that is "in recognition of complex processes of cultural mobility" (399).

The present article focuses on the dynamics of cultural encounters with US participation and their interrelation with the spaces that host or produce them. It follows Heike Paul's call for a "recognition of complex processes of cultural mobility" (399) and views region from and within a transnational perspective. Yet instead of scrutinizing the respective transnational trajectories and impacts of a region fully or partially located inside the United States, this article shifts the focus to a region fully *outside* the conventional borders of the United States and *spatio-temporalizes* the exploration of transnational trajectories into the past. As a focal point, it takes one particular region in Germany which historically has been and in the present continues to be a specific site of intense cultural contact.

This essay approaches Grafenwoehr with the idea of 'region' as a 'matrix of inquiry.' This perspective entails to acknowledge, first, that regions – albeit spatial 'units' which cannot be defined with geographical or political categories of organization such as state or nation – are entangled in discourses that transcend their own fuzzy borders and which turn themselves into dynamic contact zones. Second, an approach to Graf as a region emphasizes that cultural contact and transfer happen both on a vertical/diachronic and on a horizontal/synchronic level. Third, Graf as a region is in both dimensions defined by multiple co- and sub-constructions, i.e. diverse appropriations and projections ranging from the level of the local to the (German or US) national to the transnational. Here, 'region' refers to the unstable boundaries and fluctuating margins of a supposedly closed entity. Rather than applying the more militarily-defined and spatially-closed term, GTA-Grafenwoehr Training Area, or the German-language reference to a Bavarian rural town, Grafenwoehr, or the organizational term politically, geographically, and demographically marking the Upper Palatinate, the article uses the German-American nickname that tags the region and signifies its transcultural construction: Graf.

The cultural spectacle of the first shot reenactment is only one cultural materialization – although a double one in its characteristic as a corporeal happening turned into a visual/photographic record – that condenses the complex multi-layered and multi-sited palimpsest of Graf. Ultimately, this article argues that contemporary cultural phenomena may serve as trajectories into the complex and multifarious diachronic and synchronic appropriations and projections of Graf. Vice versa, as the smallest crystallization of the dynamics of the region, they exhibit Graf itself as a condensation and a palimpsestic prism of larger diachronic and synchronic processes of cultural mobility and transfer.

## Regional Groundwork, Conceptual Pathways

Douglas Reichert Powell "argue[s] that regionalism, despite traditionally being used to describe, define, and isolate networks of places and spaces, can provide a rhetorical basis for making claims about how spaces and places are connected to spatially and conceptually broader patterns of meaning" (4). Regions are by no means isolated from larger processes, but "the very practices of place construction that seem to exempt regional spaces from broader cultural conflicts are themselves implicated in the patterns of change they seem to defy" (14). For Graf, this means an embeddedness within a swirl of multiple local, national, and transnational discourses.[1] Analyzing Graf as a space and a region, one should thus heed the programmatic call of transnational American studies to pay critical attention to not only transnational phenomena, but also to the local and national, i.e. to different 'levels' of communal/social organization. Heinz Ickstadt argues:

> Between the local and the global there is still the 'national' as a category requiring continuous analysis. [...] [the] United States must be studied as a distinctive collective entity (however heterogeneous or divided it may perceive itself to be) within a network of global or transnational interrelatedness. (551)

Shelley Fisher Fishkin, in her often-quoted and highly programmatic 2004 presidential address to the American Studies Association and its subsequent publication in the *American Quarterly* as "Crossroads of Cultures," urges:

> We are likely to focus less on the United States as a static and stable territory and population whose most characteristic traits it was our job to divine, and more on the nation as a participant in a global flow of people, ideas, texts, and products – albeit a participant who often tries to impede those flows. (24)

While Fishkin and Ickstadt in their programmatic elaborations on the dos and don'ts of transnational American studies emphasize the impact and effectiveness of the nation (like Bryce Traister in his seminal "The Object of Study; or, Are We Being Transnational Yet?"), they nevertheless point to different levels of spatial and at the same time communal, social, and cultural organization that are to play a role in transnational American studies. Their notion of the nation displays an understanding of the nation not as an independent and unaffected stable container but as affected by and participating in transnational processes.

The example of the First Shot Reenactment in the Grafenwoehr Training Area suggests to not only acknowledge the nation as an active or passive agent in transnational processes but to also shift the focus to presumably even smaller

[1] Also see Michael McAteer in Merrett's "What Is Region and Nation? A Forum": "[T]he first question 'What is Region and Nation?' has an implicit essentialism. Any attempt to create a priori definitions of region and nation is flawed; region and nation are discursively constructed. Further, the question 'what external pressures weigh on region and nation?' implies that multiculturalism and cosmopolitanism are external to region and nation. The opposite is true: multiculturalism and cosmopolitanism inscribe themselves within the concept of region and nation" (655). See also Frampton quoted in Eggener: "Regional or national cultures," Frampton wrote in 1985, "must today, more than ever, be ultimately constituted as locally inflected manifestations of 'world culture'" (233).

spatial, communal, and cultural 'units' and to view them as involved in transnational or transcultural processes. In her "Crossroads of Cultures," Fishkin continues: "Our continued focus on local spaces will attend to the ways in which these spaces participate in global phenomena – 'internal' and 'external' migrations, the diffusion of cultural forms, the spread of capital and commodities – and all the attendant consequences" (24). Similar to her own and Ickstadt's portrayal of national spaces and in sync with Gayatri Spivak's 2007 *Who Sings the Nation State?*, which "invokes critical regionalism as going 'under and over nationalism,' a possibility between borders" (Comer 162), Fishkin illustrates the impact and impetus of transnational processes in 'local spaces.'

Such characterizations of local spaces resemble the idea of the 'contact zone.'[2] In her 1991 "The Arts of the Contact Zone," Mary Louise Pratt sees contact zones as "social spaces where cultures meet, clash, and grapple with each other, often in contexts of highly asymmetrical relations of power, such as colonialism, slavery, or their aftermaths" (34). John Carlos Rowe characterizes "the 'contact zone' as the liminal region or 'borderzone' in which different cultures meet and negotiate – violently or otherwise – their 'neighborhood'" (12). While Pratt and Rowe predominantly refer to representations of contact zones and textual debates, they nevertheless identify spaces that from the perspective of the transnational can be defined as nodes in transnational networks – or, to borrow Udo Hebel's metaphor – as 'turntables' of transnational or transcultural processes (2014b).

In this sense, Graf functions as a regional turntable of transnational and transcultural processes. The conceptual connection of 'transnational' and 'region' neither claims the 'transnational' as a fixed qualifier nor the 'region' as a clearly identifiable space, but – in parallel to Laura Briggs, Gladys McCormick, and J. T. Way's call for an investigative use of the term and concept 'transnational' – as a "category of analysis" and as a "matrix of inquiry" (Reichert Powell) that prompt the scholar to scrutinize and complicate exactly the issues the two terms entail when employed as essential denominators and categories. It understands region not as a coherent, permanent, non-porous, and clearly marked and defined geographical, cultural, or ideological unit distinguishable from the local or national, but as a flexible construct that prompts the discipline of American studies in particular to ask and investigate questions that deal with a discursive fabrication and the tension between a seemingly stable rootedness and its potential for the participation in ongoing change, exchange, transfer, negotiation beyond regional, national, or cultural borders.

The example of the Bavarian and American, of the German and the US military, of the civilian and political reenactment of the first shot at Grafenwoehr demonstrates that narratives, identities, and realities of different communal spaces

2 Also see Comer: "In an era of discourse, the contact zones of Mary Louise Pratt […] help to theorize the intersections of cultural imaginaries, everyday life, and structures of place-d feeling" (163).

overlap, intersect, and negotiate their position. At the same time, the region questions identification of home and away, of domestic and foreign by serving as a point of departure and return for US endeavors abroad, i.e. outside the United States and outside of Germany.[3] There is no clear and valid distinction of spatial 'levels' of communal identification such as local vs. national. (I.e. local places are part of national spaces; the same person may identify with a local place in- or outside a particular nation.) Moreover, assumed communal or organizational 'units' such as local places and nations do not only interact or compete with 'units' on the same spatial 'level' of communal identification. (I.e. local places may agree or disagree with national discourses of the nation they politically are a part of.) Hence, the article moves away from the juxtaposition of 'units' on a supposedly similar 'level' such as nations/national imaginaries or particular local imaginaries etc. and concentrates its attention on the intersection and interaction of discourses that happen on seemingly different levels, i.e. regional discourses and national discourses and their transnational entanglements. Consequently, it views the Graf region as a place that rather is a variety and intersection of imagined places and as a fuzzy space that participates in, is integrated into, is appropriated by, and clashes with other – local, regional, national, transnational – spatial imaginaries. 'Graf' – like Reichert Powell claims for the 'region' – must refer not to a specific site but to a larger network of sites; region is always a relational term (even when it appears not to be)" (4). For this purpose, the article draws on and adapts the concept of triangular American studies – but refrains from conceiving of 'triangular' as comparative or qualifying in regard to interactions between three (national) parties. It rather uses 'triangular' as a working term and category of analysis that prompts questions about complex entanglements – i.e. interactions between and intersections of – more than two (national) agents.

In her article "Towards a Prismatic American Studies," a long under-estimated critique of reductive uses of the concept of the 'transnational,' Jane Desmond identifies "triangulation" as the phenomenon of usually more than two parties – mostly nations – participating in transnational process. She understands triangulation as a programmatic and methodological idea for those endeavors in American studies which investigate the involvement of the United States in transnational processes. She calls for a "prismatic" perspective that extends and complicates traditional bilateral comparisons in a twofold way: it acknowledges that transnational relations may well concern more than two – here: three – parties; and it highlights that discourses about the same transnational phenomenon are multiple and defined by placed knowledges and interests. As the First Shot Reenactment shows, the GTA as a contact zone and turntable region is not only involved in diverse triangular processes between nations – for example Germany,

[3] Also see Amy Kaplan, who, in *The Anarchy of Empire in the Making of U.S. Culture,* argues that "domestic and foreign spaces are closer than we think" (1). Indeed, the contact zone GTA brings the domestic United States and the foreign into immediate local neighborhood.

the United States, and a third nation that may be the venue of US military actions; or the United States, Germany, and the bordering Czech Republic. It is also the site of more than threefold, i.e. of *multi*angular encounters and mutual constructions between the Upper Palatinate, Bavaria, Germany, the United States. Multiangular relationships blur the boundaries of international relations of presumably clearly defined (national) parties into transnational entanglements and complex systems of exchange and change. The processes and negotiations amongst them require not a simply comparative but a connective or, rather, integrative perspective. They require a *trans*angular rather than multiangular approach that recognizes the regional, the national, and the transnational as more than hierarchies or extensions and views them as in- and at the same time interdependent, as interacting, and as floating communal and cultural formations. "Transangular" as a methodological and conceptual metaphor implies the recognition of "more complicated trajectories than simply triple comparisons" and the acknowledgement of the "possibly infinite interconnectedness of all angles into palimpsestic structures" and thus purports a similarly transangular "mode of investigation" (Bauridl and Hebel 457). Moreover, in Graf these transangular encounters do not happen on the same level of spatial identification but between diverse regional, national, and transnational spatial 'units' of identification. For Graf, 'triangular' as a methodological perspective thus has to be shifted not only from 'triangular' to 'multiangular' to 'transangular,' but also from the national level to an investigation of the intersections of and negotiations between (1) regional, (2) national, (3) and transnational narratives and communal or cultural – fuzzy, dynamic, imagined, yet nevertheless effective – 'units' of identification. These three, however, cannot constitute clear-cut, sovereign and independent-from-each-other units, but they intersect, overlap, and are both individual and entangled at the same time. Transangular becomes a metaphor and conceptual perspective that points to mutliangular processes, highlights the resulting 'trans'-entanglements that dissolve clear-cut demarcations of the players in these processes, *and* highlights the intersections of communal/spatial identifications of the players between local, regional, national, and transnational.

To complicate matters, the transnational contact zone Graf extends beyond its present into the past which in turn intersects with the present. The centenntial celebration "100 Years of Grafenwoehr Training Area" shows that the GTA, as one particular spatial manifestation of Graf, was used by various armed forces, from the Bavarian Army to the German Wehrmacht to the United States after WWII to the United States in a contemporary context, and has always been a spatial foil for desires for and negotiations of military, political, imperial, and cultural power. The GTA's landsacpe is a spatial, temporal, and cultural trajectory defined by the interplay of synchronic and diachronic military displays of power, national identity, and transnational cultural encounters. The GTA, as one space within and representation of Graf, is vertically characterized by multiple, palimpsestic layers of diverse cultural and communal presences and imaginaries in the sense of Benedict Anderson's well-known idea of imagined communities – from the Bavarian Army and Upper Palatinate villages 'over'written by the Nazi era, 'over'written by the post-WWII US occupation and territorialization, 'over'written by the contemporary multinational structure led by the United States. Each layer is horizontally shaped by traces of individual and communal mobility and processes of cultural encounters and negotiations. Vertical layers and horizontal mobilities continuously intersect. They make Graf – to employ a conceptual pun on Fishkin's prominent idea of deep maps[4] – a deep space.

Douglas Reichert Powell notes that "our cultural relationships to the landscape are intimately tied with our physical (and virtual) negotiation of it" (3). Similarly, Cheryl Temple Herr in *Critical Regionalism and Cultural Studies: From Ireland to the American Midwest* asserts the intersections of cultural production – although here limited to a mere comparison with textual artefacts – and the regional space. "Like literary and theoretical works," she notes, "individual regions encompass multi-layers that host indigenous meaning, imported material, and varieties of interconnection. […] The important thing is that the restless yearning" – she writes, and I would include mutual definition, appropriation, and multiple encounters – "of one social space for another tends to expose the layering and thresholding of cultures" (9). Vice versa, the physical experience of diverse corporeal presences and past and present face-to-face encounters within one region is prismatically reflected and negotiated in the looking-glass-like cultural productions that spring from that particular region. The vertical and horizontal cultural transfer of the contact zone GTA thus becomes material in its cultural phenomena. Generated within and beyond the immediate realms of the GTA, they bear witness of these multi-communal appropriations and of "the horizontal-vertical dimension" of this particular region (Lim). Like palimpsests, they carry remnants and interact with the cultural and political past of the 'region as contact zone' which they tackle. The cultural materializations of the Graf region can be read as products and agents of the vertical and horizontal processes of cultural transfer and the resulting transangular negotiations of cultural self-definition within and against the foil of the deep space of Grafenwoehr.

## Trajectories: *Die verbotene Landschaft* GTA

A 1993 Bayerisches Fernsehen / Bavarian TV production entitled *US Army Garrison Grafenwoehr: Die verbotene Landschaft*, a documentary of some

[4] Deep Maps connect narratives, memories, imaginaries, and objects – at times overlapping, at times "conflicting interpretations" – to "the location that produced" them (Fishkin 2011: 3). "[F]ocus[ing] on topics that cross borders" (ibid.), Fishkin's digital deep maps are ever-dynamic networks at the same time archiving and shaping the traces and crossroads of past and present individual and collective movements within and outside the nation.

45 minutes, traces the 1990s activities of the US Army, the rural and natural landscape of the Training Area, as well as the communal and cultural life of not only the US military community in the GTA-affiliated towns of Grafenwoehr and Vilseck but also of the adjacent Upper Palatinate communities. The documentary records the synchronic economic interdependence of the two communities and especially the constant experience of cultural exchange: "Die andere Kultur mitzuerleben ist in Grafenwoehr Alltag,"[5] it observes, thereby nonchalantly using the term 'Grafenwoehr' to denote both the Upper Palatinate town and the US military and civil community – and thus to imply a fuzzy entanglement if not to suggest to the German audience a symbiosis. Implicitly, the documentary plays with the multiple layers of the *Landschaft*, the landscape, the natural and cultural space of the Training Area. While one may wonder, why the term *verboten* ("forbidden") was used for a documentary that in its overall tone portrays a friendly relationship and is hesitant to debate cultural, national, or military clashes, multiple possible layers of the the term nevertheless call for a closer look especially when it comes to the landscape. Ranging from possible interpretations such as border consciousness in the face of another national presence to a quasi-exotic fascination with the Other, the term particularly refers to that part of the GTA that was historically and still is used as an impact area and has not been entered since its first uses by the Bavarian Army (fig. 1). This major impact area, together with other hardly tread-upon locations, has developed into an exceptional natural habitat which has won environmental awards and houses the largest Euroepan red deer habitat (see Morgenstern passim). Already in the 1990s, the documentary speaks of a "Paradies für Fischreiher" ("paradise for common herons"), "Schwärme von Staren" ("flocks of starlings"), "seltene Kanadagänse" ("rare Canada geese"), and of a habitat for the, in this region almost extinct, "Sumpfpflanze Wollgras" ("cotton grass, a marsh plant"). After the US Army's long-term, yet in the meantime terminated shooting over the Gruenland pond, so the documentary, artillery remnants have infiltrated the habitat of the water and the fish show signs intoxication and even deformities. The fact that the American military presence has vertically continued the space's *Verbotenheit* materializes in the natural environment of the Upper Palatinate region.

The clearly-defined space of the military GTA reflects the horizontal regional dynamics and impacts of the, at any given time, contemporary encounters as well as the vertical transfer of culturally-defined visual dimensions of the space of Graf. The visual dimensions – in nature or in human architecture – themselves are never just representations but results, traces, and trajectories of human mobility whether voluntary or enforced. As "the outcome, not the backdrop, of social, cultural, political, and economic activity" – that's how Reichert Powell defines the constitution of places (4) – the GTA works like a material Fishkinian deep map

[5] Experiencing and particpating in the other culture is part of everyday life in Grafenwoehr.

that carries the signs of its past and of the pathways of mobility that crossed the region.[6] Bishop summarizes Fishkin's deep maps as

> [scholarly] open-access digital archives that collect all manner of multilinguistic primary and secondary text, paratext, ephemera, oral and written history, critical studies, and interdisciplinary and mixed media – to name just a few possibilities – in a series of overlaying and overlapping palimpsests built on a specific geolocation manifest on the surface of a digital map that serves as gateway to the archive. (2)

The digital deep map is a visual interface that allows an online digging into the multilayered pasts of particular places, thus revealing the respective layers' involvement in transnational processes. The GTA – as one condensation of the processes of the Graf region – can be approached as a non-digital, corporeal deep map. As a *deep space*, the GTA is a node in and miniature materialization of the vertical and horizontal human and cultural mobilities that have shaped the region and have produced its constructions.

Already at the beginning of the 20th century, the arrival of the Bavarian Army led to the dislocation of 300 local villagers from 10 villages. After an episode as a French camp for prisoners of war after World War I, the German Wehrmacht forcefully evacuated 144 square kilometers and 57 villages, among them Haag and Pappenberg, to the GTA's West between 1937 and 1938. On 8 April 1945, the US Army bombed the Grafenwoehr Training Area and the adjacent town before General Patten initiated the occupation of the area on 19 April 1945. The American presence led to further disclocations, for example of the village of Stegenthumbach ("Frucht der Forschung").

It is throughout the US occupation and the US presence today that the traces of the previous local villages and their forceful dislocation by the Nazi regime have remained present in the place's visual architecture. Vice versa, these ghost towns and civilian ghost structures on military ground are visual prisms into diverse cultural and ideological pasts and a marker of the present encounter of US military and former local civil identities.

The more than 500 inhabitants of the village of Haag, which Rudolf Weber identifies as a then regional infrastructural center, took their churchbells with them when they were forced to leave in 1938 (see "Frucht der Forschung"). An old junction as a symbol of civilian architecture of the pre-Nazi times is gradually taken back by nature as a result of the US military presence. Old stone cellars, products of civil procedures in food storage have become the habitat of bats. The old village pond as a previous communal space has expanded and literally grown back into the uninhabited natural environment. The old civil main street as a vibrant spot of the region's past structure has become part of the military tank trail

6 On cultural mobility, see Greenblatt, Zupanov, Paul, et al.

that also encompasses an old beer storage cellar. The remnants of an old cemetery (fig. 2) constitute the most visible culturally produced space that carries the civil traces of the regional past into the transcultural present. Gravestones guide the rare visitor back not only into pre-Nazi but into pre-1900 local times; the ornate sandstone headstones are scarce remnants of the past (Morgenstern 79). In the documentary *Verbotenes Land,* Upper Palatinate locals are shown returning to the site – previously Bavarian, civil, religiously bound to regional culture; now 'American,' international, military, foreign and domestic at the same time, yet in its structure still civil and religious. Morgenstern reports that the visit is part of an annual catholic practice. On All Saint's Day, the locals' traditional commemoration of their ancestors links the local past with past and present religious tradition and with the US or transnational present. The Upper Palatinate locals respond to the 1937 question by local poet Erhard Trummer: "Wenn wir ferne sind und weit, wer wird dann am Grabe beten, zu der Allerseelenzeit?" ("Totengedenken"). They return to the site, which was renovated in 1992 by locals and US and German military organizations in a conscious effort to continue the local religious memorial culture from the past into the future, to preserve traces of their own ancestral past.

The village of Pappenberg – its more than 800 inhabitants were dislocated in 1938 – used to be a pilgrim's destination for its Gothic church with five altars. On 13 February 1939, Pappenberg priest Wolfgang Ederer writes in the village's baptism register after the last baptism before the evacuation:

> Die Pfarrei Pappenberg wurde aus militärischen Gründen aufgelöst (Propter res militares). Die Pfarrangehörigen sind in alle Teile Bayerns zerstreut, weinend sind sie abgezogen (Flentes abierunt). / Pappenberg parish was disbanded for military reasons (Propter res militares). The parishioners are scattered around Bavaria. They left crying (Flentes abierunt). (Morgenstern 71; translation in original)

The site, now close to an Impact Area, has turned into a remnant and reminder of a cultural, in this case religious, past, whose visual and material artifact is characterized by the US military presence: shooting impacts and engravings by US soldiers mark the church ruins as a contact zone of past and present (figs. 3 and 4). Commemorative church services for which local German citizens gain access to the US military area perform present acts of commemoration in spaces that in the past had been places of religious practice, were re-defined as military training grounds, and are now re-used as religious sites by the churchgoers. The rituals of the church services dissolve present and past, regional and national cultures into mere moments in time. In 1938, the villagers took most of the church interior with them when they were relocated to the village of Wolfskofen near Regensburg. The contemporary presence of e.g. the Pappenperg St. Sebastians-Altar and the painting of saint Magreth entitled "Schwarze Margreth von Pappenberg" bear witness to the regional mobility and the intersections of past and present across space. The original of the painting of Virgin Mary had already been taken to Prague during the 1618-1648 War.

Nowadays, commemorative signs in German and English identify the spaces of Haag and Pappenberg, among others, as sites of memory. They indicate the presence of the cultural past and construct the region as a contact zone. They merge cultural, local narratives with the results of national military endeavors and, as physical objects, are smallest material spaces that, like looking glasses, open our gaze into myriad pasts and presents. Their own presence highlights a reversal of the conventional dichotomy of us and them, of domestic and foreign, when they are encountered by Upper Palatinate locals who literally tour the US military ground on guided bus rides organized for example by the German Bundeswehr, the German Forstamt, or the Grafenwoehr Folk and Military Museum (see "Im meterhohen Schnee"; Weber).

The village of Netzaberg, which was disbanded in 1937, has merged into a different present. In September 2006, the construction of the Netzaberg Housing Area for US Army members and relatives began (fig. 5) – the "largest U.S. housing area construction project in Germany" (Morgenstern 93). Previously used for military endeavors, the housing area is now part of the Upper Palatinate City of Eschenbach and features 830 housing units and a US elementary school, a US middle school, and a US child development center. Although integrated into the City of Eschenbach, the housing units are administered by the US garrison housing office. Built in less than three years, all houses follow one of just eleven floor plans and all have a garage, storage room, and garden. The result is the embedding of the architectural structure of US suburban design into the Upper Palatinate landscape. Views of the US Middle School inevitably feature views of the Speinshardt Monastery, and views of the Housing Area show views of the Upper Palatinate City of Eschenbach (Morgenstern 91-96).

(Aerial) Photographs of the Netzaberg Housing Area (figs. 5, 6, and 7) reveal the US suburban grid and can be juxtaposed with US suburban photography and art, e.g. photographs of Levittowns (see fig. 8), photographs by Bill Owens (1970s; see fig. 9) or art by Roger Brown (1990s). This juxtaposition elucidates both the interpictoriality of the images and the inter-spatiality of the area. Hebel defines interpictoriality as follows:

> Similar to concepts of literary intertextuality, the concept of interpictoriality goes beyond the mere documentation and description of relations, influence, and sources; it rather emphasizes the semantic and semiotic implications of the frame(s) of reference and act(s) of signification added to the respective image by means of its interpictorial rhetoric. The interpictorial reading of a specific visual representation underscores the functionality of the semantic surplus produced by the participation in and, particularly significant, possible transformation and resignification of conventions, repertoires and traditions.

> [...] Interpictorially charged visuals [...] complicate assumptions about the immediate accessibility and comprehension of pictures and expose the possibly manipulative structures and strategies of their own uses. (2014a: 414)

While the horizontal correspondence of the images from the German-American Netzaberg with the US suburbs reveals the transnational and transcultural mobility that both produces and finds its reflection in that particular space, the vertical juxtaposition with photographs of the area's past ranging from pre-Nazi times to its US military use to its civilian present highlights the multiple yet vertically porous layers of its past. As a space and place, the Netzaberg Housing Area is characterized by inter-spatiality – a concept used in transposition of Hebel's use of interpictoriality and describing a process that dissolves not only synchronicity and diachronicity but also the unity of the visual space. Netzaberg's interspatiality fuses past and present, German and American, civil and military spaces and imaginaries in one location representative of the dynamics of the region. At the same time it produces spatio-visual associations with US suburban spaces and depictions thereof. The Netzaberg architectural choreography is a material product of the region's existence as a turntable of synchronic and diachronic cultural and national mobility and encounters.

Since the anniversary year of 2010, the visual appearance of the GTA is also defined by a commemorative plaque fixed to a small monument which in itself serves as a prism of the dynamics of the region (fig. 10). This monument, Morgenstern explains in his 2010 *Truppenübungsplatz Grafenwöhr / Grafenwoehr Training Area* – a publication which itself is nothing but a condensed reflection and, at the same time, a segment of the transcultural and transnational processes and constructions of the region – "commemorates the events on June 30, 1910, and 2010" (225). The site of memory at Gruenhund Hill not only commemorates the original 1910 event but also the 2010 act of commemoration. Unveiled during the 2010 ceremonies, it instantly turns the commemorative procedures into a memory and thus highlights the definitional character of the joint transcultural spectacle. The "Marterl,"[7] as Morgenstern chooses to name the commemorative plaque in German with a clear linguistic regional and quasi-religious allusion, carries the logo of the 2010 celebration in its top center. This logo fuses elements of communal discourses on different levels: the Bavarian flag serves as a background for the historic water tower. The tower, which was built in 1911 in Frankonian timber-frame design, was not destroyed in the WWII bombings and continues to serve as a symbol for the GTA and Graf recognized by both German and American locals. The pictorial symbolism is topped with the English-language caption "1910. 2010. Grafenwoehr Training Area. 100 Years." The caption not only points to the

7 Regionally, the term *Marterl* fuses civil/popular and religious practice and denotes a small (Catholic) religious wayside memorial or wayside cross supposed to invite passersby to stop and pray.

American presence but also spans the connection from the Bavarian 1910s to the American 2010s, thus covering and ignoring any histories and national formations in-between.

Images of a historic Bavarian cannon and a contemporary American tank in firing action together with a textual commemoration of the three steps – Bavarian shot in 1910; commemorative reenactment in 2010 by German soldiers; and the 2010 US shot; the latter two instantly historical – stress and enhance the selective vertical dimension of the military and cultural presences from Bavarian to US-American to German as well as the contemporary transnational and transcultural dynamics of the GTA and Graf between locally Upper Palatinate, US-American, and somewhat German. The final statement on the plaque visualizes the tension – obviously not 'felt' as such – between an appropriation and fusion of multiple discourses and the simultaneous self-identification as particular communal identities: "Nur durch gegenseitige Unterstützung können wir unser gemeinsames Ziel erreichen – Frieden. It is through mutual support that we can achieve the ultimate goal – peace." While "mutual support" indicates a confident self-awareness as separate identities, the fuzzy use of the plural pronoun "we" imagines a joint community and makes it impossible to distinguish between American, German, Bavarian, or Upper Palatinate communal identities. The translation of "gemeinsames Ziel" (shared goal) into "ultimate goal" conflates togetherness with the notion of a higher, exceptional goal that is in accordance with American master narratives and ideologies of freedom, peace, and the exceptional(ist) role as the keeper of this peace. These master narratives and ideologies that are now no longer ascribed to a particular national culture but fused in the perceived togetherness that results from both vertical and horizontal cultural mobility are manifest in the region and culturally archived and condensed in the plaque. This process carries the potential to be appropriated by both parties: it may either be read as the region's emancipated and conscious appropriation of American exceptionalism for the purpose of self-elevation; or it may be interpreted as a confirmation of the US 'city upon the hill' endeavor.

## Trajectories: Veteran's Day 2010

Ickstadt claims that the "United States must be studied as a distinctive collective entity (however heterogeneous or divided it may perceive itself to be) within a network of global or transnational interrelatedness" (551). And indeed, as "a hybrid liminal space that is neither fully outside the United States nor comfortably a part of it" (11-12), to borrow Kaplan's phrasing, the GTA not only functions as a transnational contact zone but as a 'domestic space abroad.' It produces and participates in demonstrations of US collective national identity (however imagined this collectivity may be) and national military power ranging from the celebration of national holidays to promotional videos indicating physical strength and technological advancement of the US military. The Graf region as a heterogeneous, dynamic crossroads of past and present cultures and discourses is also co-constructed by US national discourses.

A particular example of a multi-layered cultural performance designed for the perpetuation and affirmation of national collective narratives and imaginaries is the 2010 Veterans Day Celebration, a spectacle that was part of the 2010 anniversary celebrations. While the material, corporeal celebrations by themselves constituted a visual and performative cultural phenomenon, they were brought to a second layer of cultural production when they were broadcast by ESPN in a Veterans Day special live from Grafenwoehr. This event ultimately complicated notions of home and abroad, domestic and foreign by bringing the United States to a US space abroad and by broadcasting the United States abroad back to the United States at home. Screenshots from this TV special continue their visual work on websites associated with the GTA.

One image frequently used in this context is that of ESPN anchors Hannah Storm and Josh Elliot in front of the Grafenwoehr water tower (fig. 11). The image unites the occasion, a US national holiday and cultural event that commemorates its military veterans, with the US military space abroad and with the Upper Palatinate setting in front of the 1911 Bavarian and now transnationally symbolic building. The caption of the banner, "America's Heroes: A Salute to Our Veterans," speaks for itself. On the occasion of the 100$^{th}$ birthday of the GTA and its installation by the Bavarian Army, American veterans of the past and American soldiers of the present stationed in Germany are celebrated via the media as American heroes, whose physical strength represents the nation's military power; as American heroes, who serve their country and especially their country's foreign and military politics not only in domestic realms but on an international level; as American heroes who are soldiers and citizens, fighters, mothers, fathers, wives, and husbands. The ESPN show appropriates if not exploits the physical, visual, cultural, and political geography of the previously occupied region that has been redefined by the US forces as home in opposition to more dangerous deployments abroad (as the following example will demonstrate) to stage national power. The US TV show stages narratives catering to US national desires against the backdrop of a regional space that simultaneously becomes defined as such: backdrop and stage.

A warrior challenge showcases the strength of US soldiers competing in military games on the occasion of the holiday while US civilians cheer and clap. In the finale, the winning 'warriors' clad in military clothing raise their cup and demonstrate US military excellence and bravery on regional grounds that have seen diverse national and cultural histories. The broadcast links these scenes of allegedly exceptional US bravery across continents and brings them to the US audience. One of the highlights of the televised spectacle is Maj. Keith Matiskella's live telephone call to his wife, Maj. Patty Hinshaw, who was then in Afghanistan with the 2$^{nd}$ Stryker Cavalry Regiment. Both Matiskella and his wife, who, via satellite, appears live on a screen, are clad in military uniform. Matiskella holds their toddler son. The scene implicates another complication of the domestic vs. the foreign, of home vs. away. Just as Reichert Powell argues for 9/11 and Hurricane Katrina, the mixture of diverse interpretations of the Graf region – as Upper Palatinate space, as US military space in the foreign Upper Palatinate, as US domestic space in the Upper Palatinate vs. the foreign space of the US war in Afghanistan – "challenge[s] our understandings of spaces and places at a bewildering variety of scales and in a range of tensions: local and global, marginal and peripheral, interior and exterior, foreign and domestic" (3-4). During the phone call, the local Upper Palatinate site of the GTA is constructed as the national home in comparison to the distant Afghanistan. The post-war image of the region as the occupied enemy site that presents the United States as redeemer nation and guardian of democracy is now adjusted into a space that via the successful occupation and democratization can be re-taken as a US home and thus used as a contrast that helps exhibit Afghanistan as a place of atrocities. The reversal of gender roles presented in the scene – the father staying 'at home' with the child – not only suggests a liberal and emancipated structure of the US Army, but is to underscore the bravery of its soldiers and the necessity of its military actions. Even mothers are shown to participate, leaving their children behind, not because they neglect their 'duties' as mothers, but because the tasks abroad are of utmost importance for the security of the child, the nation, and the transnational space of the GTA – "we're doing something good here" says Maj. Hinshaw ("ESPN DVIDS Highlights"). The ESPN broadcast exposes the Graf region as defined by, among others, discourses of transnational mobility – the US presence in Bavaria, the US presence in Afghanistan, the connection of the Afghan and German settings – and by instances of US national self-(re)presentation. It also illustrates that the Graf region – like the landscapes of 9/11 or Hurricane Katrina – is not simply a meeting ground of cultural or diverse national encounters, but a pawn and playing field for the interests of the players. If the player is by the locals (or nationals) of the region considered a powerful and desirable teammate, the region may contribute to or at least not disrupt the game.

A free steak lunch served to American families by the GTA staff, similarly, within the setting of the region, affirms and circulates images of the nation and the US military. Lt. Gen. John D. Gardner, US European Command deputy commander, and Brig. Gen. Steven L. Salazar, commanding general of the 7$^{th}$ US Army Joint Multinational Training Command, grilled and served steaks to the multi-ethnic American audience at the Grafenwoehr dining facility, Grafenwoehr, Germany, on Veterans Day, 2010. The free steak lunch is staged to emphasize diversity as exemplary and as American in Randolph Bourne's problematically exceptional sense of the transnational and conveys the idea of the US military as ethnically integrated. It constitutes a visual display of the military not serving its own purposes but the nation, i.e. American families, and stages the generals as the representatives of political and military power who are not only close to their soldiers but who participate in nurturing the nation. Again with the Upper Palatinate region and the US presence in Bavaria appropriated as a spatial point of departure, the performance of this event thus points to other well-circulated scenes and performances in 'American culture.' On the grounds of the vertically multi-layered contact zone Graf, the visual dimension of the performance reaches into present and past iconographies of American narratives and ideologies. The Graf scene is reminiscent of President Bush's visit to the American troops in Baghdad in 2003, when he, as the proverbial pater familias served a turkey to the soldiers and stressed his protective and protecting role for the US nation. Bush's carefully staged image evokes Norman Rockwell's 1943 "Freedom from Want." The region that is appropriated as a stage becomes a node in an unfolding network of multiple cultural and national narratives. Its own image is co-constructed within these narratives and, vice versa, the region itself becomes a part of these narratives.[8] In the case of the ESPN broadcast, the Graf region is used as a site for American self-definition and consequently becomes (reduced to) an American-defined space, a setting of American military and national discourses. The fact that the region figures in the ESPN American military and national narrative transnationalizes the ESPN narrative and makes obvious that the region participates in transnational processes; yet the ESPN narrative presents the region neither as an independent or equal player nor as participant in a hybrid US-German transnational formation but as a mere backdrop in a transnational *America*.

The ESPN Veterans Day broadcast culminates in the first reunion of German and American soldiers after the German soldiers had been rescued from a Taliban attack by the American soldiers in Afghanistan in 2009. It is stressed that the Americans received the Gold Cross for Valor from the German government. This example perpetuates a notion of US military bravery and excellence on a transnational level and suggests the power of the United States to create an environment of safety on a transnational level. Moreover, it creates a complex web of dependence and hierarchical structures between the American and German side. American soldiers rescued German soldiers; the German government honors the American soldiers and thus is portrayed as acknowledging the exceptional status of the United States and its soldiers; they are reunited on ground that is difficult to identify as German or American, yet whether it is German or American, it is used as the site of American demonstrations of geographical and physical power. The event is keyed by the national anthem in the beginning, and the broadcast ends not only with the words "You are strong, you are committed, serving our country" but with Toby Keith's song "American Soldier," ultimately stressing national narratives and ideologies such as hard work, freedom, liberty, heroism, and American national identity ("ESPN Veterans Day"). On a metaphorical level, the framing of the Upper Palatinate setting by the US national anthem becomes a discursive occupation of the region's cultural geography.

8 For a discussion of an interpictorial cluster of presidential photography, see Hebel 2014a.

The cultural event of the 2010 Veterans Day and its visual transmission both in its concrete live realization and in multiple images and videos that are being circulated online on military, news, and social networking portals interpret the contact zone GTA and its non-American history as a stage for American narratives. Enabling and perpetuating the image of a communal experience between ESPN anchors, American soldiers in Germany and Afghanistan, as well as with these soldiers' families as representatives of all American families and, ultimately, all American citizens, the visual construction of the Veterans Day in Grafenwoehr, Germany, creates an American space beyond borders – a transnational American space, i.e. a transnational space that is not characterized by the simultaneous presence of diverse national actors of equal standing, but a transnational space in which one national actor attempts to dominate the definition of the space and defines transnationality as its own national characteristic (see Randolph Bourne's concept of transnationality). Analogous to Turner's *communitas* and Andersons's imagined communities, the celebration enacts a collective national community and a notion of belonging by staging US military power, by justifying military actions abroad, and by portraying a military realm as a civil space of home. The actual region in the Upper Palatinate, in this event, is interpreted, appropriated, and constructed as a transnational American space – a process which reflects the notion in critical regionalism that regions are subject to and existent in multiple narratives and constructions rather than constituting one particular definable space.

## In Lieu of a Conclusion – Three Trajectories

"1800 Kilometer mit dem Panzer nach Hause in die Oberpfalz"[9] reads the subtitle of a 28 March 2015 article in the Upper Palatinate newspaper *Der Neue Tag* (Pausch 2015b). The article traces the journey of approxmiately 500 US soldiers and 100 vehicles from the so-called Dragoon Ride, a 1800 km march intended to demonstrate US solidarity with Eastern European Nato members and to create opportunities for US soldiers to communicate with local people. Alexander Pausch, in his article, announces the return to Vilseck, one of the towns and communities of the GTA, for 1 April 2015: "Am Vormittag ist auf dem Marktplatz in Vilseck ein Empfang geplant und am Nachmittag sollen alle Soldaten wieder zu Hause in den Rose Barracks sein – nach mehr als drei Monaten im Baltikum" (2015b).[10] Pausch continues the rhetoric of returning home in his 2/3 April 2015 follow-up article, now finally focusing on the return of the soldiers. He depicts American homecoming scenes on Upper Palatinate ground when he reports of fathers being reunited with their families or seeing their newborns for the first time:

9 "Going home to the Upper Palatinate, 1800 kilometers by tank."

10 In the morning, there will be a welcome reception at the Vilseck town square, and in the afternoon all soldiers will be back home in the Rose Barracks – after more than three months in the Baltic.

> Als es endlich so weit ist, fallen sich die Ehepaare in die Arme, Väter drücken ihre Kinder. Lange wiegt ein Soldat sein wenige Monate altes Baby im Arm – der Einsatz in Osteuropa war zwar nicht so gefährlich wie in Afghanistan, wo die Brigade zuletzt war. Wenn aber die Frau erst vor wenigen Wochen ein Kind bekommen hat, sind selbst drei Monate eine Ewigkeit.[11]

Pausch's articles suggest that both German and American narratives construct the region as a home for the US soldiers. US wives carry signs reading "Welcome Home," General Christopher G. Cavoli exclaims "wir könnten nicht stolzer sein, sie hier zu Hause zu begrüßen,"[12] Vilseck's German mayor Hans-Martin Schertl welcomes the US soldiers with beer and states "Für alle Vilsecker ist es ein Tag der Freude, wenn unsere Soldaten wieder zu Hause sind,"[13] ("Bier als Willkommensgruß") and the German reporter Alexander Pausch himself considers the return to the Upper Palatinate town of Vilseck a return home to the Graf region (2015b). The multiple reports surrounding the return are, moreover, accompanied by images of soldiers marching in to a warm welcome and cheers by German-American crowds or by headlines such as "Vilsecker Kavallerie kehrt zurück," "Wieder zu Hause in Vilseck," or "Nach 1800 Kilometern wieder in Vilseck."[14]

The very recent reporting is a product of and highlights the prismatic character of phenomena of cultural contact in the Graf region and the prismatic, dynamic character of the region or its constructions/representations. It stresses the diachronic dimension of the region as a node in a network of mobilities and opens trajectories into the past that led to this American presence. The headlines are eerily reminiscent of the WWII flyers bearing the title and announcement "Sie kommen" (fig. 12), secretly promoting the arrival of the US troops; the images of the marching soldiers interact (fig. 13) and form astounding interpictorial clusters with pictures of US soldiers arriving in the region in April 1945. At the same time, the articles reveal a development from an interpretation of the arrival as either liberation or occupation to homecoming – a development that either remains unquestioned, or which is consciously constructed for a US audience as a performance of a regional self-re-definition and desired elevation from US-occupied to hosting community, or which has turned into a currying favor to the admired presumably more powerful force, or which for a German national audience stages the region as acting 'on its own.' This very recent example continues the previously discussed examples. It stresses the continued productivity of the Graf system of cultural transfer in both its vertical and horizontal dimension.

[11] Finally, married couples are reunited, fathers are hugging their children. A soldier does not want to stop rocking his baby of only a few months in his arms – the deployment to Eastern Europe was not as dangerous as the brigade's previous deployment in Afghanistan. Yet if your wife has had your baby just a few weeks ago, even three months seem to last forever (2015b).

[12] We couldn't be prouder to welcome you here, back at home.

[13] It's a day of bliss, for every Vilseckian, when our soldiers return home.

[14] "Vilseck cavallary returns." "Back home in Vilseck." "Back in Vilseck after 1800 kilometers."

It highlights the multiple communities and discourses that, from multiple angles, participate in the production of images and ideas of the Graf region. It bears evidence of the region's function as a turntable and foil of diverse cultural and national appropriations and projections.

On a conceptual level, this very recent example, like the previously-discussed examples, shows that narratives about region, like auto- and hetero-imaginaries about identity/ies, are relational, flexible, possibly overlapping, possibly affirmative, possibly disruptive, possibly conflicting, or possibly conflating. Region can be understood as a cultural, social, communal state of mind,[15] a perspective, and an object and subject of projection that functions as spatial identity; i.e. region can be approached and explored as a mental, cultural, and social appropriation and construct which connects collective identity and imagined community; cultural narrative, memories, and even practices; and space. Region is located at the vertical and horizontal intersections of space, culture, and identity. It comes as no surprise then that region, and more specifically constructs of a region, are not (necessarily) identical with or correspondent to geographical or politically organizing markers of space such as state or nation. Regions may be smaller than, bigger than, or partially crossing and traversing national borders. Thus, the concept of region bears a spatial resemblance to the idea of the transcultural (see Lenz). Albeit not necessarily 'trans,' it has the potential to resist, complicate, and overcome the nation as an effective yet in analytical endeavors also restrictive category of analysis. Ultimately, region bears the structure and impact of a somewhat auxiliary yet nevertheless efficient construct – or, to return to Reichert Powell, a 'matrix of inquiry.'

The example of the homecoming US soldiers in the Upper Palatinate of the year 2015 also demonstrates that understanding a region like Graf, understanding a region in its transnational relations, means and requires approaching the region as a deep space, as a node of diverse past and present mobilities and condensations of vertical and horizontal processes of cultural transfer. Approaching the region as a vertical and horizontal prism requires and simultaneously results in approaching and investigating the region from a transangular perspective crediting the multiple local, national, and transnational (imagined) communities that use the region and the realm of cultural contact it creates as a foil of projection. Exploring a region as a prism is not limited to studying that particular region within its assumed borders. Analyzing a region as a prism that lies outside of the United States may help decenter, extend, and co(n)textualize the Americanist's perspective on America and result in further and more far-reaching insights into and about 'America.' Studying a region as a prism means studying more complex transnational and transcultural processes and America's role in them. Ultimately, scrutinizing the

[15] Not monolithically a la W.J. Cash's *The Mind of the South* (1941) or Perry Miller's *The New England Mind* (1939; 1953) as the particular state of mind that essentially defines a specific region in its entirety; but referring to the idea of a region's multiplied, dynamic existence within diverse and at times even concurring or competing states of mind.

region – and the cultural phenomena the contact zone 'region' produces as its tip-of-the-iceberg-like condensation – as a prism opens windows into and beyond its pasts and presents and unfolds exploding clusters of interconnectedness and cultural transfer across time and space.

## Illustrations

**Fig. 1**: Impact Area. 8 May 2014. Photo by author.

**Fig. 2**: Haag cemetery. 8 May 2014. Photo by author.

**Fig: 3**: Pappenberg church. 8 May 2014. Photo by author.

**Fig: 4**: Pappenberg church. 8 May 2014. Photo by author.

**Fig: 5**: Netzaberg Housing Area. 8 May 2014. Photo by author.

**Figs. 6 and 7**: Netzaberg Housing Area. Photos by Justin Ward, US Army Corps of Engineers Europe District. <http://usarmy.vo.llnwd.net/e2/-images/2010/05/05/72407/>; <http://www.army.mil/-images/2008/07/21/19586/army.mil-2008-07-24-085037.jpg>.

**Figs. 8 and 9**: Book covers depicting Levittown and a photo by Bill Owens.

**Fig. 10**: Unveiling of the Commemorative Plaque / GTA Centennial 2010.
Photo by Markus Rauchenberger. Training Support Center Vilseck <www.army.mil>.

**Fig. 11**: ESPN anchors Hannah Storm and Josh Elliot in front of the Grafenwoehr water tower. Photo by JMTC <http://www.army.mil/media/161135>.

SIE KOMMEN

mit ihren Stahlkolossen, Jabos und Flammenwerfern.

SIE KOMMEN

denn jetzt kann nichts und niemand sie mehr halten.

SIE KOMMEN

denn jetzt liegen auch Nord- und Mitteldeutschland offen vor den Anglo-Amerikanern und Russen. Der grösste Betrug der Weltgeschichte ist bald vorbei:

WO BLIEBEN die deutschen Wunderwaffen?

WO BLIEBEN die operativen Reserven?

WO BLIEBEN die Parteigenossen und „Hoheitsträger", die immer zum fanatischen Widerstand aufgerufen haben? Die alliierten Armeen nehmen Deutschland im Sturm.

SIE KOMMEN

um den deutschen Militarismus endgültig auszurotten.

SIE KOMMEN

um die Kriegsverbrecher ihrer Strafe zuzuführen.

SIE KOMMEN

um den Rechtsstaat aufzurichten, damit der Weltfrieden nicht wiederum gestört wird.

**Fig. 12**: Sie Kommen – Flyer. *Sie Kommen! – Die letzten Kriegstage in der Oberpfalz.* Ed. German Vogelsang. Amberg: Buch & Kunstverlag Oberpfalz, 2015. 17.

**Fig. 13**: *Der Neue Tag* 2/3 April 2015.

## Works Cited


Bauridl, Birgit M., and Udo J. Hebel. "South Africa and the United States in Transnational American Studies: From Comparative Approaches toward Transangulation." *South Africa and the United States in Transnational American Studies*. Ed. Birgit M. Bauridl and Udo J. Hebel. Spec. issue of *Amerikastudien/American Studies* 59.4 (2014): 455-61. Print.

Beaton, Michael. "Eyewitness to History: Grafenwoehr Training Area Reenacts Historic First Shot." ARMY.MIL 1 July 2010. Web. 9 June 2016. <http://www.army.mil/article/41665/>.

"Bier als Willkommensgruß." *Der Neue Tag* 2 April 2015. Web. 2 April 2015.

Bishop, Karen Elizabeth. "The Propositional Logic of Mapping Transnational American Studies – A Response to 'Deep Maps': A Brief for Digital Palimpsest Mapping Projects." *Journal of Transnational American Studies* 3.2 (2011). Web. 9 June 2016. <http://escholarship.org/uc/item/90r5479j>.

Briggs, Laura, Gladys McCormick, and J. T. Way. "Transnationalism: A Category of Analysis." *American Quarterly* 60.3 (2008): 625-48. Print.

Cash, W.J. *The Mind of the South*. New York: Knopf, 1941. Print.

Comer, Krista. "Exceptionalism, Other Wests, Critical Regionalism." *American Literary History* 23.1 (2011): 159-73. Web. 9 June 2016.

Desmond, Jane. "Towards a Prismatic American Studies." *Safundi* 8.1 (2007): 5-13. Print.

Eggener, Keith L. "Placing Resistance: A Critique of Critical Regionalism." *Journal of Architectural Education* 55.4 (May 2002): 228-37. Web.

"ESPN DVIDS Highlights." Excerpt from ESPN Veterans Day SportsCenter at Grafenwoehr, 2010. Video. Uploaded by 7th Army Training Command. YouTube 2011. Web. 22 July 2016. <https://www.youtube.com/watch?v=t9tcVGv0ahM>.

"ESPN Veterans Day Sportscenter from Grafenwoehr Pt. 3." Excerpt from ESPN Veterans Day SportsCenter at Grafenwoehr, 2010. Video. Uploaded by USArmyEurope. YouTube 2010. Web. 22 July 2016. <https://www.youtube.com/watch?v=24yawuJVbdk&index=3&list=PL24CAF78E307AC5BF>

Fishkin, Shelley Fisher. "'Deep Maps': A Brief for Digital Palimpsest Mapping Projects (DPMPs, or 'Deep Maps')." *Journal of Transnational American Studies* 3.2 (2011): n. pag. Web. 10 March 2015.

---. "Crossroads of Cultures: The Transnational Turn in American Studies." *American Quarterly* 57.1 (2005): 17-57. Print.

Frampton, Kenneth. "Critical Regionalism: Modern Architecture and Cultural Identity." *Modern Architecture: A Critical History*. Ed. Kenneth Frampton. London: Thames and Hudson, 1992. 314-27. Print.

"Frucht der Forschung übergeben." *Nordbayern.de* 11 September 2012. Web. 20 March 2015.

Greenblatt, Stephen, Ines Zupanov, Heike Paul, et al. *Cultural Mobility*. Cambridge: Cambridge University Press, 2009. Print.

Hebel, Udo J. "'American' Pictures and (Trans)National Iconographies: Mapping Interpictorial Clusters in American Studies." *American Studies Today*. Ed. Winfried Fluck et al. Heidelberg: Winter, 2014a. 405-35. Print. Rpt. in *Journal of Transnational American Studies* 6.1 (2015).

---. "Internationalization and International Outreach." Section of "Usable Pasts, Possible Futures: The German Association for American Studies at Sixty." Compiled by Udo J. Hebel, Carmen Birkle, and Philipp Gassert. *Amerikastudien/American Studies* 59.2 (2014b): 241-256.

Herr, Cheryl Temple. *Critical Regionalism and Cultural Studies: From Ireland to the American Midwest*. Gainesville: University of Florida, 1996. Print.

Ickstadt, Heinz. "American Studies in an Age of Globalization." *American Quarterly* 54.4 (2002): 543-62. Print.

"Im meterhohen Schnee zur Schule: Martin Schusser erinnert sich an die Zeit vor der Umsiedlung Pappenbergs vor mehr als 70 Jahren." *Der Neue Tag* 6 June 2008. Web. 9 June 2016.

Kaplan, Amy. *The Anarchy of Empire in the Making of U.S. Culture*. Cambridge: Harvard University Press, 2005. Print.

Lenz, Günter H. "Toward a Politics of American Transcultural Studies: Discourses of Diaspora and Cosmopolitanism." *Re-Framing the Transnational Turn in American Studies*. Ed. Winfried Fluck, Donald E. Pease, and John Carlos Rowe. Hanover: Dartmouth College Press, 2011. 391-425. Print.

Lim, Shirley Geok-lin. "The Shape of Transnational American Studies: Good and Excellent News." *Journal of Transnational American Studies* 3.2 (2011). Web. 9 June 2016.

Maase, Kaspar. "'I like to be in America': Zur 'Amerikanisierung' deutscher Alltagskultur nach 1945." *Amerikanisierung – Globalisierung: Transnationale Prozesse im europäischen Alltag*. Ed. Ute Bechdolf, Reinhard Johler, and Horst Tonn. Trier: wvt, 2007. 31-48. Print.

Merrett, Robert James. "What Is Region and Nation?: A Forum." *Terranglian Territories: Proceedings of the Seventh International Conference on the Literature of Region and Nation*. Frankfurt: Lang, 2000. 650-65. Print.

Miller, Perry. *The New England Mind: The Seventeenth Century*. New York: Macmillan, 1939. Print

---. *The New England Mind: From Colony to Province*. Cambridge: Harvard University Press, 1953. Print.

Morgenstern, Gerald. *Truppenübungsplatz Grafenwöhr: Gestern – heute. Grafenwoehr Training Area: Yesterday – Today*. 2010. 2nd ed. Grafenwoehr: Hutzler, 2011. Print.

Paul, Heike. "Critical Regionalism and Post-Exceptionialist American Studies." *Towards a Post-Exceptionalist American Studies. REAL*. Ed. Winfried Fluck and Donald Pease. 30 (2014): 397-424. Print.

Pausch, Alexander."Nach 1800 Kilometern wieder in Vilseck." *Der Neue Tag* 2/3 April 2015b: 8. Print.

---. "Vilsecker Kavallerie kehrt zurück." *Der Neue Tag* 28 March 2015a. Web. 9 June 2016.

Pratt, Marie Louise. "The Arts of the Contact Zone." *Profession* 91 (1991): 33-40. Print.

Reichert Powell, Douglas. *Critical Regionalism: Connecting Politics and Culture in the American Landscape*. Chapel Hill: University of North Carolina Press, 2007. Print.

Rowe, John Carlos "A Future for American Studies: A Comparative U.S. Cultures Model." *The New American Studies*. Ed. John Carlos Rowe. Minneapolis: University of Minnesota Press, 2002. 3-17. Print.

"Totengedenken im Sperrgebiet: US-Armee organisiert Friedhofsbesuch im Übungsplatz." ONETZ. 13 November 2015. Web. 22 July 2016.

Traister, Bryce. "The Object of Study; or, Are We Being Transnational Yet?" *Journal of Transnational American Studies* 2.2 (2010): n. pag. Web. 9 June 2016.

*US Army Garrison Grafenwoehr: Die verbotene Landschaft*. Bayerisches Fernsehen, 1993. Documentary.

Weber, Rudolf. "Haager Chroniken." Haag. 2014. Web. 22 July 2016. <http://www.weber-rudolf.de/haag.htm>.

"Wieder zu Hause in Vilseck." *Der Neue Tag* 2/3 April 2015: 1. Print.

# Sisterhood Is Regional? US-American Women's Activism between the Global and the Local

*Katharina Gerund*

This essay examines US-American women's activism of the so-called second wave situated between the global and the local. Taking a critical regionalist perspective, it zooms in on two seminal but equally controversial figures of mainstream US feminism: Betty Friedan and Robin Morgan. In particular, I analyze their respective foci on 'suburban sisterhood' on the one hand and 'global sisterhood' on the other as they become evident in their activism and particularly in the publication of two specific works: Friedan's monograph *The Feminine Mystique* (1963) and Morgan's edited volume *Sisterhood is Global: The International Women's Movement Anthology* (1984). Friedan and Morgan have, of course, been highly influential figures in US feminism and their works have received wide attention. While the connection between feminism and regionalism is well established, critical regionalism promises a fresh perspective on feminist activism's relations to specific places and spaces, be they real or imagined. It allows for a (re)examination of feminist activism and writing of the twentieth century in its regional, local, and global frameworks and exposes the interrelations of feminism and regionalism.

## Introduction

The connections between women's culture(s) and regionalism have long been established and discussed in scholarship on US women's literature, history, and activism – from nineteenth century 'local color' fiction to the regional contexts of feminist histories and activism in the twentieth century.[1] There have also been numerous recent attempts to (again) claim regions and regional literatures and cultures as relevant fields of study, and Wendy J. Katz and Timothy R. Mahoney have diagnosed a "simultaneous decline and revival of regionalism" in the humanities (x). Feminist approaches to (new) regionalisms can usually be located somewhere between a celebration of (specific) regions as alternative, empowering, and potentially subversive space on the one hand and a critique of regionalism's complicity in projects of nation-building and imperialism on the other. As Krista

1 Stephanie Foote notes, for example, that "[f]eminist critics have claimed that regional writing was especially hospitable to women writers, a judgment with which it is difficult not to agree" (12).

Comer has pointed out, the feminist interventions into regional studies that started in the 1970s may not have succeeded in debunking notions of regional writings as minor literature; and most feminist critics "have regarded regionalism with indifference"[2] (2003: 111), despite the fact that many feminist texts are deeply embedded in a kind of "regional thinking" (ibid. 112). My essay follows Comer's admonition that there is a "wealth of rich, new, and different feminisms that might be brought into focus were 'regionalism' taken seriously by university feminism at large" (ibid.). It engages 'critical regionalism,' as it has been introduced in architecture and adapted into cultural studies, in order to revisit the connection between feminist activism/writing and its landscapes, both metaphorical and literal. I argue not only that from a critical regionalist perspective the 'region' emerges as a useful category for analyzing and understanding women's activism of the so-called 'second wave' but also that it potentially offers a promising methodology, theoretical framework, and analytical lens to (re)evaluate feminism in the contemporary context of a 'third wave' or 'post-feminism.' My argument evolves in several stages: First, I will develop my understanding of critical regionalism (and the region) and indicate some of its possible interconnections with feminist activism. Second, I will zoom in on two central, but also controversial figures of mainstream US-American feminism in the twentieth century: Robin Morgan and Betty Friedan. My goal is to (re)read their activism and writings, particularly Friedan's monograph *The Feminine Mystique* (1963) and Morgan's edited volume *Sisterhood Is Global: The International Women's Movement Anthology* (1984), from a critical regionalist perspective. I argue that both of these books and the feminist activism they represent and perform are connected to specific regions, including the authors' individual local contexts (e.g. Friedan's 'roots' in Peoria, Morgan's connection to the New York area), the landscapes or regions – geographical and metaphorical – they focus on (US suburbs in *The Feminine Mystique*, globally embedded nations in *Sisterhood Is Global*), and the dynamics of race, gender, class, age, etc. that (implicitly and explicitly) inform their writings (Friedan's *Feminine Mystique* is concerned exclusively with white middle-class housewives, Morgan's anthology tries to give a diverse range of activists a voice without, however, compromising the discursive control of white US-American feminism). These readings indicate how critical regionalism can strengthen a critique of white US-American feminism of the twentieth century without dismissing its achievements. Finally, I will offer some tentative thoughts on the relevance of this approach in the ongoing debates about a 'third wave' of women's activism or 'post-feminism.'

[2] Feminist critics are, of course, not completely absent from the (critical) regionalist discourse and, for example, "increasingly challeng[e] the masculinist bias underpinning definitions of region and regionalism" (Wyile et al. xiii).

## Critical Regionalism and Feminism

Critical regionalism, as I understand it here, offers a methodology and a theoretical framework that allow for an analysis of the relation between the global and the local from a critical, i.e. potentially activist, perspective. While I am aware that related concepts like 'globalization,' 'transnationalism,' or 'glocalization' (as popularized by Roland Robertson) might be used and utilized in activist, resistant, or subversive ways, it seems to me that critical regionalism – as it has been developed in architecture primarily by Kenneth Frampton, Alexander Tzonis, and Liane Lefaivre,[3] and in its appropriations in cultural studies by e.g. Cheryl Temple Herr or Douglas Reichert Powell – provides a useful approach to examine the region in its cross-regional interrelations as well as its global context and to engage scholarly with an activist agenda or other forms of resistance. Furthermore, it attempts to avoid simple reductions of the region to a culturally authentic and commodifiable entity, a specific economic market, or an always already internationalized and transnationally traversed space that is nonetheless (nostalgically) reminiscent of a time before large-scale globalization. This is not to say that critical regionalism – or regionalism[4] – is generally resistant, subversive, or challenging dominant ideologies. It cannot simply do away with the tensions between the global and the local, the universal and the particular. In fact, as Lefaivre and Tzonis claim, critical regionalism does not condemn globalization outright, but rather complements "trends towards higher technology and a more global economy and culture. It opposes only their undesirable, contingent by-products due to private interests and public mindlessness" (2001: 9). In Frampton's definition, critical regionalism "mediate[s] the impact of universal civilization with elements derived *indirectly* from the peculiarities of a particular place" and it has to "maintain […] a high level of critical self-consciousness" (1983: 21). Frampton proposes that critical regionalism should "'deconstruct' the overall spectrum of world culture which it inevitably inherits" and accomplish "a manifest critique of universal civilization" (ibid.). He conceives of a critical architectural practice as an "arrière-garde" that distances itself from "the optimization of advanced technology" on the one hand and "the ever-present tendency to regress into

3 See for example Frampton 1983, 2005; Tzonis, Lefaivre, and Stagno 2001; Lefaivre and Tzonis 2012.

4 I am well aware that neither regionalism nor critical regionalism are unified fields and that there is a multiplicity of approaches that are subsumed under these labels; even the differentiation between 'traditional' or new regionalisms and critical regionalism is not always clear, even though, for example, one criterion might be that "[c]ritical regionalism's insistence on places and their cultural artifacts as dense palimpsests of broader forces represents an intentional challenge to the tradition of 'regionalism' that informs most literary and cultural criticism" (Reichert Powell 19). In the following, I draw primarily on scholarship that embraces the label 'critical regionalism' but I also rely on 'regionalist' works that critically deal with region, regional literatures, and space or place as they are relevant to develop my framework.

nostalgic historicism or the glibly decorative" on the other; this is a prerequisite for its "capacity to cultivate resistant, identity-giving culture while at the same time having discreet recourse to universal technique" (ibid. 20). Drawing on Heidegger, Frampton argues that the "precondition of a bounded domain [is essential] in order to create an architecture of resistance" (ibid. 25). It is this potential of resistance (within a limited space), the self-reflective imperative, and the ambivalent and partly paradoxical relationship between the universal and the particular, i.e. the global and the regional, that, to my mind, make critical regionalism appealing to cultural studies in general and to an analysis of feminist activism in particular.

However, this approach comes with a set of problems of its own. Keith Eggener has shown that critical regionalism – and this is also part of my understanding of the concept here – designates "a method or process rather than a product" (228). It is hard to define, (programmatically) lacks stylistic unity, and it is "a construct most often imposed from outside, from positions of authority" (ibid.). Critical regionalism critiques "universal modernism, placelessness, reactionary populism, the capitalist culture of consumption" but, as Eggener holds, it is a "postcolonial concept" (230, 234). As such, it risks affirming binary oppositions (e.g. center/periphery), being guided by an imperial nostalgia, and – even against its own agenda – prioritizing the universal over the particular (ibid. 230-34). Eggener's points indicate that the cultural capital of the discourse on critical regionalism, the power relations pervading its application, and the ambivalences arising out of its investment in both the universal and the particular have to be taken into account. Despite its possible pitfalls, I argue that a critical regionalist approach (particularly in cultural studies) can be more than a "fashionable formula" (ibid. 235). It offers, for example, a productive perspective to examine the tensions between the local and the global in US feminism. As Comer has pointed out, in order to untie the intricate connections between feminism and regionalism one has to pay close attention to the nexus between the global and the local. Too often the region is regarded merely a subset of the nation and the concept "operates in some kind of service to representations, including critical ones, of the nation-state" (2003: 112). She proposes to move beyond the nation and to focus on the region as a way to account for the transnational, postnational, or global in literary studies (ibid. 113).[5] This entails to attend to "the global *as it strategically figures in representations of the regional*" (ibid.). I share Comer's call for placing the region at the center instead of the nation-state but am aware – as I will argue in more detail later – that the nation may function or mask itself as a region and has to be analyzed accordingly.

[5] As Cheryl Temple Herr reminds us, for example, global marketing has long started to focus on the region over the nation and urges us that "[a]s the issues complicating world regionalism become more pressing, we want to be clear about how to define regions, who defines them, what the political statues of different regions will be, whether their continued emergence constitutes a step forward or an historical regression toward the violence of nationalism" (4).

Drawing on a critical regionalist perspective, I am interested primarily in regions as ideological constructs, construed and utilized by different actors for diverse purposes,[6] i.e. the guiding questions are not "what regions are but why they are that way, […] what they do as much as what has been done to them" (Reichert Powell 7). Regions are neither fixed categories nor defined through essential qualities but are subject to "ongoing debates and discourses that coalesce around particular geographical spaces" (ibid. 14). Frank Davey elaborates that regionalism as a cultural phenomenon "represents […] a strategically resistant mapping of geography in which historic and economic factors play large but largely unacknowledged parts" (4), or, to put it in Douglas Reichert Powell's words, "when we talk about a region, we are talking not about a stable, boundaried, autonomous place but about a cultural history, the cumulative, generative, effect of the interplay among various, competing definitions of that region" (5). My focus is on the construction of regions in feminist discourses and in discourses about feminism (on different levels), their individual meaning and significance, but also their mutual interrelations as well as their relations to national and global constellations as I take into account the "relationality of regionalism" (Herr 18).

Reichert Powell as well as Cheryl Temple Herr draw on Frampton's critical regionalism and adapt it "to the reading and writing of texts" (Reichert Powell 21) and to the overall agenda of cultural studies (see Herr). Both develop a critical regionalist methodology that is interdisciplinary in nature and (potentially) activist in outreach. It affirms the importance of constructions of regions and regionalist social practices, and it offers a nuanced critical take on regions and places in their multiple and interconnected dimensions. I use Reichert Powell's and Herr's methodological agendas as starting points in order to demonstrate how some of the hallmarks of critical regionalism can be employed to engage with feminist issues. There are three points of convergence that I identify as particularly crucial to such a procedure.

First of all, critical regionalism not only examines the role of regions and their boundaries for identity formation and forms of belonging but also seeks to forge new solidarities between the academy and activism. Furthermore, it can be utilized, as Herr has shown, to challenge insider/outsider tensions in cultural studies. Herr reveals critical regionalism's activist ambition when she writes about the "materials and tools" it might offer for a "cultural inquiry that can hope to participate actively in social change without falling prey to recidivist longing of the induced paralysis of an ever-consolidating market economy" (12). Along similar lines, Reichert Powell argues that "critical regionalism works in solidarity with the historically disempowered populations of its communities to transform their local material circumstances while linking their particular struggles to larger ones" (26). He claims that "[t]o understand the full effects of the impact of injustice, of uneven development, of racism, classism, sexism, and heterosexism, progressive

6 Katz and Mahoney argue that "the concept of region […] is itself an assertion of power" (xi).

intellectuals and educators must reclaim the supposedly tranquil or quiescent [...] spaces of regional culture as vital spaces of cultural strife" (21). In this regard, critical regionalism can be used as a paradigm to analyze social movements and to conceive of an engaged scholarship that potentially sides with activism and critically interrogates mechanisms of inclusion and exclusion. I am interested, however, not so much in introducing the region as yet another category for intersectional analyses (this is, however, a welcome side-effect) but more in the possibilities of critical regionalism as an approach to analyze feminist discourses of group formation. Regionalism may have "come to be accepted as a discourse or form of identification or (following Benedict Anderson's view of nationalism) a kind of kinship – if not viewed as being as significant a component of identity as nationality, then at least not far off" (Wyile et al. ix); my focus here is on examining the forms of belonging and identity formation as they come to bear on women's activism and discourses on 'sisterhood' which proclaims a kind of kinship that is at least limited in its empowering effects and applicability for feminist projects (if not outright problematic regarding its exclusionary, potentially essentialist, universalizing, and homogenizing aspects)[7] and that intersects and interacts with regional collectivities.

Second, the self-reflective imperative of critical regionalism, which we can already find in Frampton's 'architecture of resistance,' makes it a useful tool to question not only dominant spatial fields of feminist activism but also scholarship's role in creating, affirming, or challenging regionalist assumptions.[8] For my analysis of dominant white US-American feminism it is therefore crucial to keep in mind how the focus on region can become complicit in stabilizing existing power relations and hegemonic feminist regimes.[9] Critical regionalism strives toward "the best possible version of the region" and its ambition to not only produce critique but furthermore to create "new kinds of texts and images of place" (Reichert Powell 7, 22).[10] Third, critical regionalism is an approach that carefully navigates the tensions between the global and the local and seeks to account for their interactions on different levels. It emphasizes the processual and constructed character of any region and allows for metaphorical understandings of the region.

7 Chandra Talpade Mohanty, for example, contrasts Robin Morgan's universal sisterhood with Bernice Johnson Reagon's notion of coalition that is by definiton opposed to the home – and thus, we could assume – inherently at odds with sisterhood's implication of family and kinship as a basis for unity among women. While sisterhood might imply unity among women as a given, coalition has to be struggled for (see 117-18).

8 As Reichert Powell holds, critical regionalism "is about being aware of the fact that one's own work participates in that broader constellation of discourse about the region" (7).

9 While I take a critical perspective on the universalizing stance and exclusionary practices of white middle-class US women's activism, I cannot avoid to re-iterate (and thus potentially affirm) them in my analyses.

10 Herr argues similarly that "[a]s a practice, a critical-regionalist cultural studies has great potential for producing a unified but highly adaptable analysis of international flows at the local-regional level, toward the end of a more heterogeneous and tolerant future" (18).

These critical regionalist impulses inform my (re)examination of twentieth-century US-American feminism. Comer's analysis of 'second wave' feminism with regard to its spatial parameters serves as a stepping stone for my reading of Friedan's and Morgan's activism as it reveals a spatial bias in the "ruling feminist geographical imagination that retains its spatial and moral 'center' in the northeast" of the United States. This dominant

> northeastern spatial field [...] privileges particularly defined kinds of political endeavors: the writing and circulation of treatises or books [...], formation of feminist cells or women's liberation groups [...], legal challenges to the State, direct action protest [...], as well as, of course, the more informal consciousness-raising groups. This spatial field reproduces or calls upon the intellectual and activist legacy of New England-based puritanism and early republicanism, and it echoes in symbolic association with the more radical of America's later movements for social change, [...]. All of which is to say that many of the conditions for representing both feminism and political issues grow out of, and are implicated within, existing spatial relationships and their respective political roles [...] in national political history. (Comer 1999: 48)

In the following, I excavate and produce some feminist "assemblages" (in Herr's sense) around, within, and beyond specific regions and I take a close look at the different dimensions of the spatial fields involved.

## Sisterhood in Suburbia: Betty Friedan

Betty Friedan is frequently claimed as an initiator or at least major catalyst of the women's movement in the 1960s – primarily through the publication of *The Feminine Mystique*[11] in 1963 and her subsequent activism e.g. in the foundation of NOW in 1966. Her book which focused on the "problem that has no name" but that most white middle-class suburban housewives who did not conform to the "happy housewife" ideal shared has not only sparked controversial discussions but also made her work inextricably connected to a regional formation often specifically associated with the United States: suburbia. Friedan facilitated this impression by claiming that she had not only fully embraced the feminine mystique but also experienced all the hopes and perils of a suburban housewife's life. She contributed to a life narrative that capitalized on her insider status as she revealed the gap between media representations and social prescriptions for woman's role, highlighting happiness, and fulfillment as mother, wife, and homemaker and the realities of suburban housewives. However, the picture becomes more complex

[11] In fact, many historians "view its publication as marking the beginning of the modern women's movement" (Horowitz 4).

when we take a look at the different places and regions that influenced Friedan prior to her move to the suburbs and account for the multiple regional geographies that shaped her thinking, writing, and activism. As Daniel Horowitz has pointed out, "[i]n the short term, her misery in the suburb may have prompted her to write *The Feminine Mystique*; a longer-term perspective makes clear that the book's origins go back much farther – to her youth in Peoria, her education at Smith College, and her experiences with labor unions in the 1940s and early 1950s" (2). Yet, as "the women's movement's consummate mainstreamer" that she became (Siegel 75), Friedan constructed and marketed her vision of feminism as well as her own public persona and life story.

Friedan's hometown, Peoria, Illinois, figured prominently in her own life story and one might, in fact, be inclined to state that she "identified strongly with her midwestern roots, despite the fact that she would spend much of her adult life on the East Coast" (Siegel 73) and despite her assessment that "I always thought I hated Peoria, couldn't wait to get out of there" (Friedan 1976: 254). Throughout her career as writer and activist, Friedan emphasized that feminism must appeal to the 'average' American woman and that it should 'play well in Peoria,'[12] and she capitalized on her knowledge and experience of 'Middle America;' for example, when she stated that "I am not that far from everywoman (that is part of whatever political wisdom I do have – that I do come from Peoria, Ilinois)" (Friedan 1976: 159). Yet, this image of an average woman, of an insider of Middle America's mainstream, is counterbalanced by the fact that Friedan not only left Peoria as soon as she could to return only sporadically but also because she equally drew attention to the exclusionary practices in her hometown which she experienced as a Jewish girl. Her childhood and youth are usually depicted as comparatively privileged but also inflicted by anti-Semitism (see Horowitz 18; Hennessee 6-7; Friedan 2000: 15-33) and her status as an 'outsider,' which might have "intensified her sense of herself as an observer, a writer, and someone passionately committed to fighting to improve social conditions" (Horowitz 23). Friedan assumed both positions as both insider and outsider to create discursive authority and to lend credibility to her work.

By fashioning herself as 'everywoman' and furthering a feminism with mainstream appeal, Friedan opposed radical feminists and, particularly in the late 1960s, "found herself reminding sister organizers not to alienate the heartland" (Siegel 74). Friedan contends that she "continually had to fight attempts to narrow the appeal, to take positions and stands couched in the radical jargon that was okay for the East Village in New York or counterculture San Francisco, but not for the breadth of women throughout America wanting their own political voice"

12 Peoria's name was not merely a "byword for provincialism" (Hennessee 4), it "was nationally symbolic. In the vaudeville era, comics and other performers tried new stage productions in Peoria to measure audience acceptance. [...] Richard Nixon [...] reportedly imbued the phrase 'how will it play in Peoria' with new meaning – as a litmus test for how his politics would go over with so-called regular folks living in regular towns" (Siegel 73).

(1976: 175). Deborah Siegel suggests that Friedan even regarded it "her duty as the woman who had initially sold feminism to Peoria [...] to fashion a feminism that would continue to play among ordinary women in her hometown" (75).[13] In her opposition to the more radical outgrowths of the women's movement, Friedan – whether strategically or not – played down her own radical heritage[14]: As a student at Smith College she became politicized and even "radicalized" (see Horowitz 50-68) and "gained invaluable experience as a journalist, activist, and leader" (ibid. 57). Subsequently she spent a year at Berkeley and allegedly came under FBI surveillance[15] (see ibid. 93-94). After turning down a fellowship and deciding against a Ph.D. in psychology, she expanded her interest in and support of the labor movement, sought "work as a labor journalist or researcher for a union" (ibid. 103). In 1942, she took up a job at the Federated Press and later worked for the *UE News* – the "official publication of the United Electrical, Radio and Machine Workers of America, a radical union" (ibid. 121). Yet, this narrative became overshadowed by her private life[16] and Friedan claims that in 1949 "the feminine mystique began to close in on her" (Hennessee 52).

Friedan moved several times with her family, among other places, to Parkway Village in New York City, "a unique international community" (Hennessee 55), but ultimately settled in the suburbs, specifically in Grandview-on-Hudson, Rockland County. Friedan's experience as a housewife became an impulse to write *The Feminine Mystique* and allowed her to ascertain her credibility. While she stayed connected to the urban and intellectual environment of New York City, she emphasized how much she "wanted to be a happy, fulfilled suburban housewife" (2000: 85) but experienced in fact the feminine mystique first hand as a discontented housewife. Thus Friedan enabled her readers to imagine her "as a sister housewife, trapped in the gilded cage of a suburban home" (Rosen 5). Despite this emphasis, she "was not and never would be a 'suburban housewife'" (Hennessee 84); and she even "pictured herself in the years in Rockland County as

13 Friedan reflected, for example, on Ti-Grace Atkinson's "radical chic" and claimed that it "had a certain allure for young women hippies then emigrating to the East Village and San Francisco" but that Atkinson "certainly did put off the women from the cities and suburbs of Middle America who were beginning to identify with the women's movement" (1976: 109).

14 According to Horowitz, "Friedan [instead] created a second narrative in order to avoid revelations about her radical past and to project a believable persona with which her readers could identify" (217). Nonetheless, she emphasized the "inescapable sense of political responsibility" that she got at Smith College and explains how she "thought of [herself] as a revolutionary" (Friedan 2000: 55, 57).

15 Friedan "never doubted that the FBI would eventually infiltrate any women's movement" (Rosen 253).

16 She met and married Carl Friedan and gave birth to their first son in 1948. When she got pregnant a second time four years later *UE* did not grant her another maternity leave and, instead, fired her. This is, at least, Friedan's version of the events. The context and circumstances of her losing her job at *UE* may have been more complicated but I am concerned here with Friedan's self-fashioning rather than with any search for the 'true' story of her life.

a freak, an outsider, someone lonely in the provinces" (Horowitz 169). While she later became a leading figure in the nation-wide women's movement, here she first focused on "what she could do on the local level" (ibid. 179). In her activism and her life narrative leading up to *The Feminine Mystique* two regions played a central role and shaped her vision of feminism and her self-fashioning as everywoman: Peoria and the Midwestern Middle America it represents and suburbia as it signifies the dominant norms of the affluent and aspiring part of postwar American society. Her positioning with regard to both of these regions combines the assertion of authority as insider with an outsider's perspective that is able to reveal the workings of the feminine mystique and the concerns of 'average' American women. College, campus life, and labor activism, in contrast, are downplayed to shape her (regional) identity in the public.[17] However, Friedan saw the women's movement's 'promise of sisterhood' also as affecting women "across the bonds of generation, geography, race, class and man-made politics" (1976: xiv) and her book *The Feminine Mystique* was, of course, crucial to set this movement into motion. Despite this careful construction of her life narrative, Friedan claimed that "all the pieces of [her] own life came together for the first time in the writing of it" (1976: 6).

Friedan revealed 'the problem that has no name' – namely, that women were supposed to find fulfillment only and exclusively through their roles as wife and mother[18] – with which "[e]ach suburban wife struggled [...] alone" (1963: 57); and she thereby focused on a very specific regional formation, American suburbia, associated with whiteness, affluence, education, and nuclear family structures with traditional patriarchal gender roles. And while this 'problem' may have echoed in different places, the suburbs were its main stronghold. Friedan's argument consequently encompasses a salient critique of suburban space and architecture. Asserting her insider position, Friedan claims that she "sensed the problem, not as a reporter, but as a suburban housewife" (ibid. 63). However, as a writer and psychologist, she is at the same time also in the position to see the larger picture and to diagnose the problem of suburban housewives and to endow it with national significance when she states that it "may well be the key to our future as a nation and a culture" (ibid. 78); the feminine mystique is in her opinion to a large extent a uniquely US-American phenomenon (see 1963: 270-71). Though Friedan argues for the general humanity of women, her focus is very exclusive; and, based on a Maslowian understanding of needs and concerns, the problem she detects mostly

[17] Ruth Rosen points out that earlier drafts of *The Feminine Mystique* "reveal a more daring vision" but Friedan "feared her ideas would be discredited if she focused on the problems of working women" and "settled on a safer strategy, that of addressing middle-class white housewives as sister suburbanite" (5).

[18] Friedan primarily uses interviews and magazine articles to prove her point; she describes and generalizes the dominant image of women: "In the second half of the twentieth century in America, women's world was confined to her own body and beauty, the charming of man, the bearing of babies, and the physical care and serving of husband, children, and home" (1963: 83).

affects women with a certain degree of material wealth, education, and privilege. Certainly what Friedan states about Sigmund Freud holds true for her own endeavor: "no social scientist can completely free himself from the prison of his own culture" (1963: 169). It is one of the many points of criticism that have been directed at Friedan's work, that she is concerned with white middle-class housewives exclusively and fails to pay attention to issues such as race and class; and, in fact, "hers was a decidedly lily-white book" (Horowitz 208). Additionally, she has been criticized for "the derivative nature of her work" (Siegel 75), the fact that she insisted on the feminine mystique as a "mental construct" (Horowitz 221), (paid) work as a remedy for women's problems, and, not the least, her references to Nazi ideology in her comparison between suburb and concentration camp.[19] Horowitz regards this analogy as "careless and exaggerated" but also holds that it "dramatically conveyed to Friedan's readers the horrible and dehumanized feeling of women who were trapped in their homes" (205). While Friedan is concerned with the situation in the US suburbs she chooses an – highly inappropriate – other place removed both in time and space to make a point and thereby also raises questions about the comparability, specificity, and differentiation of these two places.[20] Kirsten Fermaglich contextualizes the analogy by pointing out that in the early "period of Holocaust consciousness" from the late 1950s to the mid-1960s "Nazi concentration camps became, for many liberal readers in the United States, appropriate and valuable symbols for exploring inhumanity on an American landscape" (207). These problematic aspects of *The Feminine Mystique* have been exposed from different theoretical and methodological venues, but there are a few accentuations that critical regionalism can add. First, it contributes to both a possible explanation and a thorough critique of the exclusiveness of Friedan's 'suburban sisterhood,' i.e. the establishment of a community tied to a specific region (with all of its exclusionary practices based on race, class, etc.). Friedan's limited and limiting framework can be understood as necessary for her argument and agenda but it can be countered by including regional interconnections, power relations, and global influences. Second, critical regionalism helps to contextualize

[19] While there are many reasons to criticize Friedan's argument, Rachel Bowlby, has argued in the late 1980s that "[t]he point is not to reject Friedan from some point of advanced knowledge either as simply 'of her time'" but rather to ask what we can still gain from her observations and arguments as problematic, contradictory, or twisted as they may be (71). Friedan, for example, problematized the idea of feminist progress and indicated many unresolved questions and contradictions of the feminine mystique (see 74). In essence, Bowlby's claim still – or rather again – holds true today as popular feminism has once again come full circle. In times of post-feminism, feminism been relegated to the past and has again come to be a 'dirty word' for many young women. Dorothy Chansky, for example, has more recently explained that Friedan and with her second-wave feminism is often "dismissed as dated and exclusionary, asexual, and monolithic" remains "relevant to theatre practitioners and performance analysts with feminist goals" and her argument could well be expanded into other realms of feminist analysis and intervention (341-42).

[20] For a detailed analysis of the role of Nazi imagery in *The Feminine Mystique* see Fermaglich.

Friedan's position as in- and outsider as well as her regional identities that shaped the production and marketing of the book. And, third, it contributes to the critical readings of Friedan's work in general that reveal her exclusive and universalist claims, regional and otherwise, as it asks how women were affected by the feminine mystique (and maybe also resisted it) locally and how the women's movement took shape in its different local settings while at the same time negotiating common goals on a larger – at least national – level.

Although *The Feminine Mystique* had a cross-over appeal into other regions – or at least appealed to women across the country – as it "made top-seller lists in major coastal capitals, Friedan's target audience remained suburban" (Siegel 73). Her book received mixed reviews but "few were indifferent" (Hennessee 84); and Friedan relates that she received both "angry" and "relieved letters" by women from all over the United States and from small towns (e.g. in Florida, Michigan, Georgia, Wisconsin, Massachusetts, Mississippi, or California) (see 1976: 20-27). While her own suburban community was allegedly very supportive during the years she worked on the book, it now turned against her: "suddenly I was a leper in my own suburban neighborhood" writes Friedan, who felt compelled to move back to the city in 1964 (1976: 58). While she envisioned a kind of 'suburban sisterhood' at the center of women's activism, her publication rather alienated her from her community in Rockland County. It, however, became a starting point for historical events in the women's movement and, among other things, led to the foundation of the National Organization for Women (NOW) in 1966[21] and Friedan becoming "one of the most effective popularizers and savvy marketers of the women's movement" (Siegel 75). The activities of NOW would provide another set of case studies for a critical regionalist approach to feminist activism because even though the organization was largely based and coordinated out of major cities[22], Friedan claimed: "We expected the major actions of NOW to be carried out by women in their own communities. […] We knew also that national actions were necessary to accomplish our goals – to focus, spotlight and strengthen the women in their communities" (1976: 95). While Friedan's activism around the publication of *The Feminine Mystique* was concerned with white suburban US-American women and invested in local, regional, and national issues, her work and activism resonated across the United States, as her "lecture requests began to come from unlikely cities in the Deep South, Catholic colleges, and states like Kansas, Oklahoma, Texas, Maine, and Alabama" (Friedan 1976: 137), *and* globally as the

[21] At this first conference in Washington, D.C., there were 120 women from the Midwest "which once again highlighted the indigenous female activism in this region of the nation" (Rosen 78).

[22] NOW was founded in Washington, D.C. in 1996 and one year later its first national convention also took place there. Friedan elaborates on the first years of organizing NOW: "the membership records and mailings were handled out of Caroline's office in the U.A.W. building in Detroit, the board notices and minutes out of Kay's office at the University of Wisconsin, the P.R. out of Muriel's office in New York, and the policy and organizing of the women's movement out of my apartment on 72nd street" (1976: 85).

book was translated in numerous languages and Friedan took to lecturing on an international scale. However, the global dimension of the women's movement never had the same relevance for Friedan as it later had for Robin Morgan who particularly with *Sisterhood Is Global* negotiated the inter- and transnational dimensions of US-American women's activism but who also might have never had a connection to the women in the proverbial US-American 'heartland' as she herself critically remarked with reference to her rhetoric and style: "I'm not reaching […] these women in their little Iowa dresses" (qtd. in Rosen 161).

## Global Sisterhood: Robin Morgan

Robin Morgan's three *Sisterhood* anthologies[23] are central – though certainly controversial – contributions to the women's movement. For the purpose of this essay I have singled out *Sisterhood Is Global* as an explicit attempt towards an international women's movement. Where Betty Friedan tried to foster feminism in suburbia, Morgan sought to take it global; where Friedan's efforts contributed significantly to the foundation of a nation-wide organization for women in the United States, Morgan's anthology project led to an international forum, or rather think-tank, the Sisterhood Is Global Institute, which she founded together with Simone de Beauvoir in 1984; and where we may say that Friedan was concerned to bring together women primarily across regions in the United States (even as she therefore focused on the clearly limited space of suburbia), Morgan attempted to forge connections with women from different nations around the globe though her perspective remains primarily shaped by white Western feminism. *Sisterhood Is Global* covers a comparatively long period in women's activism. It was over a decade in the making before being first published in 1984 (see Morgan 1996: xiii) and it was reissued (unchanged but with a new preface) in 1996 by the Feminist Press.

Its entries cover an impressive 70 countries plus the United Nations and Morgan proudly announces that she and her collaborators have assembled a "representative" list of nations covering "[e]very region, type of government system, and stage of 'development'" (1996: xiii). She admits to the "eclectic mix" of contributors but emphasizes that each contributor is a "native of the country about which she writes" and, though not an "*official representative*," is a "*truth teller*" (ibid. xiv, xv, xvi). Several points of criticism, which have been raised by reviewers and commentators, are of particular significance for a critical regionalist perspective on and approach to feminist activism: The organization of the book in the national paradigm, the sample of nations and contributors, as well as the

[23] *Sisterhood Is Powerful: An Anthology of Writings from the Women's Liberation Movement* first published in 1970, *Sisterhood Is Global: The International Women's Movement Anthology* which came out in 1984, and, most recently, *Sisterhood Is Forever: The Women's Anthology for a New Millenium* published in 2003.

position(ing) of the individual contributors. First of all, it is quite striking if not outright paradoxical that an anthology which tries to offer an inter- or even transnational perspective on women's solidarity and activism relies on the nation-state as its organizing principle.[24] The 'regions' of women's situations and activism here are primarily mapped through nation-states; even though Morgan herself noted early on that the project "would have to transcend standard geopolitics" (2001: 341). The nations are arranged alphabetically and this seemingly neutral and objective order contributes to the book's lack of attention to "the dissimilarity of women's oppression from region to region and the oppression of men by other axes of power" (Hackstaff and Pierce 191). In fact, as Karla Hackstaff and Jennifer Pierce suggest, the anthology "would have been better organized according to regions" because the

> attention to the similarities within regions and the differences between regions might have put to question the globality of sisterhood, but it also would have enriched our understanding of the divergent parameters that circumscribe women's lives. The constellation of factors which have an impact on women's experiences in different geographical areas – whether they be issues of race, religions, colonialism, class, urbanization, etc. – are integral to overcoming the oppression of women. (191-92)

They advocate for feminism to account for the 'region,' which may offer not only an alternative to buying uncritically into the – certainly anything but innocent – mapping of the world into geographical areas defined by nation-states but would also reveal a regional dimension to sisterhood, particularly with regard to the differences and similarities of women's lives and activism. This might jeopardize the idea of a global sisterhood as promoted by Morgan, i.e. as primarily based on victimization and oppression from similar patriarchal structures, but could reveal that 'sisterhood' is – at least to some degree – regional. The region can serve as an intermediary level between the global and the local, the universal and the particular. Amrita Basu, for example, emphasizes "the local origins and character of women's movements cross-nationally" and claims that "women's movements must be situated within the particular political economics, state policies, and cultural politics of the regions in which they are active" (68). She elaborates that local women's movements cannot "simply be subsumed by global ones" and are not sufficiently depicted by pointing out their "sustained, overt resistance to global influences" (69). Rather, global and local movements may enter into complex relationships or even "exist independently of one another and experience similar challenges and dilemmas" and while "transnational ideas, resources, and organizations have been extremely successful around certain issues in some

[24] Morgan claims in her introduction that "women seem, cross-culturally, to be deeply opposed to nationalism – at least as practiced in patriarchal society" (1996: 23).

regions, their success with these issues is more circumscribed elsewhere" (ibid. 69-70). From a critical regionalist perspective such detailed attention to the specific local and regional resonances of and impulses for a global women's movement becomes imperative. It also supports a radical critique of the hegemonic status of US feminism in *Sisterhood Is Global.* One critic has claimed that the book "is not an act of international sisterhood, but rather one of subtle cultural imperialism" (Wilson 392). Morgan acknowledges in her 1996 preface that the "real work takes place locally" and that this work has "begun to affect international forums" (1996: x); but she does not problematize the power relations involved – e.g. not all local efforts are equally influential and some do not gain attention on a global scale. The "channels of power" Morgan calls on her fellow activists to "demystify" should include those within the women's movement, the struggles for discursive authority and control, and not the least Western feminism's "totalizing effect" (Hackstaff and Pierce 197).

With regard to *Sisterhood Is Global*, it is Morgan's own position/ality as editor of the volume that needs to be taken into account. As Chandra Talpade Mohanty reminds us in her critical reading of Morgan's introduction: "A place on the map (New York City) is, after all, also a locatable place in history" (111). This white, urban, middle-class US-American perspective is part and parcel of the universalist definition of 'feminism' and 'patriarchy' in Western terms that underlie the project[25] and indicative of many of the anthology's problematic aspects. While the book seeks to let women from different countries speak for themselves, the sample of invited contributors relied on personal networks and, of course, the processes of selection, editing, etc. were in the hands of Morgan and her team.[26] Morgan's own regional identity comes into play here as does the New York area as the center of the US women's movement with all its implications. New York was the center of her early career as a child actor as well as of her work as a writer and feminist activist. Morgan writes:

> A sense of place shapes us […]. Alice Walker's rural American South, Willa Cather's Midwest prairies, Henry James's (old and New) England(s). Location, location, location – what Toni Morrison calls 'the site of memory.' For me, that place of influence is New York City, by which I mean […] Manhattan. (2001: 103)

25 Hackstaff and Pierce, for example, observe that Morgan "simply imposes the label 'feminism' on women's experiences throughout the world without considering the fact that such a label evokes divergent meanings for women within and between nations" (194).

26 Morgan emphasizes that the book was a team effort, e.g. when she writes that early on she knew that "[t]here was no way to do this one by myself. I needed a team" or when she points out that [t]he front matter and acknowledgements of *Sisterhood Is Global* read like credits for a film with a cast of thousands – with reason – given all the people who made various kinds of contributions and had assorted involvements over the years" (2001: 342, 345). However, it is Morgan's name only on the cover and her voice that frames the contributions through preface, introduction, etc.

While she acknowledges the role of her 'roots' in the New York area and particularly Manhattan, Morgan emphasizes her travels and her widespread domestic and international networks. For example, she discusses the many trips she started to take as an "itinerant political organizer" especially once *Sisterhood Is Powerful* was published (2001: 323) and the significance of these journeys and places for her own thinking and activism: "It was in small towns, on welfare lines, on factory floors during break time, in shelters, farmhouse kitchens, and student cafeterias – listening to women – that I learned a durable politics with multiple, interconnecting priorities, what I've come to call a multiplicity of feminism" (ibid. 321). Yet, New York City remains in many ways the center of her life and work. She celebrates the city's exceptionality and uniqueness and, alluding to Virginia Woolf, states: "As a woman I need no country. As a New Yorker, my city is the world" (ibid. 107). In terms of actual geographical closeness – in or around New York City – and of overlapping networks and contacts in the women's movement, Morgan was also connected with Friedan. Both were well aware of each other's work, but Morgan clearly contrasts her rather radical activism with Friedan's mainstream version of feminism (see e.g. 2001: 263, 304). Despite this self-fashioning as more revolutionary and progressive compared to white middle-class feminism à la Friedan, Morgan hardly questions or compromises her own "*positional* superiority" (Said 7) even though she admits that "[i]t's delicate to be an activist in the global context when your country is currently the only superpower" (2001: 408). She not only functions as a prominent spokesperson for (international) feminism but, particularly through her anthology projects, also turns her perspective into a filter for other women's voices and representations and, directly and indirectly, determines who can participate in a global feminist discourse. Her personal life figures prominently in all of her writings, including the anecdotes that are featured in the introduction to *Sisterhood Is Global*. Her work as an activist, writer, and editor can therefore not be viewed in isolation from her life story. Morgan elaborates, for example, how she activated and forged personal contacts to identify contributors: "In some cases […] women's-rights activists who already were my friends graciously suggested the names of sister activists in neighboring countries – a sort of national networking extended to the regional level – a 'ripple effect'" (1996: xv). This quote also points toward an aspect that is of minor relevance for the volume but of great significance for a critical regionalist perspective on feminism, namely the existing regional connections between women from different countries.

It is easy – but nonetheless valid – to criticize the selection of countries and contributors, particularly with considering that "Western countries are over-represented, whereas Third World countries are far underrepresented" (Hackstaff and Pierce 193) and that the essays were solicited via personal contacts and (pre-)established networks[27]. Similarly, it is undisputable that "[d]espite Morgan's *insistence* on the globality of feminism" the individual contributions challenge this idea of a "planetary feminism" as they expose "the various obstacles which make [...] [it] a difficult if not impossible achievement" and thus reveal the book's attempt to showcase the global dimension of sisterhood to be in parts "the editor's wishful thinking and aim to create unity" (ibid. 195, 199). What is more interesting here are the positionalities of editor and contributors as insiders/outsiders and the significance of their regional identities, local knowledge(s), and global consciousness for their activism. As 'natives' and 'truth tellers' the contributors are selected – though not as 'official representatives' – as informants whom we as readers can expect to have access to the "deep structure of local knowledge," which for Marjorie Pryse is the hallmark of (literary) regionalism and which represents "a sense of place that reflects a gap between dominant ideological and aesthetic interests and the interests and stories of persons who reside in the locale" (19, 24). While I have already pointed out the implications of Morgan's hegemonic position/ality as a white Western feminist and editor of the anthology, we could equally raise the question in what sense the contributors are 'natives' and whose 'truth' they are committed to tell.

In their critique of the volume, Hackstaff and Pierce point towards the "number of contributors that have been forcibly exiled, have 'chosen' to live in another country, or have been educated elsewhere" and consequently "have an 'outsider' status vis-à-vis their country." In the light these observations, they pose a set of questions: "Are these women fully aware of their countrywomen's present political and socio-economic situation? As outsiders, how do they differ from women inside the country? [...] does their 'outsider' status symbolize the difficulty of promoting feminist ideals and policies within their nation?" (192). It is certainly important to be aware of the positions from which the individual contributors are speaking but this does not automatically determine the credibility and relevance of their testimony. The argument regarding exiled or 'outsider' women can be construed both ways as either potentially inauthentic, and thus less attentive to the 'actual' situation in the country, or as informed by a broader horizon for comparison and endowed with a greater potential for critique. There are, of course, many ways to account for these women's contributions beyond a mere authenticity debate. If we identify the women not only via their nationality as 'countrywomen' but rather look at their regional ties and global interconnections, the simple insider-outsider dichotomy is easily complicated if not subverted; the 'native' informant may appear a construction and the 'outsider' as offering a complementary perspective that can be comparative and attentive to connections within and beyond national or regional boundaries. Many of the problems involved here have also been addressed

[27] Morgan, for example, emphasizes the importance of events like the United Nations World Conference on Women at Copenhagen, Denmark, in 1980 or a UN International Institute for Training and Research (UNITAR) at Oslo, Norway, in the same year for finding possible contributors (see 2001: 339).

in debates on anthropological research; for example, in James Clifford's by now classical critique of cultural analysis and ethnography and his call for a "comparative cultural studies approach to specific histories, tactics, everyday practices of dwelling *and* traveling: traveling-in-dwelling, dwelling-in-traveling" (36). To state the obvious: the women in exile do not necessarily have a lesser or better account of the situation in 'their' country and those who live there are not automatically more reliable as informants. With regard to *Sisterhood Is Global*, the positions of the contributors need to be taken into account including their local as well as global connections but they are not merely defined by national 'belonging' and their contribution cannot be evaluated primarily via authenticity or representativeness. Morgan later reflected on the limited approach of her early work in international feminism:

> [I]t was largely at conferences. That's all very well, but big meetings are [...] unrepresentative of most 'real people.' [...] There are international globe-trotting jet-sets of feminist elites just as there are national ones. To get at the authentic situation, you have to go *to* it – to the women in the region, in the villages, to the people who never get to go on delegations. (2001: 407)

While this statement can be read as a critical comment on her own selection process for *Sisterhood Is Global* and one that accredits greater importance to local and regional issues, it still clings to ideas of 'authentic' places, people, and experiences. The question, however, could also be how the local and global interact and come into play in a specific region and how feminism(s) can be enacted locally while being linked globally (and vice versa).

Despite its shortcomings, *Sisterhood Is Global* has been an important publication with high ambitions and numerous effects. Not only did it change Morgan's personal life – she claims, for example, that she "couldn't think in a solely national context anymore" (2001: 401) – but, as she holds, its "warm reception" by press and readers contributed to the fact that "international feminism was catching on in the United States" (ibid. 398). The anthology was translated into several languages and is now often regarded 'classic' reading in women's history; and it led to a major strategy meeting and the founding of the Sisterhood Is Global Institute, which is still active today operating out of New York City.[28] While it has been celebrated and critiqued in various ways, I believe a critical regionalist perspective on the volume in the framework of Morgan's oeuvre exposes not only its regional biases and the hegemonic strivings of white US feminism on an international scale but also offers new ways of assessing the nexus between local and global concerns, the modes of analysis, and maybe even calls for examining women's regional sisterhoods in addition to or even instead of the national, global, and local concerns raised in *Sisterhood Is Global*.

[28] See <http://www.sigi.org>, last accessed 18 April 2016.

## Conclusion

My analyses of Friedan's and Morgan's activism revolving around two of their respective publications – *The Feminine Mystique* and *Sisterhood Is Global* – and informed by critical regionalism and comparative cultural studies have indicated that the region is a category to be reckoned with in feminist practices and writing. Critical regionalism thus offers a fresh perspective to address the locations and positionalities of individual actors, to contextualize women's activism and writings, and to delineate the landscapes, literal and metaphorical, that inform, generate, or shape feminisms and that are, in turn, created through feminist activism, thinking, and writing. Not the least, Morgan and Friedan both have contributed to US-American and international feminism that with all of its laudable efforts and inevitable shortcomings remains a fundamental reference point for later feminisms. Therefore, I would like to conclude with some tentative suggestions on the productive connections between feminism and (critical) regionalism that could be explored further in feminist activism and scholarship. Though one could certainly ask whether accounting for the region does only add another factor to intersectional approaches, yet another venue for identity politics, and simply adds another differentiation (and possible barrier for women's solidarity), there are several aspects that, I propose, speak for exploring the potentials of a critical regionalist mode of cultural analysis in the constellation of feminist research and activism.

First, the region can be used as a category of analysis on different levels – referring to geographical locations in their interrelations with race, class, gender, and national(izing) discourses and in their global, (inter)regional, and local interconnections – in order to show unexpected and revealing connections e.g. between activists' geographical, social, and cultural locations and their writings and thinking. Second, critical regionalism offers a new perspective to look back at US-American feminism à la Friedan, Morgan, et al. but also an impulse to examine new regions that have so far escaped the scholarly mappings. This may be particularly relevant to the activism of a 'third wave.' Comer has argued accordingly that "feminism needs new political forms more responsive to the media-saturated culture of today, where feminism itself is a powerful player. Some of the fresher ideas in recent memory, to my way of thinking, come out of Gen. X and third-wave culture, from regions not generally studied or considered to be in the avant-garde of political movements" (2003: 126). Third, as critical regionalism can uncover (often surprising or unexpected) connections between regions, it may be enlisted as a means to contribute to solidarity and sisterhood across regions rather than contribute to adding yet another dividing line for women's activism and feminist work. Fourth, critical regionalism offers a take on global and local concerns and impulses that may be useful in contemporary debates about 'post-feminism' and 'third wave activism.' Taking up critical regionalist premises it is possible to not simply reject post-feminism (shaped by popular media and potentially global in outreach) in favor of local grassroots activism nostalgically associated to the heyday of feminism in the twentieth century. Rather, the globalized media versions of feminism could be accounted for in their tensions with regional and local concerns and this could raise the question of which aspects can be brought together in the context of a particular landscape without discounting its regional specificity or attempting to preserve its 'authenticity.'

To be sure, critical regionalism does not offer a cure-all for the many challenges and problems contemporary feminism has to face on a national, global, or local scale. A project entitled "Sisterhood Is Regional" would probably end up reproducing the problematics e.g. regarding perspective, positionality, selections, and omissions that both Friedan and Morgan enacted in their works and writings. Not the least, because while I have chosen to focus here on the respective settings and landscapes – Friedan's suburb and Morgan's globe – the notion of sisterhood itself would have to be scrutinized as well. Yet, feminisms may have a lot to gain from focusing on the 'region' and picking up on impulses from critical regionalism in order to forge new connections across regions, account for global and local concerns, and probe to what degree solidarity, coalition, and 'sisterhood' can be and, in fact, are regional. The readings of Betty Friedan's and Robin Morgan's work from a critical regional perspective has indicated how feminist activist is inevitably shaped by regional frameworks which are embedded in multi-layered local and global discourses and practices. Vice versa, feminist activism creates its own regions, interregional networks, and global connections that can be critically examined by using a critical regionalist paradigm.

## Works Cited

Basu, Amrita. "Globalization of the Local/Localization of the Global: Mapping Transnational Women's Movements." *Meridians* 1.1 (2000): 68-84. *JSTOR*. Web. 9 June 2016.

Bowlby, Rachel. "'The Problem with No Name': Rereading Betty Friedan's *The Feminine Mystique*." *Feminist Review* 27 (1987): 61-75. *JSTOR*. Web. 9 June 2016.

Chansky, Dorothy. "Usable Performance Feminism for Our Time: Reconsidering Betty Friedan." *Theatre Journal* 60.3 (2008): 341-64. *JSTOR*. Web. 9 June 2016. Print.

Clifford, James. *Routes: Travel and Translation in the Late 20th Century*. Cambridge, MA: Harvard University Press, 1997. Print.

Comer, Krista. "Taking Feminism and Regionalism toward the Third Wave." *A Companion to the Regional Literatures of America*. Ed. Charles L. Crow. Malden, MA: Blackwell, 2003. 111-28. Print.

---. *Landscapes of the New West: Gender and Geography in Contemporary Women's Writing*. Chapel Hill: The University of North Carolina Press, 1999. Print.

Davey, Frank. "Towards the Ends of Regionalism." Riegel et al. 1-17. Print.

Eggener, Keith L. "Placing Resistance: A Critique of Critical Regionalism." *Journal of Architectural Education* 55.4 (2002): 228-37. *JSTOR*. Web. 9 June 2016.

Fermaglich, Kirsten Lise. "'The Comfortable Concentration Camp': The Significance of Nazi Imagery in Betty Friedan's *The Feminine Mystique* (1963)." *Jewish American History* 91.2 (2003): 205-32. Print.

Foote, Stephanie. *Regional Fictions: Culture and Identity in Nineteenth-Century American Literature*. Madison: The University of Wisconsin Press, 2001. Print.

Frampton, Kenneth. "Epilogue: Critical Regionalism Revisited. Reflections on the Mediatory Potential of Built Form." *Vernacular Modernism: Heimat, Globalization, and the Built Environment*. Ed. Maiken Umbach and Bernd Hüppauf. Stanford: Stanford University Press, 2005. 193-97. Print.

---. "Toward a Critical Regionalism: Six Points for an Architecture of Resistance." *The Anti-Aesthetic: Essays on Postmodern Culture*. Ed. Hal Foster. Port Townsend, WA: Bay Press 1983. 16-30. Print.

Friedan, Betty. *The Feminine Mystique*.1963. New York: Norton, 2001. Print.

---. *Life So Far*. New York: Simon & Schuster, 2000. Print.

---. *It Changed My Life: Writings on the Women's Movement*. New York: Random House, 1976. Print.

Hackstaff, Karla, and Jennifer Pierce. "Is Sisterhood Global?" Review of *Sisterhood Is Global*. *Berkeley Journal of Sociology* 20 (1985): 189-204. *JSTOR*. Web. 9 June 2016.

Hennessee, Judith. *Betty Friedan: Her Life*. New York: Random House, 1999. Print.

Herr, Cheryl Temple. *Critical Regionalism and Cultural Studies: From Ireland to the American Midwest*. Gainesville: University Press of Florida, 1996. Print.

Horowitz, Daniel. *Betty Friedan and the Making of* The Feminine Mystique: *The American Left, the Cold War, and Modern Feminism*. Amherst: University of Massachusetts Press, 1998. Print.

Katz, Wendy J., and Timothy R. Mahoney. "Introduction: Regionalism and the Humanities: Decline or Revival?" *Regionalism and the Humanities*. Ed. Wendy J. Katz and Timothy R. Mahoney. Lincoln: University of Nebraska Press, 2008. ix-xxviii. Print.

Lefaivre, Liane, and Alexander Tzonis. *Architecture of Regionalism in the Age of Globalization: Peaks and Valleys in the Flat World*. London: Routledge, 2012. Print.

---. "Tropical Critical Regionalism: Introductory Comments." *Tropical Architecture: Critical Regionalism in the Age of Globalization*. Ed. Alexander

Tzonis, Liane Lefaivre, and Bruno Stagno. Chichester: Wiley, 2001. 1-13. Print.

Mohanty, Chandra Talpade. *Feminism without Borders: Decolonizing Theory, Practicing Solidarity*. Durham: Duke UP, 2003. Print.

Morgan, Robin. *Saturday's Child: A Memoir*. New York: Norton: 2001. Print.

--- (ed.). *Sisterhood Is Global: The International Women's Movement Anthology*. 1984. New York: The Feminist Press, 1996. Print.

Pryse, Marjorie. "Writing Out of the Gap: Regionalism, Resistance, and Relational Reading." Riegel et al. 19-34. Print.

Reichert Powell, Douglas. *Critical Regionalism: Connecting Politics and Culture in the American Landscape*. Chapel Hill: The University of North Carolina Press, 2007. Print.

Riegel, Christian, Herb Wyile, Karen Overbye, and Don Perkins (eds.). *A Sense of Place: Re-Evaluating Regionalism in Canadian and American Writing*. Edmonton: University of Alberta Press, 1997. Print.

Rosen, Ruth. *The World Split Open: How the Modern Women's Movement Changed America*. Rev. and updated ed. New York: Penguin, 2007. Print.

Said, Edward. *Orientalism*. New York: Vintage, 1994. Print.

Siegel, Deborah. *Sisterhood Interrupted: From Radical Women to Grrls Gone Wild*. New York: Palgrave Macmillan, 2007. Print.

Tzonis, Alexander, Liane Lefaivre, and Bruno Stagno (eds.). *Tropical Architecture: Critical Regionalism in the Age of Globalization*. Chichester: Wiley, 2001. Print.

Wilson, Elisabeth. "Review of *Sisterhood Is Global: The International Women's Movement Anthology* by Robin Morgan." *Signs* 11.2 (1986): 390-92. *JSTOR*. Web. 9 June 2016.

Wyile, Herb, Christian Riegel, Karen Overbye, and Don Perkins. "Introduction: Regionalism Revisited." Riegel et al. ix-xiv. Print.

# Over There: Willa Cather's Mobilization of Domestic Spaces in *One of Ours*

*Amy Doherty Mohr*

Born in 1873 in Virginia, Willa Cather moved to Nebraska at age nine, in April 1883. In an interview, she describes the move as a pivotal moment in her life: "I was little and homesick and lonely [...] So the country and I had it out together and by the end of the first autumn the shaggy grass country had gripped me with a passion that I have never been able to shake. It has been the happiness and curse of my life."[1] She later attended the University of Nebraska-Lincoln, and eventually became one of the great American novelists of the early twentieth century. As she writes in her 1922 preface to *Alexander's Bridge*, her novella published in 1912, she followed regionalist writer Sarah Orne Jewett's advice, "[o]f course, one day you will write about your own country. In the meantime, get all you can. One must know the world so well before one can know the parish" (viii). Cather transitioned from her work as managing editor for *McClure's Magazine* to writing short fiction to her life's work as a novelist. The most well-known of the thirteen novels published in the modernist period between 1912 and 1940, *O Pioneers!* (1913) and *My Ántonia* (1918), include lyrical depictions of the Nebraskan landscape while representing the challenges facing the original immigrants who settle the land. The protagonist of *One of Ours* (1922), Claude Wheeler, leaves Nebraska for France as a soldier in World War I. Despite their regional settings, Cather wrote most of these works from New York City, where she lived with her partner of nearly forty years, Edith Lewis (Woodress; "Chronology"). Known for her gender-bending style in her adolescence, when she cut her hair short and called herself William, expecting to follow a masculine career path as a doctor (O'Brien 1987: 96-97), her eventual work as a novelist challenged traditional gender roles, as well as constricting notions of region and nation.

Granting her protagonists increased mobility allows Cather to question the construction of central aspects of identity in her fiction. As Guy Reynolds writes in "Willa Cather's Case: Region and Reputation," Cather "simultaneously invok[es] and resist[s] the provincial" (83). With her focus on pioneers in her early novels and the American soldier in *One of Ours*, which won the Pulitzer Prize in 1923, hers was a "[n]ationalized regionalism" (84). Reynolds writes that Cather's reputation, as well as her publications and honors, placed her within a national context, "[a]nd so, perhaps, the fundamental lesson of Cather's reputation as a regional writer is that in the twentieth century region counts only so far as it figures

[1] Woodress 36. See also Bohlke 31-33. The original interview appeared as "Lure of Nebraska Irresistible, Says Noted Authoress" in the *Omaha Bee* 29 (October 1921): 2. Qtd. in Ahearn.

in the larger national story" (85). Yet the 'Late' Cather, the works published between 1927-1947, are "undeniably cosmopolitan and resolutely non-midwestern" (Reynolds 85). I would argue that Cather's war novel, *One of Ours*, published in 1922, bridges the regional and the cosmopolitan, rendering domestic spaces, considered fixed in terms of local identity and gender roles, particularly in the Great Plains in the early twentieth century, as ultimately unstable and provisional.

The novel narrates Claude Wheeler's journey from Nebraska to France, reversing the traditional belief in the domestic as peaceful and war as destructive as the protagonist, Claude Wheeler, flees his familial and marital homes to find peace among men at war. As Patricia Lee Yongue has noted of *My Ántonia*, the violence in the work, including a murder and suicide, occurs with the mass violence of World War I in the background of the reader's mind, although references to the war do not appear in the novel:

> By 1917, when she was writing *My Ántonia*, the Western world was swallowed up in war and in the vortex of verbal and pictorial messages that accompanies war. Her many references to masculine violence and killing (most of them anti-marriage and anti-family acts) in that novel set mainly in rural Nebraska are the domestic links to the stories of the violence in war-ruined Europe that families were hearing on a daily, sometimes hourly, basis. (144)

In this case, I would go beyond Yongue's identification of these acts of violence as masculine, to emphasize that Cather makes the reader think about violence in a broader sense, in terms of cultural context and belief systems. In *One of Ours*, Cather symbolically juxtaposes peace and violence in regional and international settings, leading the reader to consider the gender and sexual divisions at home and at war and the oppressive and painful effects on those outside the socially accepted norm. As Urgo writes, an "existential terror" shadows Cather's work, and the characters work to find their way to a better place: "Cather's aesthetic is built upon surfaces below which are violent and deadly depths, and above which her best lives attempt to soar" (25, 24). It is up to the reader to interpret the agent of, reason for, and resolution to this terror. In Claude's case (playing on both Cather's "Paul's Case" and Cramer's essay of this title), Claude escapes his father's acts of emotional violence which upend the seemingly stable home of a nuclear family with three sons, and eventually finds a companion in violinist and soldier David Gerhardt at war, providing a respite from the actuality of its horrors. In her depiction of his family and his experience at war, Cather refutes the typically heterosexual and masculinist model of male identity associated with the Middle West, as well as the homosocial but not homosexual standard of the military (Boxwell 289-91). Claude's unusual experience at war led to the criticism of this novel by male writers H.L. Mencken, Sinclair Lewis (Trout 2002: 32), Edmund Wilson (Woodress), and Ernest Hemingway, as she had written on a masculine topic with which she had no personal experience (O'Brien 1989: 186). Merrill Maguire Skaggs has also addressed the issues of Cather writing "a manly battle yarn," drawing on Cather's observation in *The Kingdom of Art*: "When a woman writes a story of adventure, a stout sea tale, a manly battle yarn, anything without wine, women, and love, then I will begin to hope for something great from them, not before" (qtd. in Skaggs 1990: 26). Although such scholars recognize the irony of its patriotism as Cather crosses gender boundaries (Skaggs 1990: 43-44), very few have addressed Claude's sexuality in detail. However, Timothy Cramer argues that "the tension between what to reveal and what to conceal [...] is one of the most fascinating aspects of Cather's art" (151). He references Cather's "The Novel Démeublé," to address the coded representation of sexual orientation in her work. In this suggestive modernist statement on literary style, published in the same year as *One of Ours* (Anders 75), Cather writes, "[i]t is the inexplicable presence of the thing not named, of the over-tone divined by the ear but not heard by it, the verbal mood, the emotional aura of the fact or the thing or the deed, that gives high quality to the novel or the drama, as well as to poetry itself" (6, also qtd. in Cramer 151). Indeed, the evocative symbolism of *One of Ours* sets into motion the emotional conflict beneath the surface of an American narrative of a young man who goes to war. In *Willa Cather's Sexual Aesthetics and the Male Homosexual Literary Tradition*, John Anders argues for a "homosexual paradigm in *One of Ours*, *The Professor's House*, and *Death Comes for the Archbishop*," with the Greek references in these novels and their homoerotic imagery supporting his reading of the evolution in the search for and achievement of an ideal friendship between men (71-74). I am interested in the ways in which Cather, as a regional writer with an international, cosmopolitan sensibility writes gender and sexuality through the transnationalism of her male protagonist in *One of Ours*. I would argue that his disorientation in his home community underlies his desire for mobility, and that the influence of European characters within his region, and French and European-American characters at war, changes his perspective on his role and place in the world. As Claude becomes more 'worldly,' he, and in turn, the reader, becomes more cognizant of the intrinsic connections between domestic and international spaces, undermining a fixed local identity. The question of his outsider status is often expressed in local terms, but suggests the challenges facing both men and women in a period of changing gender roles, as well as his apparent preference for the company of men. Claude's "imprisoned spirit" is initially shared with the local women of the novel, including his mother, Mahailey, and Gladys Farmer, women "whose wish was so beautiful that there were no experiences in this world to satisfy it" (170, 171). Ironically, his spirit is set free at war.

Cather's destabilization of seemingly stable settings and themes have led to a focus on the modernist, transnational elements in her apparent celebration of regional identities (Homestead and Reynolds). Her interest in *Europe* arises from her own European tours ("Mapping"), common to many American writers of the modernist period, along with the Lost Generation, and America's involvement in

World War I. Her research into the experience of her cousin, G.P. Cather, "the first Nebraska officer to die overseas" (Trout 2002: 31) whose reburial in his tiny town of Bladen, Nebraska drew two thousand mourners (Trout 2002: 26), inspired her modernist depiction of World War I in *One of Ours* (Trout 2002: 66), which, as Skaggs notes, is "bathed and saturated in irony" (1990: 40). A central irony of this novel is the focus on the domestic beneath the gloss of war patriotism. Although her focus on domestic spaces in the United States and Europe allows for an international comparison of private realms rather than a focus on the 'theater of war,' her preoccupation with domesticity prompted the ire of many male critics of her time. The intersection of mobility studies and gender studies allows for a closer look at the ways in which violence at home and abroad figures into Cather's depiction of masculinity. Through her attention to domestic spaces, Cather examines the ways in which masculinity functions within a gendered social context within the United States and then introduces different dimensions of gender and sexuality at war, reflecting on their constructions.

During World War I, the call to become a soldier, as Mary Ryder demonstrates in "As Green as Their Money: The Doughboy Naïfs in *One of Ours*," played on the 'innocence' associated with soldiers from the Middle West, who were believed, as their name suggests, to have been largely protected from urban and international influences of modernization, seeing the war as an adventure and opportunity for patriotism, to be heroes of democracy, an extension of American values derived from the Heartland. As Bohlke notes, "Cather's citation [for the 1923 Pulitzer Prize] was 'for the American novel published during the year which shall best present the wholesome atmosphere of American life, and the highest standard of American manners and manhood'" (57). However, her work is more deeply divided than the national narrative of the innocent who goes to war would suggest. In her international perspective on literature, evident in her speech on the novel genre at the Pulitzer Prize ceremony in 1933, she praised Russian and European literary traditions, lamenting that "in America, until within the very last few years, novelists have confined themselves almost entirely to two themes: first, how the young man got his girl, whether by marriage or otherwise; second, how he succeeded in business" ("On the Novel"). Certainly, this speech was neither nationalistic nor patriotic, but emphasized the significance of new forms of expression. Consistent with her views on the novel, she gives her war story its own form by devoting most of the narrative to Claude's experience at home, while refuting traditional heteronormative domestic narratives.

For this novel is not what one would expect of a war novel. It is not only about international conflict, but the confluence of war and domestic spaces, both the home of origin and the series of homes across cultural and national boundaries – Claude's search for a home takes him on a journey through the family home, the married home, the series of homes which provide refuge to soldiers in France, and the temporary home at war he makes with David Gerhardt. While criticism of this novel was initially gendered through Hemingway's comment that she did not serve in the war, Cather's attention to domestic spaces reveals a significant aspect of war (Yongue 151-52) beyond what is now called 'collateral damage' to identities that are formed through private spaces, across geographically determined identities, whether of region or nation. As part of a larger project, I am interested in the development of scholarship on domestic spaces within mobility studies, as Homi Bhabha called for in his "The World and the Home," to account for the transience of homes in both *One of Ours* and *The Professor's House* (1925) for two young men associated with the Middle Western and Southwestern United States who are unexpected precursors of the Lost Generation. Since both protagonists die at war, Cather prevents an expatriated transnational alternative to their lives. Indeed, they exist only in the memories of those who knew them through domestic associations; in the case of Claude, through his mother and their servant, Mahailey, and in Tom Outland's story, through Professor Godfrey St. Peter and his family. Consistent with her earlier novels, Cather focusses on domestic affiliations in international contexts, and continues with the multifaceted theme of domesticity and its gender and sexual codes in perhaps her most masculine novel.

Countering Gertrude Stein's use of the term Lost Generation to refer to literary expatriates who resettled in Europe after World War I, used as an epigraph to Hemingway's *The Sun Also Rises*, Cather suggests that young men such as Claude are not lost in the aftermath of war, but lost before in that they do not fit into the domestic spaces of American life, represented by the American Heartland, the Great Plains, with Nebraska officially recognized as part of the Midwest, but imaginatively seen as part of the West ("Census Regions"; O'Connor). While this region does not receive as much critical attention as New England, the South, or the Southwest – in fact, Mahoney and Katz, in their volume *Regionalism and the Humanities*, call the Midwest "a classic example of a nonexistent region" (xxii) – the Heartland's strong connections with its pioneer and agricultural roots has created its own sense of identity, one that is often read as embodying a masculine strength. In actuality, Nina Baym writes in her work *Women Writers of the American West, 1833-1927* the settling of the west was a "shared narrative" between men and women (3). Furthermore, as Cather indicates through the tensions between nature and industry, Nebraska's origins derived from a mobile national economy based in agriculture. As Kurt E. Kinbacher writes in "Imagining Place: Nebraska Territory, 1854-67," "urban and rural spaces in the territory became symbiotic components of an economy that required both agricultural surpluses and urban entrepôts to distribute them" (259). Claude's malaise, which in part derives from a modernist sensibility, also seems a fitting response to the capitalist industry and mobility inherent in modern agriculture. From her groundbreaking works set in rural Nebraska, *O Pioneers* and *My Ántonia*, Cather's protagonists increasingly resist the rural, with Claude Wheeler of *One of Ours,* choosing to enlist in World War I rather than continue the increasingly industrialized work of the family farm. In contrast to the antipathy towards nature represented by his father and his brother Bayliss, with their emphasis on land speculation and machinery, Cather presents Claude as extraordinarily sensitive, one of the "children of the moon" (171), evoking a feminine aspect which places him outside the stereotypically masculine realm. He often seeks time alone in spaces between farm and home:

> The people whose hearts were set high needed such intercourse – whose wish was so beautiful that there were no experiences in this world to satisfy it. And these children of the moon, with their unappeased longing and futile dreams, were a finer race than the children of the sun. This conception flooded the boy's heart like a second moonrise, flowed through him indefinite and strong, while he lay deathly still for fear of losing it. (171)

Being a child of the moon, Claude has difficulty finding a place on earth that would allow him to find solace and companionship. As Leonard Dawson, a friend who seems fully assimilated to the masculine norms of the region, states, Claude does not seem to "fit in right" despite his physical strength, because his sensibilities do not conform to the traditional masculinity associated with the region and the work of the farm (116).

For Cather, this region represents the American mainstream cultural notion of home, including marriage (presumptive heterosexuality), Protestantism, home ownership, and effective land management. In sum, this region, as the term 'Heartland' suggests, is a synecdoche for a specific construct of home at the core of American identity. In her earlier works, Cather focused on the complicated domestic spaces of female protagonists, whether inside the home, in *My Ántonia*, or outside, as in Alexandra's management of her family farm after her father's death in *O Pioneers!* There are many feminist readings of her novels, including the scholarship of O'Brien, Rosowski, and Romines but the study of the masculine relationship to domestic spaces in this region has not received as much analysis. Claude's brother Bayliss, who has inspired Cecilia Kingsbury's comparisons with the dictatorial German *Kultur* in propaganda of the period as well as American industrialists, and his father, who resents Claude's sensitivity, are men cut of the same cloth, with a cruel streak and dark humor reminiscent of Faulkner. In her study of Cather and Faulkner in *Axes*, Skaggs writes of the similarities between *One of Ours* and Faulkner's *Soldiers Pay*: "One very startling similarity between the two, however, is their agreement that war itself can be heaven, even preferable to peace, if peace is too static to bear" (2007: 7). However, Cather shows that it is both the predictability of regional life and the controlling impulsivity of his father that is too much to bear. In *One of Ours*, a disturbing scene of Claude's troubled home occurs when his father cuts down the cherry tree, symbolic of the legend of George Washington who cut down his father's cherry tree and then said he could not tell a lie, admitting his guilt and establishing himself as truthful to generations of American children. Thus through ironic allusion, Cather's depiction of Claude's father suggests that his openness masks complicity with violent norms within

American culture. When the father cruelly encourages his wife and son to pick some cherries, they discover that the "beautiful round-topped cherry tree," his mother's favorite, lies next to a "bleeding stump" (25). While his mother tries to excuse his father's actions, which could be considered a form of symbolic domestic violence to the family and physical violence to the environment, Claude flies into a rage. Far from following in his father's footsteps, he will try to make his own way by matriculating at the state university.

The Midwest is home to some of America's premier land grant universities, which Cather's protagonists in *One of Ours* and *The Professor's House* attend before going to war. The presence of the universities in both of Cather's war novels, as Trout argues, speaks to the impact of the war on intellectual life, and its incomprehensibility to both European and American scholars as well as the loss of artists, writers, and intellectuals in World War I (150). Claude's sensibilities set him apart from his family, yet he remains in limbo, caught between the regional emphasis on the nuclear family and traditional gender roles, and his own inclination for a more wide-ranging existence and liberation. He finds this in the state university, which he elects to attend temporarily and independently over the denominational college of his parents choosing, inspired by a devoted professor of European History. This decision represents a deeper intellectual existence, inspired by an international perspective, that attracts Claude's attention and offers him respite from the parochial constrictions of his home and locale.

Claude only realizes his change of perspective when he is confronted with the difference from accepted norms when he goes away to study in Lincoln, Nebraska, which, relative to Frankfort, *is* the city. Along with his studies, he is accepted into the intellectual and culturally vibrant home of a German-American family of intellectually curious young men, drawing the attention of the attractive widowed mother, Mrs. Erlich. Notably, when he visits the Erlich family, he realizes his family never enjoys the kind of life that he begins to find at their home. Although the Wheelers have the means to enjoy their lives, they would rather spend their money on the timesaving devices developing in the United States while living in an atmosphere of emotional and intellectual repression. As Claude notes, "[h]e had grown up with the conviction that it was beneath his dignity to explain himself" (Cather *One of Ours*: 38). Claude begins to realize that his alienation reveals more about the character of the region as defined by his family and local community than his own inclinations and longing, which have not found a place, or a person, where and with whom he can find comfort and acceptance.

For a time, his visits with Europeans and his study of European History (32), which challenge his internalized American ideology, provide the perspective he needs to question the values of his place of origin as he comes to understand the problems and limitations of his existence. In Frankfort, Nebraska, an obvious alteration of the German city, suggestive of its European roots, Cather reveals the construction of the American region as always already showing its international interconnectedness, and the character of a region including a combination of choice and chance, rather than a stable identity as suggested in American cultural history. Cather's interest in the effects of mobility arose from her own transition from Virginia to Nebraska and the immigrant influence on Red Cloud, Nebraska. She listened to the stories of European immigrants as a young girl (O'Brien 1987: 72-73), and eventually wrote her own stories of pioneers rising from European roots, succeeding or failing depending on their past experience in their country of origin and their own ability to adapt to a new way of life. The cultural make-up of the region, she shows, is not a given, but created by the integration of generations of settlers with their distinct cultural backgrounds, personalities, and stories. Even Claude's own parents are not native to the area, but are transplants from New England; his father from Maine, his mother from Vermont (Cather *One of Ours*: 9), with his father representing the worst of Manifest Destiny expansionism, replacing the Indians who originally settled the land, narrated in the ideologically highly charged subtle imagery of settlement, with nature falling to the background:

> He had come to this part of Nebraska when the Indians and the buffalo were still about, remembered the grasshopper year and the big cyclone, had watched the farms emerge one by one from the great rolling page where once only the wind wrote its story. He had encouraged new settlers to take up homesteads, urged on courtships, lent young fellows the money to marry on, seen families grow and prosper; until he felt a little as if all this were his own enterprise. (ibid. 7-8)

Despite Mr. Wheeler's seemingly easy assimilation through his aggressive social and land management, reminiscent of Slotkin's studies of violence and enviromental destruction on the frontier, the authoritiative position he enjoys actually derives from his cultural status. The integration of newcomers varies, Cather demonstrates, with migrants within the United States and immigrants from countries at peace with America faring better than those who come from countries on the wrong side of international conflict. For example, the initial acceptance of the German restaurant owner, Mrs. Voigt, turns to discrimination (ibid. 200-02), and of the farmers Yoeder and Oberlies, to charges of disloyalty (ibid. 194-98), respectively, after World War I begins. The domestic region of the Heartland and its social order, seemingly firm and unwavering from an outsider's perspective, becomes more tense and unstable with the influence of these cultural prejudices and the reminders that its façade of stability was created on a violent foundation. The antidote to human intervention, social conflict, and alienation, always in Cather's novels, is the land, and there is very little freedom left within it, save for the quietness of Lovely Creek or a bubbling spring, "a wise unobtrusive voice, murmuring night and day, continually telling the truth to people who could not understand it" (ibid. 127). Nobody stops long enough to listen, except for Claude in brief moments, and they become increasingly removed from their natures and instincts. In her impressionistic references to nature, Cather suggests the focus on industry, development, and social conflicts remove people from their origins; socially constructed divisions have taken over.

The 'truth' that the spring suggests but people do not understand, refers to those sitting nearby, Claude and Gladys, who intends to marry Bayliss Wheeler, despite her attraction to Claude, who will marry Enid Royce. In this novel, Cather follows a pattern of questioning the institution of marriage as she does in her earlier works. The legal unions are most often portrayed as undesirable, ranging from incompatibility in many cases, to murder, in the most extreme case of Frank Shabata's shooting of his wife Marie and her lover Emil in *O Pioneers!* (also see Handley). While this in itself could be an example of realism, and Cather's unwillingness to write a typical romance, the closest relationships she describes exist in same-sex friendships. Earlier queer readings of Cather's work, notably by Eve Sedgwick, most often addressed "Paul's Case," her short story of a young man, coded as gay through her references to a difference and style reminiscent of Oscar Wilde, who flees the staid heterosexuality and lurking violence of his father in his Pittsburgh home. This led to a full consideration of queer sexuality in her novels in Marilee Lindemann's *Willa Cather: Queering America* and Scott Herring's *Another Country: Queer Anti-Urbanism.* While both works develop Cather scholarship within gender studies, neither takes a close look at sexuality in this novel. As these critical works suggest, sexuality, in Cather's novels, is connected with place; either expressed in urban centers, as in Paul's escape from an oppressive environment in a Pittsburgh suburb to New York City in "Paul's Case" (Herring 2007) or coded in her rural novels. In *Another Country,* Herring writes that "Cather's corpus suggests a cross-identification with men as well as a counter-identification with lesbian-based literary metronormativity" (37). Rather she sought to represent gay partnerships, though coded, that could exist peacefully in rural spaces (Herring 41). She creates this 'space apart' in Claude's experience both in Nebraska and in France.

Then, as today, such relationships are more subtly coded than in "Paul's Case," representative of the more conservative ethos of the time and place and striking a balance which would allow her to reach a broad range of readers. I would argue that Cather's approach to these relationships is not motivated by a fear of coming out either personally or fictionally (Cramer 159), but rather that she seeks an artistic balance that allows all elements to exist simultaneously, the landscape, domestic relationships, and the local ways of life. To return to the reference to "the thing not named [...] the emotional aura of the fact or the thing or the deed" in Cather's "The Novel Démeublé" (6), Cather allows the domestic to exist beyond its material to encompass its emotional existence. In her novel, the domestic is not gendered per se as feminine or heterosexual, as defined by the locale, but exists in a more cosmopolitan setting, suggestive of a home in the world, indeed a sense of home in the best sense of the word, which has the potential to exist in all places. The modernist introduction of new social norms, through changing national and international influences at war, as indicated by Claude's friendships with the Erlich boys and Ernest Havel, makes Claude begin to question his parents' cultural norms as well as the strictness of his locale.

Cather deals with the intersection between regionalism and transnationalism in the references to Bohemians in her novels, drawing on the stereotypes of the time (Ross). For example, the Bohemian Marie Shabata in *O Pioneers!* possesses an impulsiveness which contrasts the Swedish Alexandra Bergson's methodic, stoic approach to life, leading to their friendship, which Elizabeth Ammons suggests is a "same-sex romantic attraction" (128). In *One of Ours*, Cather also posits a free-spirited Bohemian, Ernest Havel, a "free-thinker" (106) who counters Claude's malaise and allows him to consider his own feelings about religion and marriage, which run counter to those of his family and community. Notably, his discussions with Ernest take place outside of his home of origin or his married home, with the friendship becoming a space that allows him to be free of the constrictions of social expectations. As Anders notes, Ernest and Claude meet together for "a quiet afternoon outside of town": "The stream trickled by under the willow roots with a cool, persuasive sound. Claude and Ernest lay in the shade, their coats under their heads, talking very little" (12). I would add that this stream along Lovely Creek seems to echo the spring that spoke the truth to those who could not understand, when Gladys and Claude were alone. The repetitive natural imagery within her work allows her to contrast scenes thematically, allowing for a comparison of the consciousness of the 'persuasive' sound in this scene with their deafness to truth in the other. Through such friendships, Claude realizes that his parents' social norms, his father's aggressive land management and man about town behavior and his mother's religious fervor and her constricted life as a wife devoted to a cruel man, have created a domestic culture in the private sphere that exemplifies the oppressive potential of a patriarchal ideology. Claude waivers between fleeing from and succumbing to this culture. As he reveals to Ernest, whose desire for security (perhaps meaning marriage) he laments, he "imagines that there was something splendid about life, if he could but find it!" (86). This image of something splendid leads to his false choice to marry Enid, and continues to elude him, until he goes to France, serves in the war, and meets David Gerhardt.

Despite his obvious proclivities toward an intellectual life – in choosing to study under a Classics professor and in his conversations with the Erlichs and Ernest – he eventually marries, in one of many anticlimactic marriages in Cather's work – Enid, a Prohibitionist. As an early feminist, she drives her own car, which makes Claude uncomfortable, with the automobile symbolizing the "values of an oppressively insular small-town world where technology is valued over art, total compliance to social convention is demanded, and intellectualism is scorned" (Trout 2010: 215). Despite the warning of Enid's father, Claude, who continually seeks a stable relationship to the world and a purpose in life, decides to marry her when she nursed him back to health after an accident when ploughing a field with his mules. Both questioned the decision to marry; Enid originally rejected his proposal, and Claude consciously reflects on his desire for a sense of purpose rather than, necessarily, a wife (122). Rather, "he thought how she was to be the one who would put him right with the world and make him fit into the life about him" (122). Mahailey, their servant from Virginia, a Southern survivor of the Civil War and a victim of domestic violence, wonders at the wedding ceremony "what it was the preacher did to make the wrongest thing in the world seem like the rightest thing in the world" (158). Claude eventually must admit that their marriage doesn't exist as such. In a moment of dark humor, Enid closes him out of the sleeping car on their honeymoon, leaving him to admit to her, in overdone *double-entendre*, that sometimes he left things on the train, the meaning of which is apparently lost on Enid. Eventually, she leaves to become a missionary in China, and he goes to war, leaving their perfect house, built from his construction and her domestic efficiency, empty.

Claude, then is not a stereotypical American soldier. Neither fully innocent of the world nor devoted to a single cause, he uses his mobility as a soldier for other purposes; in short, he seeks a home that meets his needs. As he says of his family home, he "both loved and hated to come home" (40). Of his home with Enid, he distinguishes between the material objects of the house and the elusiveness of home in the "sick feeling of his soul" and the aborted attempt to follow tradition epitomized in "the crooked trees with empty birds' nests in their forks" (184). His provisional relationship with home suggests that rather than being rooted, home is unstable, dependent on social context, and defined by personal relations. Claude belongs to several different kinds of homes simultaneously, countering common notions of home in this period as local and regional, and war as an extension of national values, by creating a space in which people meet amid violent conflict, irrevocably influence each other, a space in which divisions are not so easily maintained, ultimately making it impossible to return to the enclosed home of origin, either physically or psychologically. In fact, the impossibility of returning home effectively results in his death. Thus, Cather maintains several threads of narrative associated with the domestic: one, the generic tale of the Lost Generation, that after having experienced the horrors of war, one can never go home again; two, an underlying belief, that the domestic costs of war, both at home and abroad, should count as much as the lauded deaths of the soldiers; and three, that home can be experienced elsewhere, outside of the established boundaries of region and nation.

Claude finds in his travels a series of homes that temporarily meet his needs. In Frankfort, Nebraska, Claude ends up finding his own space outside the home: "The timber claim was his refuge. In the open, grassy spots, shut in by the bushy walls of yellowing ash trees, he felt unmarried and free; free to smoke as much as he liked, and to read and dream" (174). Despite his antipathy towards industrialization, represented by his wife, brother, and father, he decides to leave behind their home to become a soldier in World War I. On the troop ship from New York, Claude's mobility allows a psychological flexibility; as he "moved away" from conversations about "sweethearts and war-brides," he does so "with the happy feeling that he was the least married man on the boat" (247). Ironically, he finds his place when he is literally at sea, treating those on the warship who suffer from the influenza epidemic, effectively inverting the nursing role that Enid played, which as Pearl James argues, could be seen as a threatening New Woman role in its time, to gain a new, sanctioned position in a homosocial environment (Boxwell 302). Recognized for the first time for his leadership, Claude finds a sense of purpose, which seems lacking throughout his life. This sense of military duty slides in domestic scenes, when Claude seems practically blissful in France, where he and David stay with a French couple, the Jouberts. Significantly, the presence of the cherry tree as the refuge where Mme. Joubert sews and they share their meals undoes the symbolism of the bleeding cherry tree of the Wheeler home with a scene of domestic harmony (280, 286). Furthermore, this compatibility extends to him and his friend: "To be so warm, so dry, so clean, so beloved!" (326). Far from 'the doughboys' who spring from comfortable homes in the Midwest and Great Plains to find unimaginable horrors at war, Claude has experienced psychological violence in the United States and temporarily finds security and comfort in his identity on the warship and in France, before engaging in warfare and quietly facing his own death. As it did for Cather, the cultural life of Europe represents an antidote to his constricted American life; the uniting of these contrasts at the university and at war suggests the beginnings of an internationalizing dynamic later associated with the Lost Generation, which would influence the full spectrum of modernist writers, including both Cather and Hemingway.

To say that Claude 'finds himself' in peaceful settings at war while the families who take him in have suffered the violent deaths of their loved ones may make Cather's version of World War I seem somewhat unrealistic and self-serving. However, while she does not engage in lengthy battle descriptions, she includes many examples of deaths affecting families in Europe, the deaths of the Joubert's two sons (286) and Mlle. de Courcy's brother (313), the young Belgian refugee who remains traumatized by the death of her mother (288), the girl on the street eating chocolate, only to die violently, "blood and brains oozing out in her yellow hair" (346). The 'shellhole' turned swimming hole that turns into a soldier's grave also serves as a reminder of the battles and their horrible ends (295-96). Despite the focus on heroism in US war memorials (Trout 2002), Cather does not depict Claude as a war hero who purposefully joins the war to spread democracy; he is attracted to the study of the martyr Joan of Arc and has a vague sense of purpose in going to war. Instead, she focuses on his individual experience, which is not contained within a national, consistently patriotic context; his goal is fulfilled in companionship rather than in battle. Cather certainly risked losing part of her audience with Claude's ambivalent reflections in this war narrative; her focus on the individual shifts the war narrative from patriotism to a modernist reflection on the role of the individual in relation to the group, striking a careful and at times an uneasy balance between heroism and alienation.

For Claude functions largely outside the group and its social norms, both at home and at war. However, he never consciously awakens to his desires within the voice of the narrative except in his own admiration of David Gerhardt, an accomplished violinist and soldier, an American with a German family name, an artist reminiscent of the German family who provided shelter and culture to Claude in his time at the state university. A conversation when Claude finally questions his reasons for enlisting takes place in an "open glade like an amphiteatre" surrounded by forest (327), an intimate environment, reminiscent of Claude's timber claim and his talks with Ernest (Anders 88-89). David enters the war in a more determined way than Claude, in his decision to prove his manhood by going to war: "I didn't feel I was a good enough violinist to admit that I wasn't a man" (329). "I've sometimes wondered whether the young men of our time had to die to bring a new idea into the world [...] something Olympian" (330-31). Since David has already rejected the notion that he is serving "to make the world safe for Democracy, or any rhetoric of that sort" (330), this "new idea" remains undefined, but suggests something that unites them for this cause, which associates them with Greek gods (Anders 89) rather than the future, with a suggestion that ideas which do not exist now could exist after their deaths. Claude's image of David suggests his infatuation: "he was always hunting for someone whom he could admire without reservations; someone he could envy, emulate, wish to be." The idea of someone like David seemed to have already existed somewhere within him: "Now he believed that even then he must have had some faint image of a man like Gerhardt in his mind." In the final sentence, the ellipsis suggests, that it would be difficult for them to exist anywhere together otherwise: "It was only in war times that their paths would have been likely to cross; or that they would have had anything to do together ... any of the common interests that make men friends" (332). Of course, the notion of strong homosocial bonds within the military have existed since antiquity; the significance here is that David seems to fulfill a dream not of a generic male bonding like in military comradeship but an individualized relationship, an image that Claude has always sought (Cramer 158). The home, and the ideals represented by a sense of place, which seem to elude him, he finds, temporarily, with David. The sense of "physical well-being" he finds in France (282), the sensual descriptions of the house he and David share as boarders within the military setting, even the dugout seems to have a romantic air about it (Cramer 159): "Between the two bunks was a soap-box table, with a candle stuck in a green bottle, an alcohol stove, a *bain-marie*, and two tin cups" (294-95). Although Claude has attractions to women over the course of the novel, including Gladys Farmer, whom he admires for her desire for something greater than her place in town or society, or Mlle. Olive, the French woman he has an affinity for (316-17), their quick and rather factual conversation with a deeper emotional response suggests expatriate writing of the superficial yet intense relations of travel and expatriation, while the moments with David suggest a deeper and stronger emotional bond, which he had not previously found, one as he admits would not have been possible in his previous life.

While Claude's sexual orientation is never identified, the most overt representation of the possibility of homosexual attraction occurs when a German soldier is shot by Officer Hicks, after Claude "caught him in the back with a bayonet" (348), visually his first violent act at war, notably as Boxwell states, "an act of killing an effeminate homosexual" (305). As he goes through the "very handsome" officer's effects, an official act turns voyeuristic: Claude opens a locket he is wearing, and sees a "young man, pale as snow, with blurred forget-me-not eyes" (349). He muses aloud, "[i]t looks like a poet, or something. Probably a kid brother, killed at the beginning of the war" (349), closing off the possibility of a romance with another man. David, more knowing than Claude, confirms "Probably," distracts him with "the inlay work on the handle of the officer's revolver," a combination of aesthetic pleasure and masculine violence, and then "looked at him as if he were very much pleased with him, – looked indeed, as if something pleasant had happened in this room; where, God knew, nothing had" (349). This scene, then, is reminiscent of the ways in which gay sexuality temporarily enters social discourse and then is shut down. As in other cases of ambiguity regarding sexuality or sexual orientation in Cather's work, Claude's naïveté could be accepted within the context of a traditional heterosexual narrative with a plausible interpretation offered. However, to a knowing reader, and certainly to contemporary scholars of Cather, the locket, a sign of a romantic gift and a cherished relationship, is likely that of a lover. David, already coded as more worldly than Claude, seemingly protects him from acknowledging his attractions while admitting to himself his own. Anders notes that "Cather's German officer is an ambiguously emblematic character, both 'one of ours' in his homosexuality and 'Other' in his demonization, a position not unlike the one in which some of Claude's German-American neighbors find themselves back home" (93). Through this scene, Cather reveals the constructions of nation, gender, and sexuality, which structure social divisions, and the uneasy interpretations, self-deceptions, and manipulations that sustain them.

Through the deaths of Claude and David, Cather suggests the personal, as well as cultural and social, losses incurred by war. Their friend says, "[t]hank God I never told him […] Thank God for that!" Their friendship ends ironically, with "three clean bullet holes," which may be seen as parallel to the national desire to evade the actualities of the horrors of war, not only as artifice but also to question the sanitized narratives that are told (Trout 2002: 15, 33-34, 54-55). The more complicated narratives, of ugly deaths, violent homes, and attractions beneath the surface of military brotherhood remain largely unspoken. Cather broaches a subject of gays in the military that was absolutely unspeakable in her time, and only very recently legally addressed in our own. In short, the domestic spaces he encounters at war in his friendship with David and in the Joubert home allow an alternative to the unsatisfying domestic spaces of Claude's local experience.

Claude's restlessness and psychic homelessness lead to a transnational choice that then allows for reflection on the relationship between home and the world, not through an easy cosmopolitanism but through a realignment, clash, and seriality of domestic spaces. In "The World and the Home," Homi Bhabha writes "[i]n a feverish stillness, the intimate recesses of the domestic space become sites for history's most intricate invasions. In that displacement, the border between home and world becomes confused; and, uncannily, the private and the public become part of each other, forcing upon us a vision that is as divided as it is disorienting" (358). I am interested in the ways in which these "intricate invasions" occur in the domestic space of home as well as abroad at war, so that the private and public become part of each other. The violence at home is not separate from the violence of war; and the peace that Claude ironically finds at war is also indicated in quieter moments, alone in a timber claim or with a friend, outside of the domestic space of his home, and often influenced by cultural differences, including his own difference from 'the all-American' culture.

The cultural differences between Europe and the United States, often referenced as generically 'Western' in our own time, stood in contrast in Cather's time, a division emphasized through the literature of World War I, expatriation, and the 'Lost Generation.' Claude's discomfort with home resonates with Bhabha's notion of the "unhomely":

> In the stirrings of the unhomely, another world becomes visible. It has less to do with forcible eviction and more to do with the uncanny literary and social effects of enforced social accommodation or historical migrations and cultural relocations. The home does not remain the domain of domestic life, nor does the world simply become its social or historical counterpart. The unhomely is the shock of recognition of the world-in-the-home, the home-in-the-world. (358-59)

Although Bhabha's work has obvious references to postcolonial immigration narratives, 'the shock of recognition,' symbolized by Claude's entry into war, also allows for reflection on 'enforced social accommodation' experienced at home, and the 'literary and social effects' of historical migrations and cultural relocations." The modernist period and World War I, in particular, a time of increased international mobility, allow for reflection on the meanings of home and mobility.

While Claude's 'home' in Europe and European homes would seem to suggest what the Lost Generation expatriates discovered, Cather includes a character whose American regional identity 'places' Claude and calls him home through personal and cultural memory, after his death. A lingering figure in the book is that of Mahailey, a Southern servant to the family, who experienced a brutal marriage, and finds shelter in the family's home, providing companionship to his mother, with both often working side by side in the kitchen. Ann Romines, a scholar of

Cather's Southern origins, notes that Mahailey stands in for a Cather family servant, Marjorie Anderson, who moved with them from Virginia to Nebraska (2006). Mahailey, a Southern regional character without a formal education, speaks in dialect, often dropping the endings of her words, and as regional and minority characters often do, providing the most direct and heartfelt observations on the family dynamic. Though her name and Southern dialect might lead to the assumption that she is a black servant (her race is not mentioned), Mahailey is effectively an untouchable because of class associations with her poor whiteness as an Appalachian, which continues today. Romines details Cather's childhood connections: "Willow Shade, Cather's childhood home, literally had its back to the economically depressed Appalachian Mountains" (2003). Claude's connection with her, shown by Mahailey's noting that he "never avoided touching her" and her ability to "read" him despite her own illiteracy (20-21) suggests that they come from a similar place, figuratively if not literally; both have experienced a kind of violence, emotionally and physically, and alienation from their homes. Along with her experience of domestic violence, she is the only character in his family who has experienced war, through her family's involvement in the Civil War (177). The final lines of the novel allow the omniscient narrator to interpret Mahailey's consciousness from a respectful distance: "Mrs. Wheeler always feels that God is near, – but Mahailey is not troubled by any knowledge of interstellar spaces, and for her He is nearer still – directly overhead, not so very far above the kitchen stove" (371). Uttering these words after his mother's reflection that her son was "safe, safe" (370) from the suicides of returning soldiers, the narrator offers a religious statement from a backwoods character with a deep spirituality, someone who recognizes that Claude ultimately escapes the domestic reality which defined her own. Her sentimental reflection would also appeal to the patriotic readers of Cather's time, as it provides a positive interpretation of his death, countering the actual complexity of his experience at war. However, this novel challenges sentimental or categorical readings. Claude's experience of the world outside of his home is not presented as an easy adventure, nor does it end with the lingering malaise of the returning soldier, nor the rejection of everything American. The novel rather demonstrates the difficulty of finding a home in a place and time defined by its desire for stability. Claude pursues the freedom to choose what he wants for himself, something outside the American Dream. In tracing Claude's emotional journey, Cather shows the limitations of regional and national identities in a soldier who does not fit the typical American narrative, but temporarily finds a home in the world after leaving the world at home.

## Works Cited

### *Primary Texts*

Cather, Willa. "Preface." *Alexander's Bridge*. 1912. New York: Dover, 1922. viii. Print.

---. *Death Comes for the Archbishop*. 1927. New York: Vintage, 1990. Print.

---. *My Ántonia*. 1918. Boston: Houghton, 1995. Print.

---. "The Novel Démeublé." *The New Republic* 30 (12 April 1922): 5-6. *The Willa Cather Archive*. Web. 9 June 2016.

---. *O Pioneers!* 1913. New York: Penguin, 1994. Print.

---. "On the Novel." Pulitzer Prize Awards Ceremony. Plaza Hotel, New York, NY. 4 May 1933. *Willa Cather in Person: Interviews, Speeches, and Letters*. Ed. L. Brent Bohlke. Lincoln: University of Nebraska Press, 1986: n. pag. *The Willa Cather Archive*. Ed. Andrew Jewell. University of Nebraska-Lincoln. Web. 7 April 2016.

---. *One of Ours*. 1922. New York: Vintage, 1991. Print. All page numbers reference this edition.

---. *One of Ours*. Lincoln: University of Nebraska Press. New York: Knopf, 1922. *The Willa Cather Archive*. Web. 9 June 2016.

---. *The Professor's House*. 1925. New York: Vintage, 1990. Print.

### *Secondary Sources*

Ahearn, Amy. "Willa Cather: Longer Biographical Sketch." *The Willa Cather Archive*. Web. 9 June 2016.

Ammons, Elizabeth. *Conflicting Stories: American Women Writers at the Turn into the Twentieth Century*. New York: Oxford University Press, 1992. 121-39. Print.

Anders, John P. *Willa Cather's Sexual Aesthetics and the Male Homosexual Literary Tradition*. Nebraska: University of Lincoln, 1999. 71-96. Print.

Baym, Nina. *Women Writers of the American West, 1833-1927*. Urbana: University of Illinois Press, 2011. Print.

Bhabha, Homi. "The World and the Home." *The Domestic Space Reader*. Ed. Chiara Briganti and Kathy Mezei. Toronto: University of Toronto Press, 2012. 358-62. Print.

Bohlke, L. Brent. Introduction. "1923: Paris." *Willa Cather in Person: Interviews, Speeches, and Letters*. Ed. L. Brent Bohlke. Lincoln: University of Nebraska Press, 1986. Print.

Boxwell, D.A. "In Formation: Male Homosocial Desire in Willa Cather's *One of Ours*." *Eroticism and Containment: Notes from the Flood Plain*. Ed. Carol

Siegel and Ann Kibbey. New York: New York University Press, 1994. 285-310. Print.

"Census Regions and Divisions of the United States." US Census Bureau. 7 September 2000. Web. 19 August 2013.

"Chronology." *The Willa Cather Archive*. Ed. Andrew Jewell. University of Nebraska-Lincoln. Web. 19 August. 2013.

Cramer, Timothy R. "Claude's Case: A Study of the Homosexual Temperament in Willa Cather's *One of Ours*." *South Dakota Review* (1993): 143-73. Print.

Handley, William R. "Unwedded West: Cather's Divides." *Marriage, Violence, and the Nation in the American Literary West*. Cambridge, UK: Cambridge University Press, 2002. 125-58. Print.

Herring, Scott. *Another Country: Queer Anti-Urbanism*. New York: New York University Press, 2010. Print.

---. "Willa Cather's Experiment in Luxury." *Queering the Underworld: Slumming, Literature, and the Undoing of Lesbian and Gay History*. Chicago: University of Chicago Press, 2007. 67-103. Print.

Homestead, Melissa J., and Guy J. Reynolds (eds.). "Introduction." *Cather Studies* 9: *Willa Cather and Modern Cultures* (2011). ix-xx. Print.

James, Pearl. "The 'Enid Problem': Dangerous Modernity in *One of Ours*." *Cather Studies* 6 (2006): n. pag. Web. 9 June 2016.

Jewell, Andrew (ed.). *The Willa Cather Archive*. University of Nebraska-Lincoln. 2004-16. Web. 9 June 2016. <http://cather.unl.edu/>.

Kinbacher, Kurt E. "Imagining Place: Nebraska Territory, 1854-67." Mahoney and Katz 251-73. Print.

Kingsbury, Cecilia. "Squeezed into an Unnatural Shape: Bayliss Wheeler and the Element of Control in *One of Ours*." *Cather Studies* 6 (2006). Web. 9 June 2016.

Lindemann, Marilee. *Willa Cather: Queering America*. New York: Columbia University Press, 1999. Print.

"Mapping a Writer's World: A Geographic Chronology of Willa Cather's Life." *Willa Cather Archive*. Ed. Andrew Jewell. University of Nebraska-Lincoln. Web. 9 June 2016.

Mahoney, Timothy R., and Wendy J. Katz (eds.). *Regionalism and the Humanities*. Lincoln: University of Nebraska Press, 2008. 79-94. Print.

O'Brien, Sharon. "Combat Envy and Survivor Guilt: Willa Cather's 'Manly Battle Yarn.'" *Arms and the Woman: War, Gender, and Literary Representation*. Ed. Helen M. Cooper, Adrienne Auslander Munich, and Susan Merrill Squier. Chapel Hill: University of North Carolina Press, 1989. 184-204. Print.

---. *Willa Cather: The Emerging Voice*. New York: Oxford University Press, 1987. Print.

O'Connor, Daniel. "East is East, West is West, but Midwest?" *New York Times* 3 May 1987: Opinion. Web. 9 June 2016.

Reynolds, Guy. "Willa Cather's Case: Region and Reputation." *Regionalism and the Humanities*. Mahoney and Katz 79-94. Print.

Romines, Ann. "Willa Cather's Civil War: A Very Long Engagement." *Cather Studies* 6 (2006). Web. 9 June 2016.

---. "Admiring and Remembering: The Problem of Virginia." *Cather Studies* 5 (2003). Web. 9 June 2016.

Rosowski, Susan J. *Birthing a Nation: Gender, Creativity, and the West in American Literature.* Lincoln: University of Nebraska Press, 1999. Print.

Ross, Edward Alsworth. "Racial Consequences of Immigration." *Century Magazine* 87.4 (February 1914): 615-22. Print.

Ryder, Mary R. "As Green as Their Money": The Doughboy Naïfs in *One of Ours*." *Cather Studies* 6 (2006). Web. 9 June 2016.

Sedgwick, Eve Kosofsky. "Across Gender, Across Sexuality: Willa Cather and Others." *South Atlantic Quarterly* 88 (1989): 53-72. Print.

Skaggs, Merrill Maguire. *Axes: Willa Cather and William Faulkner*. Lincoln: University of Nebraska Press, 2007. Print.

---. *After the World Broke in Two: The Later Novels of Willa Cather*. Charlottesville: University Press of Virginia, 1990. Print.

Slotkin, Richard. *The Fatal Environment: The Myth of the Frontier in the Age of Industrialization, 1800-1890*. New York: Atheneum, 1985. Print.

Trout, Steven. *On the Battlefield of Memory: The First World War and American Remembrance, 1919-1941*. Tuscaloosa: University of Alabama Press, 2010. Print.

---. *Memorial Fictions: Willa Cather and the First World War*. Lincoln: University of Nebraska Press, 2002. Print.

Urgo, Joseph R. "Existential Terror in Cather." *Violence, the Arts, and Willa Cather*. Ed. Joseph Urgo and Merrill Maguire Skaggs. Madison: Fairleigh Dickinson University Press, 2007. 11-30. Print.

Woodress, James. *Willa Cather: A Literary Life*. Lincoln: University of Nebraska Press, 1987. *The Willa Cather Archive*. Ed. Andrew Jewell. University of Nebraska-Lincoln. Web. 9 June 2016.

Yongue, Patricia Lee. "For Better and for Worse: At Home and at War in *One of Ours*." *Willa Cather: Family, Community, and History (The BY University Symposium)*. Ed. John J. Murphy, Linda Hunter Adams, and Paul Rawlins. Provo, UT: Brigham Young University Humanities Publications Center, 1990. 141-53. Print.

# Blue Northers and Barbed Wire: Modernization and the Village in Larry McMurtry's *The Last Picture Show*

*Rachael Price*

Beginning in 1969, in the wake of the postmodern era in popular culture, the American television network CBS instigated what was known as the "rural purge," cancelling all of its previously popular rural-themed programming (with more popular examples being *Petticoat Junction, The Beverly Hillbillies, Green Acres,* and the Andy Griffith spin-off *Mayberry RFD*) in the space of just two years. Indeed, the anti-pastoralism of CBS's head of programming, 33-year-old Fred Silverman (often billed as "the first executive who grew up on television"), was so vehement that it led Pat Buttram, who portrayed the bumbling salesman Mr. Haney on *Green Acres*, to quip that CBS cancelled "everything with a tree in it," and the "casualties" extended to even *Lassie* and *Mutual of Omaha's Wild Kingdom* (Berman). The reason given at the time for such a move involved what was seen as the increasing irrelevance of such settings to modern life, and the following years at CBS saw these programs replaced with the likes of heavier, more urban fare such as *All in the Family*, *The Mary Tyler Moore Show*, and *The Bob Newhart Show*. And with that, simple portrayals of small-town life were all but exorcised from the television landscape for a number of years, and those depictions that did thrive (such as CBS's drama *The Waltons* and NBC's *Little House on the Prairie*) often did so by setting their stories in bygone eras, thereby fueling Raymond Williams's (*The Country and the City* was published just the year before, in 1973) assertion that Western civilization tends to conflate the rural with a sense of nostalgia. Glimpsing the rural life on television was a way of looking backward, not forward.

Though there is no similarly dramatic term for trends in American literature at that time, a look at popular bestsellers and even the American canon of this era supports the idea of a comparable "rural purge." During the previous fifty years writers had worked to challenge simplistically pastoral evocations of small-town America, beginning *en masse* with the initial spark of the literary "revolt from the village" between 1915 and 1930, which was spearheaded by such luminaries as Edgar Lee Masters, Sherwood Anderson, and Sinclair Lewis. Bestsellers over the intervening years continued to challenge these (mis-)conceptions, such as Henry Bellamann's *Kings Row* (1940) and Grace Metalious's *Peyton Place* (1956). An important bridge between the success of these novels and the "rural purge" of the late sixties and early seventies is Larry McMurtry's 1966 novel *The Last Picture Show*. While works such as Sinclair Lewis's *Main Street* sought to show what lurked beneath the postcard-perfect exterior of the American small town, by the time we get to *The Last Picture Show*, there is no postcard-perfect exterior left in representation to disrupt. McMurtry shows us the inevitable consequences of the increased emphasis on urbanization and modernization in the twentieth century; not only does he undermine the heretofore established bucolic ideal of small-town America, but he turns established notions of rural beauty and morality on their heads. While earlier efforts shocked readers in the modern era by suggesting that not everyone in a small town is a paragon of virtue, *The Last Picture Show*'s Thalia, Texas is a community where little virtue is to be found at all. In fact, there is hardly any real community to speak of; everyone exists in their own solipsistic universe, and the tenuous connection to any kind of civic-minded altruism rapidly dissipates when the novel's moral center, pool-hall owner Sam the Lion, dies a little more than halfway through the narrative.

While we can certainly link the novel to the modernist notions of critiquing a simplistic evocation of rurality, McMurtry's work, typical of David Harvey's description of the "anti-modern movement of the 1960s" (38), also critiques this very critique by showing us the logical outcome of a society devoted to ever-increasing urbanization. In *The Condition of Postmodernity: An Enquiry Into the Origins of Cultural Change*, Harvey writes that "[i]f the modernist has to destroy in order to create, then the only way to represent eternal truths is through a process of destruction that is liable, in the end, to be itself destructive of those truths" (17). In this vein, the small postwar Texas town with which McMurtry presents us (while the novel first appeared in 1966, the story takes place circa 1953) is a far cry from what Carl Van Doren infamously deemed the "cult of the village" in his initial characterization of the literary "revolt," but there is ample textual evidence that it is a far cry perhaps because of the very forces that initially challenged the cult (146). *The Last Picture Show* shows a community that presents us with a kind of *reductio ad absurdum* picture of the consequences of striving to continually 'make it new,' which is, of course, a total abandonment of that which we deem as 'old,' i.e., any kind of tradition. With this tension, the text, unlike the town itself, becomes a kind of liminal space, acknowledging the modernist tradition but also signaling a more postmodern rendering of small-town America.

Within this seemingly contradictory space, *The Last Picture Show* also utilizes numerous regional tropes as aids in demystifying and deconstructing glorifying accounts of the advent of ubiquitous modernization and its accompanying economic practices, yet it does so with a self-consciousness that can only come about as a result of this same process of change. The text mourns the loss of a way of life while simultaneously acknowledging that its characters can't go 'home' again. In this sense, the novel is suggestive of a kind of critical regionalism, itself a term that began to gain ground in the world of architecture in the early 1980s through the work of first Alexander Tzonis and Liane Lefaivre and then Kenneth Frampton. Frampton, who has devoted a substantial portion of his career to exploring this phenomenon, writes that critical regionalism "is a dialectical expression. It self-consciously seeks to deconstruct universal modernism in terms of values and images which are locally cultivated, while at the same time adulterating these autochthonous elements with paradigms drawn from alien sources" (149). In fleshing out her own definition of critical regionalism from a literary perspective, Cheryl Herr explains that "[a]s a practice, a critical-regionalist cultural studies has great potential for producing a unified but highly adaptable analysis of international flows of capital and resistance to the negative effects of those flows at the local-regional level, toward the end of a more heterogeneous and tolerant future" (18). McMurtry presents us with a desolate rendering of the effects of such flows of capital on rural Texas, since the town of Thalia is not an island, physically or metaphorically. The text uses regional tropes and myths associated with historic conceptions of the American West not merely to glorify days gone by, but ultimately to show the failings of not just the small town, but the nation and even the world as a whole in the face of late-capitalist practices. In honing his own definition of late capitalism, referring to the global economic practices that first gained a real stronghold in the aftermath of World War II, Fredric Jameson explains that the use of the word "late" here refers to "the sense that something has changed, that things are different, that we have gone through a transformation in the life world which is somehow decisive but incomparable with the older convulsions of modernization and industrialization, less perceptible and dramatic, somehow, but more permanent precisely because it is more thorough-going and all pervasive" (xxi). This kind of amorphous, less "dramatic" change for the worse is certainly evident in the tone throughout *The Last Picture Show*. In showing us these failings McMurtry explores the options of resistance to which Herr refers in fiction. He uses the culture of a specific American region to exemplify the problems created by forces larger than those of the region alone. In the introduction to *Critical Regionalism: Connecting Politics and Culture in the American Landscape*, Douglas Reichert Powell writes that critical regionalism addresses "this kind of place, this kind of contradictory moment where something unique and isolated seems to be going on, but something else – something complex and interconnected – is also happening" (18). The isolation that permeates *The Last Picture Show* is largely connected to the town itself, but there are numerous instances in which the reader can glean this sense of "something else"; indeed, other "complex and interconnected" processes are to be uncovered behind the textual unraveling of this "unique and isolated" rural locale.

Nowadays, one might dare argue that when most people think of *The Last Picture Show*, if they have heard of it at all, they conjure up the image of Peter Bogdanovich's 1971 film adaptation of McMurtry's tome. As a prominent member of the set labeled the "New Hollywood," directors such as Bogdanovich wrestled with the tensions of a changing America in the aftermath of the advent of late capitalism. Much like Larry McMurtry's novel, and like critical regionalism itself, these films embrace inherent contradiction; they rebel against the excesses of modernity but, in conveying their sense of rebellion, necessarily embrace some of these same excesses. According to Alexander Horwath, "these conflicts create a magnificent richness and enormous internal tensions and an incoherence, which lays bare their conditions of production and, consequently, the contradictions in American culture" (13). From the very beginning, Bogdanovich's auteurist choice of visuals highlights the desperate situation that fosters anti-pastoralism in the novel. In an era in which popular audiovisual entertainment relied on the use of color more than ever before, *The Last Picture Show* is tellingly shot in a stark black and white. Rather than utilize a Hollywood set, Bogdanovich shot the film on location in Archer City, Texas, McMurtry's own hometown and the not-so-secret inspiration for the novel's Thalia. In addition to the lack of color, Bogdanovich highlights the loneliness and desolation of the landscape by frequently panning across the town's main streets, with such shots being commonly accompanied by rolling tumbleweeds and loud, howling winds.

Such effects emphasize the anti-bucolic sentiment that permeates the novel. In Leo Marx's *The Machine in the Garden*, published just two years before *The Last Picture Show*, Marx underscores what he deems two different types of "pastoral" (one that is "popular and sentimental," and one that is "imaginative and complex") by emphasizing that both embody "the yearning for a simpler, more harmonious style of life, an existence 'closer to nature'" (6). And, in the popular imagination of most of the modern era, that was the consolation prize for living apart from the ever-increasing urban centers of the United States, a simpler way of life, and proximity to the beauty of nature. But in Thalia, Texas, life is not simple, nor is there any beauty in nature; indeed, the tumbling tumbleweeds are about as good as it gets. In his article "Doing Without," Tom Pilkington writes that, "*The Last Picture Show* indicts Thalia in about every way possible for deadening and constricting the lives of its citizens, for making those lives as drab and gray as the West Texas sky during a spring duststorm" (120). The town's own moniker takes on a very ironic quality with this landscape, as Thalia was, in Greek mythology, the muse of both comedy and pastoral poetry. The fact that this dusty postwar town could ever be associated with pastoral poetry in any way does lend itself to a kind of comedy, specifically to the black humor that trickles in throughout the narrative.

Larry McMurtry specifically ties this desperate landscape to the novel's Southwestern locale in the 1989 preface to his essay collection *In a Narrow Grave: Essays on Texas*, explaining that

> [b]efore I was out of high school I realized I was witnessing the dying of a way of life – the rural, pastoral way of life. In the Southwest the best energies were no longer to be found in the homeplace, or in the small towns; the cities required these energies and the cities bought them. The kids who stayed in the country tended to be dull, lazy, cautious, or all three; those with brains, zip, and daring were soon off to Dallas or Houston. (xiii)

Such sentiments echo Raymond Williams's problematization in his exploration of the process of urbanization in Industrial-Revolution England of stereotypes regarding those who 'stayed behind' in the more rural environs: "It is often said of the whole process of industrialisation and urbanism that all of the able people went off to the factories and the towns, or decided to emigrate, leaving only the slow, the feckless, and the ignorant" (184). While Williams does present such sentiments as stereotypes, both he and McMurtry are emphasizing that industrialization does necessarily steal human resources, in addition to natural resources, away from the rural locale.

While the brain-drain phenomenon that McMurtry describes is certainly not endemic to Texas, Thalia's own particular brand of desolation is also closely linked with the regional prevalence of the oil industry. Decades before national conversations turned toward hydraulic fracking or the Keystone XL pipeline, McMurtry shows us the adverse consequences that our dependence on oil has on the natural landscape. Texas-based historian Walter Prescott Webb, in 1951's *The Great Frontier*, already acknowledges the voracious oil consumption of the late-capitalist era, noting that "[t]he story of oil and its derivatives is much shorter and more extreme than that of coal. The source supplies only 7.8% of fossil fuel energy. Its use dates from about 1850, but its consumption has been so accelerated that we have already used up 5.7% of the estimated total of petroleum and natural gas" (297). Oil is big business in Thalia, and the continual exploitation of natural resources puts a strain on the town in a number of ways. The importance of the commercial oil business over the natural landscape is illustrated particularly tellingly in a scene in which Sonny Crawford, the novel's teenaged protagonist, first shares an illicit kiss with Ruth Popper, the forty-year-old wife of his high-school football coach, at a Christmas dance at the local Legion Hall: "For a minute they were too silent – Sonny looked over her head, beyond the town. Far across the pastures he saw the lights of an oil derrick, brighter than the cold winter stars. Suddenly Mrs. Popper lifted her head and they kissed" (81). Here McMurtry subverts the association of romantic and sexual acts with unblemished nature; not only is the oil derrick part of the local landscape, but its lights actually shine brighter than those of the stars, thereby visually emphasizing the importance of commerce over nature in the era of late capitalism. It also calls to mind the prologue of McMurtry's first novel, 1961's *Horseman, Pass By* (later made into the 1963 film *Hud*), in which the protagonist, seventeen-year-old Lonnie Bannon, climbs to the top of the windmill on his grandfather's ranch to watch the scene below:

> When I knew Granddad was in bed I went back to the windmill and stopped the blades, so I could climb up and sit on the platform beneath the big fin. Around me, across the dark prairie, the lights were clear. The oil derricks were lit with strings of yellow bulbs, like Christmas trees. The lights were still on in the kitchens of the pumpers' cabins, the little green-topped shacks scattered across

> the plain, each one propped on a few stacks of bricks. Twelve miles away, to the north, the red and green and yellow lights of Thalia shimmered against the dark. I sat above it all, in the cool breezy air that swept under the windmill blades, above it all, in the cool breezy air that swept under the windmill blades, hearing the rig motors purr and the heavy trucks growl up the hill. Above the chattering of the ignorant Rhode Island Reds I heard two whippoorwills, the ghostly birds I never saw, calling across the flats below the ridge. (5-6)

While *Horseman, Pass By* deals more with ranch life than town life in west Texas (note the use of "Thalia," which McMurtry uses as a locale in not only *The Last Picture Show* and *Horseman, Pass By*, but also in his second novel, *Leaving Cheyenne*), it presents a similar conflict between the region's cowboy, pioneer past and its (post-)industrial present. Here young Lonnie physically stops the motion of the windmill, which represents an older mode of power, one more often associated with the agrarian past, and gazes out not on pure, unspoiled nature but on the lights of modern industry. The line between nature and industry is blurred further with the anthropomorphic characterization of the rigs "purring" and the motors "growling," while he depicts the real animals as "ignorant" and "ghostly." This grotesque core image seems to have sprung from Larry McMurtry's own childhood in the same region, during the same time period. In his essay "Movie-Tripping: My Own Rotten Film Festival," he paints a similar picture while recalling his Texas upbringing:

> I did as a boy sit on the barn my uncles sat on to watch the last trail herds go by, and from there, or, as had been more common (it not being easy to climb barns), from the top of the windmill I could see a long way, into some great sunsets and far back into the mythic reaches of the West, to which, try though I might, I could never belong, nor ever fail to respond. (148)

This scene perfectly encapsulates this tension between past and present; he knows that he can "never belong" to that mythic vision, yet he also can't "fail to respond." It is a process that haunts the psychological landscape of *The Last Picture Show*.

In keeping with the simultaneously anti-pastoral and yet anti-modern tone of *The Last Picture Show*, the juxtaposition of these 'machines' with the desert landscape shows us the inability of modern industry to fully subvert the natural landscape of the desert Southwest. In the introduction to their edited collection *Regionalism and the Humanities*, Timothy R. Mahoney and Wendy J. Katz explain the importance of the Southwestern United States to studies of critical regionalism, noting that "[i]ts desert, as a supremely harsh environment, provides reassurance of the overriding importance of nature in a culture that otherwise flaunts its ability to escape nature, through means such as air conditioning or irrigation" (xxii). Or oil derricks, for that matter. Yes, the oil derrick does shine more brightly than the stars, but the stars are still there. Most of the nature with which McMurtry presents us, though, is far more challenging than stars in the night sky; again and again, the text emphasizes this "supremely harsh environment."

One way in which it does this is via the regular presence of strong winds that the townspeople deem "blue northers;" one particular early passage, in which Sonny performs his job of delivering butane to inhabitants of the surrounding countryside, aptly describes the power of such a phenomenon on multiple levels:

> Out in the open country the norther gusted strongly across the highway, making the truck hard to hold. Once in while a big ragweed would shake loose from the barbed-wire fences and skitter across the road, only to catch again in the barbed-wire fence on the other side [...] It occurred to Sonny that perhaps people called them "blue northers" because it was hard not to get blue when one was blowing. (16)

Here, Sonny's mental connection renders the wind as a kind of cyclical objective correlative, an entity that both makes the townspeople feel "blue" and also symbolizes the largely "blue" feelings that permeate the emotional landscape of the novel. We can also examine this phenomenon through the lens of critical regionalism. This powerful wind pushes against the butane truck, making it "hard to hold." The ragweeds are described as "shaking loose" from the barbed-wire fences that hold them back, only to be caught again. This struggle between elements of the natural realm (i.e., winds and ragweed) and those of the modern industrial realm (i.e., butane trucks and barbed-wire fences) highlights the struggle that is life in Thalia. In the desert Southwest, nature is a force to be reckoned with, and attempting to subvert it inevitably leads to struggle. Though it is not merely the landscape itself that makes the area so bleak, but also what modern industry has turned this landscape into.

The tension is also enumerated in the text's characterization of Sam the Lion, the elderly proprietor of the local pool hall, the local diner, and the one eponymous "picture show" in Thalia. He espouses an old-fashioned sense of stability that is found in no other characters in the novel; Christopher Baker, in his article "The Death of Frontier in the Novels of Larry McMurtry," refers to him as the town's "last remnant of the frontier cowboy culture of the plains" (168). In the novel's first chapter, McMurtry furnishes some background on Sam in the form of a brief but tragic biographical synopsis:

> Sam the Lion was the man who took care of things, particularly of boys, and Sonny did not like to think that he might die. The reason Sam was so especially good to boys was that he himself had had three sons, none of whom lived to be eighteen. The first was killed when Sam was still a rancher; he and his son were trying to drive a herd of yearlings across the Little Wichita River one day when it was up, and the boy had been knocked loose from his horse, pawed under, and drowned. A few years later, after Sam had gone into the oil business, a gas

> explosion knocked his second son off a derrick. He fell over fifty feet and was dead before they got him to town. Sam sold his oil holdings and put in the first Ford agency in Thalia, and his youngest son was run over by a deputy sheriff. His wife lost her mind and spent her last ten years rocking in a rocking chair. Sam drank a lot, quit going to church, and was said to be loose with women, even married women.
>
> He began to come out of it when he bought the picture show, or so people said. He got lots of comedies and serials and Western and the kids came as often as they could talk their parents into letting them. Then Sam bought the pool-hall and the all-night café and he perked up more and more. (7-8)

When McMurtry presents Sam as a man who "took care of things," this is realized in the text on a number of levels. Not only does he take care of the townspeople (mostly the young townspeople, as this passage indicates) in providing the town's main sources of entertainment, but he is also described as someone who takes particularly good care of young boys. We see this in his relationships with many young men in the text, particularly Sonny and Sonny's best friend Duane. Both Sonny and Duane live not with their own parents, but in a local boarding house:

> People thought it a little strange, because each had a parent alive, but the boys liked it. Sonny's father [who, after a terrible car accident that resulted in the death of Sonny's mother, has become a prescription drug addict] ran the local domino parlor and lived in a room at the little hotel, and Duane's mother didn't really have much more room. His grandmother was still alive and living with his mother in their two-room house. (15)

He also takes care of Billy, a mentally disabled boy who has already been abandoned by several guardians and who earns his keep by sweeping out Sam's three places of business each day (9). But perhaps what is most striking about this passage are the tragic deaths of his three sons. Here the text carefully links each death to a different capitalistic venture: Sam's experience as a rancher leads to the death of one son while herding cattle; his stint in the oil industry leads renders another son dead in a gas explosion, and a third child is run over by a car shortly after his father opens a car dealership. This unfortunate series of events suggests an important connection between modern forces beyond the confines of the rural town (such as large-scale cattle ranching, the oil industry, and automobile traffic), death, and depression. It is only when Sam changes his priorities, when he buys the picture show, pool hall, and café, that his depression begins to lift. Sam elaborates on the financial outcome of his decisions when he tries to dissuade Duane from his dream of becoming wealthy: "'Once you got rich you'd have to spend all your time staying rich, and that's hard thankless work. I tried it a while and quit, myself. If I can keep ten dollars ahead of the bills I'll be doin' all right'" (52). This statement further connects Sam's previous ventures to larger channels of modern capitalism, while investing his money within the community, even if it does not lead to a huge payoff, is, according to Sam, much more worthwhile. This again underscores the idea that the problems in Thalia are not always due to the town itself, but to the larger processes of modernization and industry that threaten the community from beyond. According to Reichert Powell, "a commitment to inhabitation forged out of a working relationship to the land and to other people [...] augments the cultural and material resources that people use to counter unjust forces and pressures" (171). In developing a close relationship with the land itself and the people of the community, rather than focusing on channels that cause energy and capital to flow outward to the modern economy, Sam seems to become a kind of critical regionalist himself. The fact that his energies encompass such modern conveniences as a movie theater and an all-night diner speak to critical regionalism's complex stance that simultaneously rejects the placelessness of modernity while embracing the necessity of its effects. Though Sam represents, in many ways, Texas's cowboy past, his solution to the conflicts of the modern era does not entail complete eschewal of modernity. Rather, he finds a way to experience community despite the pressures of a global economy.

Speaking more broadly, the rural tableau that the text creates is very much tied to popular conceptions not just of the Southwest, but of the American West as a whole. In her essay "The Realization of the American West," Patricia Nelson Limerick asserts that one of the defining characteristics of the region known as "the West" is aridity: "The West is more prone to aridity, and aridity is the most significant factor in producing what we now refer to as 'the wide open spaces.' Aridity, moreover, puts a conventional strain on conventional Anglo American notions of proper landscapes and land use" (73). This reference to "conventional Anglo American notions" itself refers back to conceptions of that institution known as "the American frontier." In his landmark historiography *Virgin Land: The American West as Symbol and Myth*, Henry Nash Smith presents what he terms "the myth of the garden," explaining that, in so many eighteenth-century writings about the American continent, "the physical fact of the continent dominates the scene. The American interior is presented as a new and enchanting region of inexpressible beauty and fertility" (11). As settlers continued to take advantage of this beauty and fertility, many politicians thought it necessary, Smith argues, to migrate further westward, beyond the verdant fertility of the Middle West and into harsher landscapes, in an effort to establish American domination over the continent, to conquer more "virgin land." This very migration led to another kind of myth, as Smith notes:

> But in the decade following the Civil War the impetus of the westward movement and the implied pledge of the victorious Republican party to develop the West were uncontrollable forces urging the agricultural frontier onward. On the level of the imagination it was therefore necessary that the settler's battle with drought and dust and wind and grasshoppers should be supported by the

> westward extension of the myth of the garden. In order to establish itself in the vast new area of the plains, however, the myth of the garden had to confront and overcome another myth of exactly opposed meaning, although of inferior strength – the myth of the Great American Desert. (174-75)

In presenting the town of Thalia, McMurtry utilizes a "Great American Desert" motif throughout the narrative that is directly antithetical to any kind of garden image. In presenting us with a landscape marked by tumbleweeds, mesquite, and oil derricks, McMurtry offers up a kind of "machine in the garden" scenario without any sign of an actual garden. This not only refutes generalizing of a pastoral conception of American rurality (which is based on this very 'Anglo American' idea of the national landscape as a kind of green, fertile 'garden of the world'), but also serves as a means of de-mythologizing the region; in connecting the desert landscape with modern American industry, McMurtry suggests that some myths surrounding the American West are just that: myths. In the era of late capitalism, the West, despite its strong winds and tumbleweeds aching to break free from their restraints, has never been entirely wild and "untamed" but also functions as another type of environment ripe for exploitation. And its small towns are just as domesticated and desperate as those of the Midwest in the 1920s (the era and region most associated with the "revolt from the village"), perhaps even more so. Thus, the paradigm shift that began with the "revolt from the village" finds in *The Last Picture Show* its peak chronologically as well as geographically; this rejection of simplistic pastoralism extends even into the "wild" and "untamed" West.

Metaphorically speaking, the desert landscape continually serves to underscore the loneliness and desperation experienced throughout the text by the citizens of Thalia, that "blue" feeling that Sonny experiences as he drives his butane truck along the desert roads. This sense of desolation is apparent even from the very first lines of the novel, as McMurtry first introduces the character: "Sometimes Sonny felt like he was the only human creature in the town. It was a bad feeling and it usually came on him in the mornings early, when the streets were completely empty, the way they were one Saturday morning in late November. The night before Sonny had played his last game of football for Thalia High School, but it wasn't that that made him feel so strange and alone. It was just the look of the town" (1). Not only do these lines set up the neo-existentialist nature of the novel in emphasizing the stark loneliness of the character, but they also tie this loneliness directly to the rural, exploited landscape, thereby immediately establishing the anti-pastoral tone that dominates the narrative. Of course, it also alludes to regional myths by playing upon the tradition of the Wild West hero of the dime novels of the previous century. In capturing the essence of this particular trope, Smith invokes Charles Averill's rendering of Kit Carson as an archetype for the burgeoning Western frontiersman of the nineteenth century, depicting him as an "anarchic and self-contained atom [...] alone in a hostile [...] universe" (89).

These words aptly describe Sonny's situation as well, although, here, McMurtry's ironic use of this trope serves not so much to denote any heroism on Sonny's part, but to emphasize his loneliness and isolation, and the harshness, both physically and metaphorically, of the surrounding rural environs; in a modernized society in which the forces of late capitalism have attempted (but not entirely succeeded, as noted earlier) to drill the environment into submission, the novel's protagonist can only reflect on his surroundings with a profound sense of isolation.

The text continues to emphasize Sonny's loneliness, ironically, by introducing the reader to the various relationships in his life. At the beginning of the novel, he has a girlfriend, with the lackluster moniker of Charlene Duggs, but McMurtry makes it clear early on that Sonny is only with Charlene because he feels that his options are extremely limited in the small town of Thalia:

> Of course Sonny had often considered breaking up with Charlene, but there weren't many girls in the town and the only unattached girl who was any prettier than Charlene was an unusually prudish sophomore. Charlene would let Sonny do anything he wanted above the waist; it was only as time wore on that he had begun to realize that there really wasn't anything of permanent interest to do in that zone. As the weeks went by, Sonny observed that Jacy [the girlfriend of his best friend, Duane Jackson, and the most popular girl at Thalia High School] seemed to become more and more delightful, passionate, inventive, while by contrast Charlene just seemed more of a slug. (11)

Despite the fact that the two of them, at the novel's beginning, have been dating for a year, here McMurtry's use of the term "slug" not only objectifies Charlene but also certainly shows the absence of any real emotional connection.

Sonny's desire to do things "below the waist" gives us an inkling of what becomes a large and almost obsessive theme in the novel, and that has to with the text's emphasis on sex, an emphasis that is even more present in the novel than in the then notoriously racy film. Yet the many sex acts that happen in Thalia, Texas, serve not to show us the scandal and corruption that lurks beneath the perfect small-town exterior, as was the case with novels such as *Kings Row* and *Peyton Place*, but rather serves to further emphasize the overt loneliness and alienation that permeate the exhausted Texas landscape. In the world of *The Last Picture Show*, sex serves as a desperate attempt for people to alleviate their existential loneliness, but these attempts fail nearly every time. In his article "Anatomy and *The Last Picture* Show: A Matter of Definition," Donald E. Fritz writes that "[v]irtually all the characters we see may be consumed by their absorption with sex, but none of them derives anything resembling substantive pleasure from it… Of the numerous sexual relationships in the book, not one is a mutually rewarding experience; sex is a matter of giving and taking, never sharing" (189). The sexual activity that takes place in the town is just as exploitative as the economic activity that takes place in the local landscape.

It is in the sex lives of these characters that we can glean another dimension to the "aridity" which Limerick describes. In a manner somewhat reminiscent of T.S. Eliot's modernist classic "The Waste Land," McMurtry's depiction of sex in Thalia corresponds much more with the desert metaphor than with any "beauty and fertility" notion associated with the myth of the garden. As a matter of fact, the sex acts rendered in the text are distinctly infertile, as, despite the prevalence of sexual activity in the novel, no pregnancies result. Nor does the text take care to describe a great deal of beauty in any of these pairings, with many encounters leaving one or both partners noticeably unsatisfied. Not only do these experiences of sex mirror the myth of the desert, but they also, in their often exploitative nature, mirror the process of exploiting the land that is such an important component of the regional oil industry. Even some of the language used to describe sexual acts mirrors this process. After the reader finds out that Lois Farrow, one of the wealthiest women in town, is carrying on a relatively open extramarital affair with the oil driller Abilene, the text visits an evening at home with the bored Lois, who calls Abilene hoping for a tryst. When he rebuffs her, she ridicules his sexual ability by scoffing at him: "'Well, drill hard,' she said. 'You're better at oil wells anyway'" (50). Lois's daughter Jacy, the most beautiful and popular teenager in Thalia, repeatedly refers to sex as "screwing" after learning the term from her more urban friends in the nearby city of Wichita Falls. Describing sex in terms such as "drilling" and "screwing" not only serves to undermine any romance or eroticism, but it also reminds of the drilling and screwing of the land that is happening on a continual basis.

Jacy's own sexual activities are particularly indicative of this "give and take" brand of sexuality. When it comes to her own sexual relationships, Jacy Farrow does display an element of sexual agency not often associated with teenage girls in the 1950s, but she always uses sex as a means to an end, and appears to derive little enjoyment from the act itself. After attending a naked pool party at a mansion in Wichita Falls, she is nearly seduced by Bobby Sheen, the unofficial leader of the popular set in Wichita (as the locals call it), but when he finds out that she is a virgin, he stops short of having sex with her. She then loses her virginity to Duane on a class trip to San Francisco, only to break up with him right afterward, content that she can move on to Sheen. She then embarks on a sexual relationship with Sheen's friend Lester Marlow, for "she was getting ready to be in love with Bobby Sheen, and she regarded Lester as a necessary stepping-stone" (160). After spending some time with Lester, Bobby does finally seduce her, and she does experience some degree of sexual pleasure, as the text notes that "Jacy tried to concentrate and do everything right but it was actually pretty arousing, screwing Bobby Sheen, and she couldn't keep her head clear" (162). But this pleasure is short-lived, as within a week she finds out that Sheen has eloped with another young woman.

Her next partner is Abilene, her mother's lover. If Sam the Lion is the town's last viable connection to its cowboy past, then Abilene represents the diametrically opposing qualities of the oilman; Clay Reynolds, in "Showdown in the New Old West: The Cowboy vs. the Oilman," writes that

> [o]pposed to the horseman is the oilman or modern rancher, a ruthless individual to whom rules are absurd, romantic obstacles. His vision is defined in the most base, materialistic terms: money, land, bigger cars, more of everything. The horseman, to him, is a bothersome antique, out of place in a modern world of profit and exploitation. (157)

Abilene's overt materialism is clear from his first appearance in the text, as he rolls into town in his fancy car: "Abilene was coming into town in his Mercury. Abilene was the driller Duane worked for. He had spent a lot of money souping up the Mercury, and in Thalia the sound of his exhausts was as unmistakable as the sound of the wind" (6). McMurtry goes on to tell the reader that "Abilene had only the best car in the country, he also shot the best stick of pool. Drilling and pool shooting were things he did so well that no one could decide which was his true vocation and which his avocation" (6). The text emphasizes the tension between the horseman and the oilman in this same scene, when it notes that "[t]hough [Abilene] was the poolhall's best customer, he and Sam the Lion had almost nothing to say to one another" (7). When Abilene seduces Jacy, their act of intercourse takes place in the middle of the night, on a pool table in the very pool hall where we first met Abilene. Though one of the most famous scenes of Peter Bogdanovich's film version involves the lithe, young Cybill Shepherd sprawled out on a pool table, the sex itself is distinctly unerotic, with the text characterizing Abilene as "just going on, absorbed in himself, moving, nudging, thrusting – she was no more than an object" (174). Greg Giddings, in "The Love Song of Larry J. McMurtry: *The Last Picture Show*," notes that "[e]ven by Jacy's selfish standards, Abilene's behavior is distant and self-centered" (61). This scene highlights not only the futility of sex as a means of alleviating the existential loneliness that permeates Thalia, but it also connects this loneliness to the landscape itself. Abilene's self-absorbed behavior echoes his behavior toward the landscape; as an oilman, his job is to take what he can from the land, and to make the most money for it, without regard to the environmental consequences. McMurtry depicts Jacy as "no more than an object" as her body becomes like the land itself; she is both "drilled" and "screwed" as Abilene takes what he wants from her. The pool-table locale adds to Abilene's self-absorption, as we see him partaking in his aforementioned two best skills: drilling and playing pool. Like pool, she is no more than a game. After their encounter is over, Abilene drops Jacy back off at her house, where he displays similarly callous behavior:

> They pulled into the Farrow driveway and he glanced at her. She leaned over and kissed him but he turned his face away. Jacy got out, very puzzled, and walked across the yard. When she was halfway across, Abilene raced his motor

> and made his mufflers roar, so that anyone in the neighborhood who was awake would know what car was in the driveway. Then he backed out and left. (220)

Here Abilene invokes the sound of those distinctive mufflers not only to let Jacy's mother Lois know of his actions, but to let the town in general know that Abilene was here, and Abilene, the modern-day oilman, takes what he wants.

By the last chapters of the novel, when Jacy begins dating Sonny, she has reverted to her formerly chaste lifestyle:

> Necking with him might even be fun, but she made up her mind right away that she wasn't going to let him screw her. She had had quite enough of that for one summer – it didn't really work out. She was nostalgic for the days when boys necked with her and wanted her desperately and didn't get her. That was better than actually screwing, somehow. (177)

While Jacy is sexually liberated by conventional 1950s standards, her sexual activity does not serve her much good in the end, not for any moral reasons, but because it fails to alleviate her problems, shallow as they may be. For Jacy, sexual activity, like Thalia itself, is not so much a fertile garden to be discovered as an exhausted desert.

Regarding Sonny himself, the closest that he ever comes to a mutually satisfying sexual relationship are his continuing liaisons with Ruth Popper. Their trysts begin shortly after Coach Popper asks Sonny to drive his wife to a doctor's appointment in the nearby town of Olney. The fact that we soon learn that her appointment is related to breast-cancer treatment underscores the lack of caring that Coach Herman Popper (himself alluded as an outwardly homophobic closeted homosexual) displays for Ruth (460). This lack of connection between husband and wife is emphasized in the grotesque manner in which McMurtry portrays their own sex life, and in one scene in particular, which takes place not long after Ruth observes her husband gorging himself on "yellow canned peaches, one of his favorite desserts":

> Ruth clenched her fists at her sides. Her chest and abdomen felt crushed, but it crossed her mind that she had crushed herself. What was crushing her was the weight of all the food she had fed Herman through the years, all the steaks, all the black-eyed peas, all the canned peaches. It was particularly the canned peaches: she had never until that moment realized how much she hated them. It seemed to her that pyramids of cans of slimy peaches piled on her abdomen. After a moment the weight became intolerable and she moved a little, to try and ease it. She moved from side to side and stretched her legs, to try and escape it. Herman sweated easily and his sweat was already dripping down her ribs, but what bothered her was the weight of the cans. (119)

This encounter not only serves to highlight the lack of sexual connection between the two partners, but it also presents a starkly grotesque take on the machine in the garden. While the garden myth correlates sexuality (i.e., the "fertility" of the "virgin land") with nourishment (in the physical fruits of the garden), the scene combines these aspects in a bizarre tableau that reinforces the fate of rural America in the era of late capitalism. In this scene, Ruth clearly associates sex with food, but not in the sense that sex is nourishing. Rather, she is repulsed by the images of the canned peaches that she has fed her husband; she conjures up no whole fruits but canned fruits, the mass-produced, industrial version of the garden's bounty. All of this combined with the distinct lack of sexual attraction that Ruth feels for her partner reinforce the text's depiction of intimacy as exploitative and unreciprocated.

Regarding Ruth's encounters with Sonny, Sonny's feelings for Ruth are complicated at best (he initially refuses to tell anyone about their encounters, partly because of her marital status, but also because she is "so old"), she possesses a genuine if unsettling affection for him. Even though he is the younger and more sexually inexperienced one, it is Ruth who experiences a sexual awakening, as it is not until she sleeps with Sonny that Ruth is able to experience any kind of real sexual pleasure, although even these encounters do not include the component of physical orgasm. As she becomes more and more comfortable with their affair, McMurtry writes that

> [s]he soon made terms with lovemaking itself, though for a time they were not the best possible terms. She thought that once they relaxed with one another the beautiful thing would happen, the whole moment toward which all the sharp little individual movements tended. She had read about it, she expected it, she longed for it, and came very close to it, but it eluded her. (101)

After one incident in which she comes particularly close to achieving such a state, her frustration is evident to Sonny, who does not come back to see her for three days and then, when he does come to see her, she is "so thrilled and relieved that she resolve(s) not to seek the moment if it was going to put everything else in danger" (101, 102). This abandonment of the pursuit of pure pleasure makes clear that Ruth's main goal in the affair is emotional, and not sexual, thereby reinforcing the fog of loneliness that permeates the community. Ruth herself encapsulates this sentiment as she reassures Sonny regarding his own sexual capabilities: "No, look… Nothing was your fault. You have to remember that I've been lonely for a long time. Loneliness is like ice. After you've been lonely long enough you don't even realize you're cold, but you are. It's like I was a refrigerator that had never been defrosted at all – never. All these years the ice has just been getting thicker" (102). While the image of ice is, on the surface, oppositional to the desert metaphor, it accomplishes the same effect, negating an ideal of community and cohesion in small-town America.

As the story of Sonny and Ruth continues, Ruth's newfound freedom eventually becomes a kind of burden to Sonny as it physically and emotionally wears him out; it explains that "[a]ll she wanted was Sonny, and he began to feel strangely washed out and restless," going on to say that "[a]s he grew more tired and less certain of himself, Ruth seemed to grow fresher, more self-possessed, and more lovely, though it was only at odd, oblique moments, lying beside her or coming into her room, that he noticed she was lovely" (114). Sonny's figurative wasting away as Ruth feeds on him sexually suggests a kind of parasite/host-relationship, and especially given the age difference, a kind of predator/prey aspect to their already complicated relationship. This is compounded as Ruth's feelings for him are portrayed as disturbingly entwined with regrets over her own childlessness, a fact that McMurtry highlights in another grotesque sex scene that takes place the day after Ruth has a dream in which she actually gives birth to Sonny:

> The next day Sonny came, and while they were spreading the blue quilt on the bedroom floor Ruth remembered the dream. It was very vivid in her mind as she undressed. She lay quietly, her eyes closed, as Sonny began, but almost before she knew it she became excited, so much so that she could not be still. She thought of the dream again, hoping the excitement would die before she became completely possessed by it, but instead of dying it became keener. Because of the dream, pleasure took her over: with her eyes shut she could pretend she was giving birth. Sonny was inside her but in truth she was bringing him out – it was that which excited her. She grabbed his hands and put them on her thighs, so that he would force them wider. She was filled with a strength she had not suspected and held him with her thighs, just at the entrance, just connected, both of them struggling, until she was finally seized, rent by what she felt. Then she took Sonny back to her, her heart was pounding, her eyelids fluttering; she almost fainted with the relief of delivery. (101)

While Sonny is, at this time, eighteen years old and not a legal minor, Ruth's childbirth fantasy certainly suggests a kind of pedophilic undertone to their encounters. This again reinforces the notion of sexuality as exploitative, but the most obvious motivator in their relationship is certainly loneliness. This sense of loneliness is reinforced again and again, culminating in the final scene in which Sonny, having abandoned Ruth when he gets the opportunity to date Jacy Farrow, comes back to her after Jacy ends their relationship. At this point in the novel, both characters have acknowledged the ways in which their relationship is unhealthy. Sonny has certainly expressed his doubts, and we have glimpsed the myriad ways in which his union with Ruth is more depleting than sustaining. And, by this point, even Ruth has her doubts; as she contemplates the possibility of reconciling with Sonny, she acknowledges that "[e]ven if the springs in her would start again it would only be a year or two or three before it would all repeat itself. Something would take him from her and the process of drying up would have be endured again" (219). The fact that, in this final tableau, the text makes it clear that they will both endure this difficult process again reinforces the pervasive loneliness and isolation of rural modernity. Here McMurtry's use of "drying up" connects Ruth's emotional state to the land around them, which is not only a desert but also a landscape that has been sucked dry even further by modern exploitation.

This continual linking of sexuality with the oil industry constitutes not only an important extended metaphor, but also a performance of astute critical regionalism. Heike Paul explains that "[c]ritical regionalism (re)turns scholarly attention to the region and interrogates the discursive 'production' and the role of regions in larger geopolitical constellations – often under the conditions of colonialism/empire and/or modernism, neo-liberalism, and globalization" (398). While the novel does present modern-day rural Texas with a sense of loss, it does not yearn simplistically for an earlier time. Rather, the text revamps the modernist trope of salacious sexuality to call attention to the environmental and social depletion of a region in the name of global capitalism. Thus, in many ways, *The Last Picture Show* does presages the idea of a "rural purge," as there is no doubt that its picture of small-town Texas is a bleak one, and that Thalia is a place that has been damaged by the onset of global modernity. By the end of the novel, the picture show has closed down, and both Sam the Lion and young Billy have died tragically. Jacy has broken things off with Sonny after a failed elopement, and it appears that the only thing that comes close to sustaining him is his fragile and ultimately unsatisfying relationship with Ruth. This town is certainly no pastoral idyll, and in this sense the novel certainly does represent a climax in the paradigm shift that began with the "revolt from the village." But, by the time when we get to *The Last Picture Show*, the "revolt" has been watered down by the realities of modernization; there is no need to "revolt" from the village as the village, by this point, lacks even the outer veneer of respectability that made earlier texts in the tradition so shocking. McMurtry's pushback against pastoralism not only laments a lost era, but is also reifies the actualities of modern Texas and oil production. While it does this via focusing on regional specifics and tropes, it also brings the story to a wider audience; it's important to not only lament any perceived loss of the frontier days, but also to make this modern-day plight real and raw for people across the globe who take part indirectly in the exploitation of the this particular geographic region every day.

## Works Cited

Baker, Christopher. "The Death of the Frontier in the Novels of Larry McMurtry." *Taking Stock: A Larry McMurtry Casebook.* Ed. Clay Reynolds. Dallas: Southern Methodist University Press, 1989: 164-73. Print.

Berman, Marc. "The Rural Purge." *TV Media Insights*. 27 April 2012. Web. <http://www.tvmediainsights.com/fun-stuff/the-rural-purge/>.

Frampton, Kenneth. "Prospects for a Critical Regionalism." *Perspecta* 20 (1983): 147-62. Print.

Fritz, Donald E. "Anatomy and *The Last Picture Show*: A Matter of Definition." *Taking Stock: A Larry McMurtry Casebook.* Ed. Clay Reynolds. Dallas: Southern Methodist University Press, 1989: 186-92. Print.

Giddings, Greg. "The Love Song of Larry J. McMurtry: *The Last Picture Show*." *JASAT: Journal of the American Studies Association of Texas* 44 (November 2013): 57-64. Print.

Harvey, David. *The Condition of Postmodernity: An Enquiry into the Origins of Cultural Change*. Oxford, England: Blackwell, 1989. Print.

Herr, Cheryl. *Critical Regionalism and Cultural Studies: From Ireland to the American Midwest*. Gainesville: University Press of Florida, 1996. Print.

Horwath, Alexander. "The Impure Cinema: New Hollywood 1967-1976." *The Last Great American Picture Show: New Hollywood Cinema in the 1970s*. Ed. Thomas Elsaesser, Alexander Horwath, and Noel King. Amsterdam University Press, 2004. 9-18. Print.

Jameson, Fredric. *Postmodernism, or, the Cultural Logic of Late Capitalism.* Durham: Duke University Press, 1991. Print.

Limerick, Patricia Nelson. "The Realization of the American West." *The New Regionalism*. Ed. Charles Wilson Reagan. Jackson: University Press of Mississippi, 1998. 71-104. Print.

Mahoney, Timothy R., and Wendy J. Katz (eds.). *Regionalism and the Humanities*. Lincoln: University of Nebraska Press, 2008. Print.

Marx, Leo. *The Machine in the Garden: Technology and the Pastoral Ideal in America*. New York: Oxford University Press, 1964. Print.

McMurtry, Larry. *In a Narrow Grave: Essays on Texas*. New York: Simon and Schuster, 1989. Print.

---. *Film Flam*. New York: Simon and Schuster, 1987. Print.

---. *Horseman, Pass By*. College Station: Texas A & M University Press, 1985. Print.

---. *The Last Picture Show*. New York: Dell, 1966. Print.

Paul, Heike. "Critical Regionalism and Post-Exceptionalist American Studies." *Towards a Post-Exceptionalist American Studies. REAL*. Ed. Winfried Fluck and Donald Pease. 30 (2014): 397-424. Print.

Pilkington, Tom. "Doing Without." *Taking Stock: A Larry McMurtry Casebook.* Dallas: Southern Methodist University Press, 1989: 113-27. Print.

Reichert Powell, Douglas. *Critical Regionalism: Connecting Politics and Culture in the American Landscape*. Chapel Hill: University of North Carolina Press, 2007. Print.

Reynolds, Clay. "Showdown in the New Old West: The Cowboy vs. the Oilman." *Taking Stock: A Larry McMurtry Casebook*. Dallas: Southern Methodist University Press, 1989: 156-64. Print.

Smith, Henry Nash. *Virgin Land: The American West as Symbol and Myth*. Cambridge: Harvard University Press, 1950. Print.

Van Doren, Carl. *Contemporary American Novelists (1900-1920)*. Middlesex: The Echo Library, 2007. Print.

Webb, Walter Prescott. *The Great Frontier*. Boston: Houghton Mifflin Company, 1951. Print.

Williams, Raymond. *The Country and the City*. New York: Oxford University Press, 1973. Print.

# Reality Television, Critical Regionalism, and Low Theory: Paranoid and Reparative Readings of Representations of Class and Race in the US South

*Tanja N. Aho*

Reality television is awash in representations of region/alisms: *Here Comes Honey Boo Boo, Redneck Island, Swamp Pawn, Deadliest Catch, Chainsaw Gang, Ax Men, Swamp People, My Big Redneck Wedding, My Big Redneck Vacation* – the list continuously expands. Central to most of these is the region of the South, albeit a South vague enough to encompass even the rural areas of Pennsylvania and Michigan.[1] Less a geographical place than a socio-economic and cultural space, the South as represented in reality television centers around the figures of the 'hillbilly' and the 'redneck.'[2] These figures are easily contestable not just from an academic perspective; their stereotypical presentation and, as others have coined it, rednexploitation,[3] is also readily apparent to the lay viewer.

Nevertheless, academics and journalists alike have become fond of practicing what Eve Kosofsky Sedgwick calls "paranoid readings" of these cultural figurations that are informed by a Ricœurdian "hermeneutics of suspicion" (124). The many articles that have been published on the topic of representations of Southernness in reality television – mostly in major newspapers, magazines, and in some online journals – serve as sites of meaning making for the performative nature of knowledge production. These readings have much in common with traditional notions of regionalism as an epistemological project in which the allegorical or essentializing function of certain regions is deconstructed. Such

1 The television channel TMC, which offers everything 'country,' routinely conflates any type of 'redneckery' under the label Southern, a move that reflects Michael Denning's hypothesis of the "'southernization' of American culture" (35) that he locates in the second half of the twentieth century.

2 Anthony Harkins provides in his 2004 study *Hillbilly: A Cultural History of an American Icon* a cultural history of the 'hillbilly' that speaks to the central concerns surrounding critical regionalism. Figures such as the hillbilly and the redneck provide multi-layered cultural scripts through which a more nuanced reading of the overlap, intersection, and contestation of concepts such as the region, the rural, the local, and of course, specific regions such as 'the South' could be developed. While Scott Herring points to the slippage between these terms, he – along with much of critical rural and critical regionalism studies – refrains from exploring this nexus in more depth (26-27).

3 While many contemporary commentators believe this to be a new trend, shows such as *The Dukes of Hazzard* and other television and film productions of the 1980s speak to a longer history of this type of cultural script and draw our attention to the fluctuation and apparent cyclicality of the importance of region/alisms.

studies have tended to focus on revealing the dynamics through which certain conceptions of a specific region are embedded within ideological frameworks that attempt to erase the material realities of the US imperialist project, racial apartheid, and Native genocide in their constructions of a region's specific history, authenticity, and exceptionalism (see Jackson; Mahoney and Katz). In other words, their paranoid impetus has been to reveal the ways in which social imaginaries of regions function to efface "interlocking systems of oppression" (Combahee River Collective).

Paralleling Douglas Reichert Powell's call for a 'critical regionalism' methodology, I explore the effects of extending paranoid inquiries of representations of Southern regionalism with materialist, reparative readings of the cultural work that the critiques of and audience engagements with these representations perform. In other words, this chapter applies critical regionalism's methodology via Sedgwick to viewer engagements with reality television's representations of one particular region in the United States, the US South. Motivated by Sedgwick's call to inquire into "the motive each has *for looking*" (138; italics in original), I provide discussions of both paranoid and reparative reading practices in order to advance the materialist methodology of critical regionalism.

In his 2007 publication *Critical Regionalism: Connecting Politics and Culture in the American Landscape*, Douglas Reichert Powell develops a materialist pedagogy of critical regionalism, in which "critical regionalism self-consciously shapes an understanding of the spatial dimensions of cultural politics in order to support projects of change" (8). Challenging the locational lacuna of elitist cosmopolitanism, which has, according to Reichert Powell, elided its proponents' own locatedness – oftentimes because academics tend to ignore their own class positions and lives of mobility (20) – Reichert Powell calls for a rethinking of critical regionalism as a "transdisciplinary ethic that link[s] cultural criticism to material social change" (23), in which local participants are as much included as academic thinkers and public intellectuals. Critical regionalism's "vernacular sensibility" thus offers a methodology of "dialogic openness" (Jackson 20) that centers local participants' subjugated knowledges (see Collins; Foucault) in its materialist concern for the realities of social justice projects.

Local participants – here broadly defined as those who see themselves as stakeholders in constructions of the US South – provide materialist analyses and perspectives through various sites. I expand critical regionalism's use of literature, ethnography, and popular culture to include what might be considered the least local site of all, the internet. I argue that online commentaries in web 2.0 spaces such as Facebook pages, blogs, and interactive websites should be regarded as part of the rich regionalist archives that studies of the US South can engage. As Stuart Hall and Alan O'Shea emphasize, despite their ubiquity in today's world, such sites of meaning making have garnered little attention in academic analyses. Drawing on these "low theory" (Frith) sites of knowledge production can, however, offer avenues to reparative reading practices that would complicate academic approaches to representations of regionalism as, in this case, they manifest in viewer responses to the US South.

Through the application of Sedgwick's and Frith's methodologies I seek to contribute to a larger discussion about "sitpoint theory" (Garland-Thomson 1570) in cultural studies, highlighting the ways in which knowledge production is itself oftentimes implicated in the paradigms it seeks to challenge. I thus offer an extension of Sedgwick's critique of paranoid reading practices as not just limited in their epistemic reach, but as complicit in hegemonic discourses. While Sedgwick's writing is well-known for inspiring work in queer and affect theory, I showcase how her thinking can also be useful in reconsidering epistemological approaches based on a materialist critique of knowledge production in media/television and critical regionalism studies. Following Robert Jackson's demand that "American regional theory must clarify its own aesthetic bias" (22), I use audience engagement with reality television's regional scripts to discuss the classism of paranoid reading practices and the ways in which it can hinder a fuller development of critical regionalism's "language of possibility," since, as Reichert Powell asserts, "the function of critical regionalist cultural scholarship ideally should be not only to criticize but also to plan [...] the construction of texts that can envision more just and equitable landscapes" (24-25). Employing reparative reading practices that inspire a low theory from local knowledges can extend the insights of paranoid deconstructive analyses – of reality television, of region/alisms, of the function of representation – while challenging their complicity in hegemonic discourses.

## Eve Sedgwick's Reparative Reading Practice and Frith's Materialist Low Theory

I begin my inquiry with a number of questions that Sedgwick outlines in *Touching Feeling* (2003), in which she calls upon us to

> open a space for moving from the rather fixated question: Is a particular piece of knowledge true, and how can we know? To the further questions: What does knowledge *do* – the pursuit of it, the having and exposing of it, the receiving again of knowledge of what one already knows? *How*, in short, is knowledge performative, and how best does one move among its causes and effects? (124; italics in original)

To Sedgwick, it is quite clear that the 'hermeneutics of suspicion' have become the modus operandi for most practitioners of deconstructive, feminist, queer, psychoanalytic, and New Historicist criticism, which she delineates via Paul Ricœur from the "fundamental categories of consciousness" that underlie Marxian,

Nietzschean, and Freudian theory, namely "false consciousness and the method of deciphering" (qtd. in Sedgwick 125). As Sedgwick posits herself, "to theorize out of anything *but* a paranoid critical stance has come to seem naïve, pious, or complaisant" (126; italics in original), a charge that seems disconcertingly familiar to those who have attempted to read reality television against the scholarly and/or even popular grain. A reparative reading, according to Sedgwick, "inaugurates ethical possibility" through a focus on the "*seeking of pleasure*" (137; italics in original), and it advances the productive potential of surprise and hope (146). I see the ethical possibility of reparative readings reflected in Simon Frith's materialist 'low theory,' which he introduces in his contribution to the anthology *Marxism and the Interpretation of Culture*. In "Art Ideology and Pop Practice," Frith outlines an organic, materialist approach to popular culture in which, "rather than using cultural theory to illuminate cultural practice, I want to examine certain cultural practices and suggest ways in which they can help us refine cultural theory" (461). Such approaches have become, thanks to the work of the Birmingham Centre for Contemporary Cultural Studies and the vast field of cultural studies that it inspired, more prevalent today, and many take their inspiration from Stuart Hall's tireless reconceptualizations of cultural theory and cultural practice.

Most recently, Jack Halberstam has reintroduced the idea of 'low theory' in his 2011 publication *The Queer Art of Failure*. Even though Halberstam does not acknowledge the work of Frith, he does attribute a major intellectual debt to Stuart Hall and his famous postulate that "theory is not an end unto itself but 'a detour en route to something else'" (1991: 43; qtd. in Halberstam 2011: 15). I evoke and build on Frith's approach over Halberstam's not just for the sake of originality, but because Frith's materialist methodology centers questions of political economy that in Halberstam's postmodern embrace of failure and naivety are given less centrality, which can reinforce a liberal logic vis-à-vis the classist captivation with 'unproductive' forms of resistance. And yet, Halberstam's reintroduction of low theory into queer studies as a field has to be appreciated for the ways in which it could inspire conversations about academic approaches to "knowledge from below" (Halberstam 2011: 11) and "critique 'from the ground up'" (Reichert Powell 26). While academic discussions about epistemology in general and sitpoint theory in particular are ongoing, I explore the productivity of materialist methodologies despite their reinforcement of hierarchies of knowing (high v. low theory) and their erasure of the racialized spatiality of knowledge production (center v. margin) in the hope of illustrating the importance of continuing the intersectional analysis of epistemological hierarchies in fields such as media studies, television studies, and critical regionalism.

Frith's low theory offers an approach to reception theory that can complicate the ubiquitous paranoid readings that both cultural studies and popular responses to reality television have advanced. Next to paranoid readings' "extraordinary stress on the efficacy of knowledge per se – knowledge in the form of exposure" (Sedgwick 138), paranoid positions are also "inescapably narrative" (138) and to a fault trusting in the good such explanatory narratives will do. In this vein, reality TV scholars and journalists often frame their articles not just with detailed exposures of all the Southern stereotypes and the constructedness of reality television productions, they also appear appalled when viewers remain invested in watching after they have been told explicitly how 'bad' these shows are. Such a paranoid position can only be built on a strong misconception of viewer engagement – it presupposes both that the viewer is not aware of these 'facts,' and that their only pleasure derives from their seemingly banal functions. These paranoid readings also reveal an oftentimes pervasive class bias and a classed aesthetics that values auteur television over reality shows, postmodern novels over realist fiction, syncopated compositions over pop music.[4] Such paranoid reading practices of Southernness in reality television can be juxtaposed with a reparative position based on audience feedback and engagement. Be it Facebook comments, blog posts, or op-ed articles, the variety with which so-called consumers of reality television engage with representations of regionalism speaks to a productive site of what Frith has labeled low theory. As Frith concludes in his study of popular music,

> [p]op music is not revolutionary (or even liberating) as such. It matters because it is an important way in which people, young people in particular, accommodate themselves to capitalism, accommodate themselves, that is, to the contradictions of capitalism. To study pop music is to study a way in which common sense (including our own common sense) is shaped; to discover places, moments, where that common sense breaks down, cannot deal with needs and desires via straightforward consumerism, sets up alternative fantasies and demands. (472)

Twenty-five years later Stuart Hall and Alan O'Shea still call for a more pronounced inquiry into the construction of common sense under neoliberalism. Juxtaposing two ways of producing and reproducing common sense understandings of the region of the South through responses to reality television, this chapter draws attention to the involvement of both popular and academic discourses in supposedly counter-hegemonic critiques of neoliberal common sense. In other words, through my analysis of paranoid and reparative readings of constructions of Southernness in reality television, I want to both trouble the often

4 Wood and Skeggs have developed a detailed reading of British reality television and its audiences based on Bourdieu's insights about class, habitus, judgment, and value that speaks well to this pervasive perception of reality television as sentimental 'trash' (2011). More recently, Wood and Skeggs have published a detailed study of viewer responses that delineates the ambiguous pleasure of the viewer who is aware of the television show's ideological function and yet enjoys its format and content, the pleasure viewers experience when locating moments of 'inauthenticity' in television shows, and the pleasure of resisting and playing with the messages that shows transport (2012).

unspoken investments in hegemonic positionalities that paranoid readings advance, in this case through the lens of classism, and sketch a reparative position based on web 2.0 local participants.

## Paranoid Readings of Southernness: Judging Pleasure

Andrew Ross in *No Respect: Intellectuals & Popular Culture* delineates the relationship of intellectuals to popular culture and investigates the central role that pleasure plays at this particular nexus. Ross states that "pleasure may yet become a popular political issue" (207), and it certainly has in the context of queer studies. But what about cultural studies?

According to Ross, pleasure is largely ignored by those trained to deconstruct, criticize, and uncover the forces of capitalism, patriarchy, and colonialism in cultural products. Since popular culture "trades on pleasures which a training in political rationality encourages us to devalue" (Ross 231), its function in knowledge production remains undertheorized. This lacuna reappears in Sedgwick's discussion of paranoid reading practices, where the pleasure of exposure replaces the primacy of reparative understanding:

> What makes pleasure and amelioration so 'mere'? Only the exclusiveness of paranoia's faith in demystifying exposure: only its cruel and contemptuous assumption that the one thing lacking for global revolution, explosion of gender roles, or whatever, is people's (that is, other people's) having the painful effects of their oppression, poverty, or deludedness sufficiently exacerbated to make the pain conscious (as if otherwise it wouldn't have been) and intolerable (as if intolerable situations were famous for generating excellent solutions). (144)

Pleasure is inadmissible in paranoid readings because it is 'merely aesthetic' and thus cannot possibly produce demystification. Upon closer inspection there are really two types of pleasure at play here: on the one hand, there is the naïve pleasure that critics accuse viewers of enjoying, and on the other hand there is the pleasure of exposing that supposed naivety. While television scholars such as Helen Wood and Beverley Skeggs have provided a nuanced critique of scholarly assumptions about naïve viewer engagements (2012), other cultural theorists, from Andrew Ross' early work to Daniel Horowitz's latest study of intellectuals and their relationship to pleasure, have inquired into the results of omitting paranoid positions' own pleasure production.[5] Paranoid readings provide pleasure in and of

[5] Cultural and media studies scholars have attempted to reconfigure the question of pleasure and/or bliss, but have mostly remained invested either in a rethinking of the epistemological process for the scholar (see Ott), the normative function of academic readings of pleasure and value (see Shumway), or the gendered experience of television-produced affect (see O'Connor and Klaus' extensive summary). Few scholars seem to be ready to allow viewers access to

themselves, and oftentimes do so by 'uncovering' (read: constructing) the 'naive pleasure' of reality television viewers.

In December 2011, NPR ran a segment on depictions of Southernness on reality television and interviewed TV critic Eric Deggans on his interpretation of regionalisms depicted in reality television. His reading is representative of many media critics in its focus on the stock characters and stereotypes employed in depictions of the South, the supposed mono-racialization, ruralization, and povertization that only leaves room for a very small segment of Southerners in reality television.[6] As Deggans remarks:

> More than anything, these series feed an odd sort of racial stereotype. They're hard-partying, not particularly intellectual, and connected to the land in ways we Yankees can only guess; real-life descendants of the Dukes of Hazzard who wave around the rebel flag and embrace the term redneck as a badge of honor. […] They show a South with no people of color, and weirdly lacking contact with sophisticated Southern cities such as Atlanta or Dallas. I guess it's tough to play the bumpkin card when you're looking at skyscrapers and a booming technology corridor. (NPR)

In the ubiquitously condescending and metronormative tone (Halberstam 2005; Herring) of these paranoid critiques, Deggans reinforces the well-worn dichotomy of "sophisticated Southern cities" (n. pag.) that is juxtaposed with the uncivilized spaces of rurality, evoking the quintessential US-American racialized trope of degeneracy, barbarism, and immorality that marks the rural as margin to the metropolitan center. Deggans's reading of representations of Southernness in reality television ends with the observation that "[o]n these shows, decades of stereotypes about the South have risen again, ready to make a new generation laugh at the expense of real understanding" (NPR).[7] The ulterior motive of the

multiple positions and readings at the same time; a notable exception is the work of Wood and Skeggs.

6 Other articles that discuss the rednexploitation of contemporary reality television and address these issues include Roger Catlin's "Reality TV's Explosion of Southern Stereotypes" in *The Washington Post*, Karen L. Cox's "The South Ain't Just Whistlin' Dixie" in *The New York Times*, Carol Memmott's "'Rednecks' Swamp TV as Viewers Seek Grittier Reality" in *USA Today*, Shelley Fralic's "Television's Southern Fried Reality: Viewers Are in Love with 'Redneckonized' Stories Set in Swamps, Backcountry Moonshine Stills and Duck Blinds" in *The Vancouver Sun*, and Tricia Romano's "'Duck Dynasty,' 'Buckwild,' 'Honey Boo Boo,' and the 99 Percent" in the online *The Daily Beast*.

7 Karen Cox, author of *Dreaming of Dixie: How the South Was Created in American Popular Culture*, in her blog devoted entirely to representations of the South in reality television, makes a very similar remark in her discussion of MTV's *Buckwild*: "You see, this hillbilly stereotype goes back for more than a century and has often been used for purposes of humor. Very often this stereotype highlights the urban and rural divide in American culture. The city slicker versus the country rube. So, 'Buckwild' just continues to perpetuate that long held stereotype, so that urban dwellers can get a cheap laugh at hick culture and feel superior about

shows' producers, argues Deggans, is profit, which apparently banks on the pleasure of condescending dis-identification that the regional stereotypes provide.[8] According to Deggans, a more in-depth engagement with Southern regionalism that would lead to 'real understanding' seems to be a pleasure- and profit-less path that reality television producers do not want to follow. In Deggans's paranoid reading of representations of Southernness in reality television, stereotypes are evoked for the pleasure of the viewer and a 'real understanding' of the South is thus foreclosed. Such a limited analysis of representations of Southernness in reality television elides both other ways of understanding and of finding pleasure through these productions.

Karen Cox, one of the most prominent scholars on representations of the US South in popular culture, constructs a very similar argument in a 2011 op-ed article in *The New York Times*, but adds to Deggans's paranoid critique of viewer dis-identification a moral judgment about the ways in which these representations condone questionable behavior. Not only are stereotypes of Southern people constructed to profit the producers and provide a cheap laugh at Southerners' expense, but such representations also have two 'morally dangerous' results: on the one hand, according to Cox, non-Southerners can supposedly ignore their own deficiencies and revel in their *schadenfreude* about the South's ignorant and backward rednecks; in other words, Cox interprets these representations as a *carte blanche* for any discriminatory behavior that differs in its regional specificity. On the other hand, she argues that the same ignorant and backward rednecks can employ their televisual representations as an easy excuse for not changing their ways – even if, as Cox is at pains to point out, these ignorant and backward rednecks are fictional stereotypes that do not exist. Despite the logical fallacies

it while they do. If MTV, or any other reality show (like 'Moonshiners') truly wanted to represent the diversity of Appalachian culture they would. But they are content to make money by striking the same note – over and over – much to the chagrin of so many people who live far richer lives there, in those same mountains, than what is presented. That's a shame, but I doubt we've seen the last of shows like these" (*Pop South*).

8 I do not mean to invoke the type of outsider 'disidentification' as José Esteban Muñoz has theorized it for queer of color subjects located outside of mainstream cultural production, but engage the much more dichotomous thinking about dis-/identification as media studies has theorized it. Despite important interventions such as Beverley Skeggs and Helen Wood's study of affective responses by reality television viewers, in which their extensive work with focus groups showed "mixes of community and misanthropy, connection, disconnection, reach and distancing, at different moments, […] oriented not only by time as a sense of immediate present but also by time and space in terms of our respondents' classed and gendered histories and location" (*Reacting to Reality Television* 180), much of reality television studies remains invested in a simplified understanding of viewer engagement. As much as one would like to think Skeggs and Wood's insights into the varied and oftentimes contradictory reactions of television viewers should not feel like groundbreaking news in media and cultural studies, the tendency for scholars to universalize their specific analytical position and concomitant reactions to reality television remains a common occurrence.

permeating such paranoid readings of representations of Southernness, they remain common fare in critical receptions of Southern reality television.

Shelley Fralic's article for *The Vancouver Sun* introduces important nuance into the discussion of reality television's commercial success vis-à-vis its representations of Southern regionalism, suggesting – albeit only at the very end and rather hesitantly – an extension of the explanatory paranoid reading with a possible reparative perspective. Considering the importance of a materialist analysis of class and taste in audience studies, Fralic's comments should be approached through Reichert Powell's larger call for a critical regionalism that remains acutely aware of its own "spatial and political idiosyncrasies" especially as they become manifest in an "attenuated cosmopolitanism" (8) that influences not just what texts we choose to study, but how we value and appraise their contributions. Fralic notes:

> And make no mistake: While critics denounce reality television as lowest-common-denominator entertainment and long for more Masterpiece Theatre-style fare, the great unwashed are tuning in by the millions [...]. The reality audience, truth be told, often surpasses that which tunes into the traditional critics' favourites – last fall, the critically reviled and overtly distasteful *Here Comes Honey Boo Boo* drew 2.8 million viewers for its season finale; the critically acclaimed and stylishly smart *Mad Men* attracted 2.7 million for its finale.

Fralic's tone could be read as an attempt to engage ironically with the blame media critics have heaped on reality television viewers, the "great unwashed," as she mockingly calls them. Pointing out the classist dichotomy of reality v. auteur television, Fralic emphasizes the importance of engaging with popular reality television because of its wide reach. Fralic's thinking encourages a resistance to the easy classism that many reality television critics succumb to, and suggests a more nuanced approach to televisual texts that approaches the multilayered messages beyond the stereotypes contained within them. Thus Fralic emphasizes the "emerging Southern ethic" of familial bonds over consumerism, a work ethic of community building and local pride that resists liberal labor-normativity, and a politics of regional "unfashionability" (Herring).[9] Following bell hooks' emphasis on the "connection between poverty and personal integrity" (1994, 167), the poor's "value system [...] which emphasized the sharing of resources," and their "ethic of communalism" (170), Southern reality television shows that represent the poor can

[9] Labor-normativity as I develop the concept elsewhere in more detail (see Aho) denotes the mainstream centralization of remunerated work as a driving force of one's life, its importance as a significant site of identity construction, and the ways in which it is understood as the major influence on one's life cycle, daily rhythm, personal psyche, and imagined future. In other words, labor-normativity denotes the various axes along which labor functions as a disciplinary regime and ontological force under liberal capitalism.

be understood to trouble classed dichotomies of space, moral values, and human worth even while they reinforce specific regionalized, classed, and racialized stereotypes.

Fralic's article ends with the following words that suggest a reconsideration of the simplifying, classed analyses of reality television through a possibly reparative reading practice, as it can extend paranoid interpretive paradigms:

> And while the danger is that the contrivance that often comes with unblinking television cameras can interfere with the so-called realism of the sub-genre – in too many of these shows there is an unsettling focus on the rural-living, moonshine-swilling, uneducated white southern stereotype, living it up in hillbilly heaven while whistling Dixie – the reality is that many of these shows have also opened a window on an ethnically diverse, culturally vibrant and politically progressive south that swells with pride in its sweet tea, shotguns, NASCAR and good old boys named Bubba.

Fralic situates her inchoate reparative reading within the more traditional paranoid practice that focuses on stereotypical representations of Southernness in reality television, the "rural-living, moonshine-swilling, uneducated white southern stereotype" (n. pag.). The final sentence, however, speaks to Fralic's desire to rethink these representations and their analyses. While Fralic does not expand on the importance of her observation and the many analytic roads it could offer, her statement does open the possibility to move away from simplifying paranoid readings. Overcoming the easy dichotomization that paranoid readings tend to favor, Fralic's more nuanced analysis mirrors Reichert Powell's call for critical regionalist scholarship that attempts to understand "how the identity of the place is rooted in conflict and change as much as in permanence, stability, and continuity" (14). Provincialism is an easy register to fall into, as these examples that range from radio interviews to scholarly articles and journalistic essays showcase. Following Reichert Powell's call for an awareness of the ways in which academic writing about regions not only constructs, but also invents their characteristics, I juxtapose these simplifying, paranoid readings of Southernness on reality television with viewer comments that offer more nuanced, low theoretical perspectives through which we can consider the role of attenuated cosmopolitanism in shaping dominant readings of the production and reception of the US South in reality television.

## Reparative Readings of Southernness: Viewers Write Back

Following Stuart Hall and Alan O'Shea's call for a more in-depth engagement with online viewer feedback, I provide an initial foray into viewer reactions to one specific reality television show that is situated in the US South (*Here Comes*

*Honey Boo Boo*, in the following *Honey Boo Boo*) in order to showcase the rich 'low theory' archive that such sites of meaning-making can provide for a materialist, reparative reading practice within critical regionalism studies. I especially trouble the notion of 'naive pleasure' that viewers of television shows supposedly engage in, and instead offer a more nuanced understanding of viewer positionality and engagement vis-à-vis televisual representations of the South. Following Helen Wood and Beverley Skeggs, I argue that viewers derive different forms of pleasure from reality television and that questions about viewer engagement should never be framed in exclusively binary terms (such as identification v. dis-identification or exploitation v. education), but that at any time viewers engage with a variety of discourses and perspectives that make their experience of reality television a site of low theory.[10] As Henry Jenkins claims in *Convergence Culture*, audiences have undergone a significant shift from "individualized and personalized media consumption toward consumption as a networked practice" (244). The web 2.0 comments of local participants can thus be read as exemplary of "new forms of participation and collaboration" (245) that this convergence culture makes possible. In many ways the *Honey Boo Boo* Facebook page becomes a communal space in which local participants, here defined as all those who lay claim to subject positions attached to the construction of the US South, engage in dialogue, emotional support, and identity work that, if analyzed in its placement within larger structures of oppression, can provide an impetus to

[10] I realize that the choice to focus on one reality television show's Facebook page limits the argumentative validity of my argument to a very specific group of viewers, namely those who are invested enough in the show to like its Facebook page and who have access to Facebook in the first place. Commenters on the page – according to their self-identification, which should of course not be read as a simple reflection of 'reality' – seem to represent a specific section of US-American society, including the young and old, working and middle class people, but mostly white women. An analysis of the perceived demographics of these commenters should consider the 'white-washing' of Southernness in reality television, especially as it functions through the racialized trope of the redneck. Furthermore, the perceived gender imbalance speaks to the show's concern with quotidian, read femininized, issues, since most of the air-time is devoted to the female family members and their everyday activities. Reality television has for a long time been read as a feminized form of television (see Glynn 22; Helsby 1; Johnston), although many recent shows, including those focused on the South, have countered this trend with a hyper-masculinization (e.g. *Ax Men*, *Ice Road Truckers*, *Deadliest Catch*, etc.). As some media journalists have argued, many producers have attempted to draw in the hard-to-reach segment of men in their 40s and above through these shows, and if one compares *Honey Boo Boo* to male-centered Southern-based reality shows, the gender imbalance is indeed reversed for these other shows. The newest trend seems to be a convergence of both gendered formats into a 'family-friendly' show that is supposed to appeal to all audiences; *Duck Dynasty* has been lauded as successfully appealing to both target groups. See the recently published *Reality Television: Oddities of Culture* for more in-depth analyses of many of these shows (Slade, Narro, and Buchanan).

reconsider the classist dismissal that many cosmopolitan, paranoid readings perform.[11]

*Honey Boo Boo* is a reality television show that aired for four seasons on TLC from 2012-2014, focusing on the youngest family member Alana Thompson, who first came to public attention through the TLC reality television show *Toddlers & Tiaras*. The show centers the family's quotidian activities alongside various beauty pageant-related pursuits, but capitalizes on the family's resistance to any self-improvement plots that are otherwise a staple of the "entrepreneurial ethics of self-care" of makeover TV programs (Ouellette and Hay 6). Instead, the Shannon-Thompson family prizes familial time over everything else, exemplify non-normative interdependence, and resist heterosexist norms through their queercrip, fat pride that is squarely located in a regional, rural Southern identity (see Aho; Cavalcante; Friedman; Parkes). As Scott Herring suggests, the Shannon-Thompsons's "unfashionability" pride resists heteronormative scripts and "can be a supreme site of queer critique given that stereotypical images of the region or the rural can be used for unexpected ends" (12-13).[12] However, audience engagements with the show, while providing reparative readings that are rarely found in academic spaces, simultaneously complicate an all too easy lionization of the show's queer potential. In their engagement with *Honey Boo Boo*, viewers oftentimes perform a reclamation of their region's "ethical past" (Dainotto 493) that reinforces white supremacist, exceptionalist narratives of naturalized authenticity and romanticized community. From a paranoid perspective, this "pastoralization" (Jackson 5) could be read to uncover larger discourses of white supremacy, heteropatriarchy, and liberal capitalism that become manifest in viewer comments. Expanding from this paranoid project of "the detection of hidden patterns of violence and their exposure" (Sedgwick 143), I address in the following how a reparative focus on interdependence, happiness, and pleasure in the face of a "culture surrounding it [that] is inadequate or inimical to its nurture" (Sedgwick 149) can speak to alternative visions of "radical possibility" (Reichert Powell 26) within a critical regionalist project.

One way in which *Honey Boo Boo* has been praised by its viewers as changing perceptions that shape our understanding of reality is that it centers on a Southern, white, working poor family that can otherwise not be found on television. Between *Roseanne* in the nineties and *Raising Hope* in the early 2010s two decades saw a dearth of televisual representations of white, working-class families. Meanwhile, non-white working poor families were ubiquitously vilified in the media and on

[11] *TLC* stopped airing *Honey Boo Boo* in 2014, which is also when it deactivated the show's Facebook page. This chapter draws on an archive of comments on the show's Facebook page from the first six months of its existence. For a more detailed discussion of the cultural work that the show's Facebook page performs, see Cavalcante's insightful analysis that advances a reparative reading much along the same lines as I suggest here.

[12] Queer rural studies has seen an exponential increase in recent publications; see M. Gray; Herring; Johnson; Thomsen.

television in particular while a Democratic president was disassembling governmental support structures, black women were notoriously constructed as 'welfare queens' in popular discourse, and the exponential increase in the incarceration of non-white people was justified by the War on Drugs, which retained popularity in part because of televisual representations that cast black men as criminals (see H. Gray; Hunt; Torres). The reintroduction of a white, working poor family into televisual production is celebrated in many early comments on the show's Facebook page. Most prominently, commenters laud the fact that *Honey Boo Boo* represents the working poor and their daily struggles. As Glenda Sabo comments:

> Most people do not live in mansions and most people in America fit the poor side of town, just trying to make it in the real world. Imagine .just barely finishing school and never having more than 7 an hour job .where would you be? Happy like this family????????? Most people are never happy unless they are spending huge amounts of money. (11 September 2012 at 5:15am)[13]

Similar to Sabo, many viewers comment on the connection they see between themselves, their own lives or their friends' and relatives' lives, which are strongly informed by poverty, structural injustices, and economic exploitation. The show serves to create a communal identity for many viewers based on a classed identification that has a long history of vilification in the United States. As Erin Hatton's work on the temp economy outlines, the past decades have witnessed a devaluation of workers as assets, and cultural texts have contributed to the identification of workers as liabilities. Spaces such as Facebook sites offer alternative scripts about workers, and, as we see in Sabo's comment, about issues such as minimum wages, consumerism, and the growing wealth disparity in the United States. Of course many comments remain invested in liberal scripts of hard work and individual responsibility, and even the delinking of wealth and happiness that Sabo performs can be troubled for its elision of structural forces that produce forms of psychological suffering. Nevertheless, these critiques should not delegitimate the important work that such comments do engage in.

Many viewers situate *Honey Boo Boo* within a tradition of representations of working-class characters that lay claim to pleasure as a way to resist both liberal labor-normativity and white, bourgeois investments in containment, restraint, and thrift (see Cavalcante). Most often, references to the iconic working-class family on fictional television – *Roseanne* – place *Honey Boo Boo* as a continuation of representations that advance strong, female-centered working-class social structures in which characters stubbornly continue their claims to laughter, joy, and

[13] Since all comments were made on an online social media site, I object to the notation of grammatical or spelling errors in quotations, as typographical and lexical styles vary greatly from standardized English in these forums.

pleasure in the face of structural oppression and exploitation – a reclamation that is continued by viewers of the show and emphasized in their comments on Facebook. This "happiness of the oppressed" (Cavalcante) is not just praised by viewers, but refracted in their own enactments of pleasure in reaction to the show. The following conversation thread is representative of numerous exchanges in which female-identified community is enacted through laughter:

> Sue Williams: It makes me laugh, and anything that makes me laugh right now, is great in my book. (1 September 2012 at 11:09am) / Amanda Clark Larson: I agree with Sue ..this show makes me laugh .i love it! (3 September 2012 at 3:46am) / Lizzy Esposito: Me too ladies ! (4 September 2012 at 7:21pm)

Not only do Williams, Larson, and Esposito stress the importance of laughter in their lives, they also enact a female-identified community around their need for laughter. Numerous comments on the page point to the importance of laughter, and challenge the notion of the show's actors as exploited for cheap laughs – a position that assumes a viewer's simplified disidentification. To an outside observer who cannot identify with the social position, material reality, and cultural roles that the Shannon-Thompsons inhabit, their representation might seem like exploitation, slumming, and an overdrawn caricature of 'hicks' and 'hillbillies,' but to many of the show's viewers *Honey Boo Boo* reflects their personal experiences, life challenges, and provides a positive example of pleasure in the face of struggle. In other words, reactions to *Honey Boo Boo* continue to show how "selves and communities succeed in extracting sustenance from the objects of a culture – even of a culture whose avowed desire has often been not to sustain them" (Sedgwick 151).

The laughter and pleasure that both the Shannon-Thompson family and their viewers engage in can be understood from a reparative position as a political enactment of not just survival, but of drawing sustenance from a socioeconomic system that has relegated the working poor to the 'trash' heap of the scales of human worth. Emphasizing the "seeking of pleasure" and the "ethical possibility" that it inaugurates (Sedgwick 137), viewers' pleasure, joy, and laughter – as well as the pleasure represented on the show itself – can be read as another signal of an alternative politics of human worth and a "postwork imaginary" (Weeks) in which the connection of value and labor is resignified.[14] As Helen Wood and Beverley Skeggs have amply proven, viewers derive pleasure from resisting "expert advice," from detecting moments of "inauthenticity," and from simultaneous identification and dis-identification with characters represented on reality television (2012).

[14] This is not to suggest that the Shannon-Thompson family does not engage in traditional, liberal capitalist labor structures (Mike Thompson works as a chalk miner) or that they do not contribute to society, from the nuclear family care work and reproductive labor performed by June Shannon and her daughter Anna to communal care work such as their annual food charity drive for their neighborhood.

Resisting labor-normative demands and heternormative valuations of human worth, which Ouellette and Hay claim reality television is suffused with in its governmental paradigms of an "entrepreneurial ethics of self-care" (6) produces scales of pleasure that a reparative reading can engage in order to refine its theorization of viewer consciousness and popular hermeneutics. In other words, it can provide a low theory of popular pleasure that is still largely absent from media and cultural studies.

Given *Honey Boo Boo*'s camp politics of "unfashionability" that flies in the face of "regional shame" (Herring), the ubiquitous moral trope of 'white trash' that is continuously leveled at the Shannon-Thompson family is rejected by most viewer comments. As Matt Wray and Annalee Newitz summarize in their field-shaping anthology of whiteness, class, and rurality, the concept of white trash helps to "understand how tightly intertwined racial and class identities actually are in the United States" (4). As the most visibly marked form of whiteness, bell hooks argues (2000), white trash does not just contain moral judgments based on one's class status, but employs racialization in order to condemn the non-normative rejection of white middle-class values of thrift, containment, and (sexual) propriety that is also enacted on *Honey Boo Boo*. The rejection of "white liminality" (Wray) that these Facebook comments perform, however, is oftentimes refracted through the non-white other in a displacement of class consciousness into racial anxiety; we can find this same refraction in the transference of liberal notions of individualized effort and the concomitant meritocratic American Dream onto non-white 'success' families, from the Cosbys to the Kardashians. As Chrissy Markley Sorace, for example, states:

> I don't see how the show is trashy. It's just a real freaking family. Real people are over weight, not everyone is smart with an extensive vocab. Thats why Roseanne was such a great show. People were tired of seeing successful couples like The Cosby Show. (6 September 2012 at 5:20am)

The rejection of the white trash label as it is performed by Facebook commenters recaptures working poor resistance to bourgeois norms, but does so repeatedly by transferring classed anxiety into racial resentment. These dynamics that manifest at a low theoretical level provide important impulses as to how a critical regionalist methodology needs to engage with the intersection of white supremacy, heteropatriarchy, and liberal capitalism in order to address how cultural texts about rurality, whiteness, and poverty and their academic and popular analyses can overcome "a suspect localism" for a more "transformative cultural politics" (Reichert Powell 30) that can advance reparative readings despite the obviously problematic discourses within which these cultural texts are situated.

Remaining mindful of the structural matrix of interlocking systems of oppression (Combahee River Collective; Crenshaw) that analyses of reality television should be located in, viewer feedback can provide a more nuanced understanding of already existing audience awareness and the ways in which it manifests in popular reactions that celebrate regional unfashionability over the exploitative participation of non-poor reality television families in capitalist structures of consumerist circulations. Reality shows oftentimes face the critique that they draw attention away from structural issues and focus on the quirky but lovable personal intimacies and everyday occurrences of the people on the show. Some commenters on Facebook, however, offer thoughts that disprove the supposed lack of awareness of larger structural forms of exploitation. Elaine DeWese Simmons, for example, comments that "[t]hey are a family and I would much rather watch them than give the Kartrashian's any more airtime. At least they haven't come out with a clothing line that is made in China by child laborers" (14 September 2012 at 6:40am). Simmons compares the Shannon-Thompson family to another notoriously famous television clan, the Kardashians, who are, however, socio-economically far removed from the Shannon-Thompsons. Situating the Kardashians within the realities of global capitalist circulations of consumer goods and the neo-imperial violence they enact, Simmons' comment can be read as a statement not just about the commodification of personal stories that reality television enacts, but as a critique of global capitalism that displaces much of the exploitation of contemporary production processes into the Global South. Reappropriating the term that is most often leveraged against working poor whites, 'trash,' Simmons links its inherent moral judgment to the exploitation advanced by the upper classes, as represented by the "Kartrashians" here, instead. The Kardashians's uneasy racial status again complicates any simplified celebration of viewer resistance to bourgeois governmentality; instead, from a low theoretical perspective, Simmons' comment contributes to a more nuanced understanding of the complicated co-constitution of white supremacy, liberal capitalism, and heteropatriarchy as they manifest themselves at the intersection of the production of reality television texts and consumer goods.

Finally, reactions to *Honey Boo Boo* on its Facebook page offer insights into how regional identification is constructed through notions of rurality, whiteness, and classed, gendered, and embodied non-normativity. The very first posts on the Facebook page are exemplary of this; in reaction to the new banner picture many viewers comment positively on Alana's dirty feet that are prominently displayed:

> Love my Georgia family and the good ole Georgia clay […] honestly y'all if dirty feet is all you have to pick on with my Honey then she's got this! Shes cute, a typical 6 yr old with a good attitude about herself and her family and they all have love and each others back! How many families these days can say that! (Anne Gordon Vest, 26 August 2012 at 10:36pm via mobile)

Others who are not from Georgia still identify with a certain Southern way of thinking that they see showcased on *Honey Boo Boo*. Thus Darla Dike comments that "I have to agree that June is a solid-HOOT! I'm from East Texas and I think just like June, only she gets to say and do it!!" (27 August 2012 at 5:04pm). Many commenters link their regional pride to June Shannon's resistance to bourgeois norms of bodily containment, her fat pride, her rejection of self-improvement plots, her unabashed jouissance, and her visceral pleasure at quotidian games and the interdependence with her daughters that is celebrated through daily care work located in the queercrip temporality of their "postwork politics" (Weeks). The Shannon-Thompsons evoke a regional way of being that many viewers can identify with and from which they draw pleasure. Such identifications should of course be regarded carefully, especially as they have oftentimes served to reinforce a racialized regional identification that continues white supremacist investments that need to be carefully parsed out. Reparative readings should not become yet another vehicle through which questions of racism, sexism, and disablism can safely be relegated to analytical sidelines. Critical regionalism has yet to face these questions thoroughly, and I would argue that a low theory could contribute to a more nuanced understanding of these intersections. And yet, reparative readings can expand the classist paranoid perspectives that are so ubiquitous in reality television and regional studies, which all too often dismiss the low theoretical potential of those sites of resistance. Focusing on the material scales of pleasure that reality television as a site of dis/identification and its concomitant reception and circulation provides can open analytical avenues that remain underutilized in cultural studies. A materialist critical regionalism that draws on the low theory of alternative archives can advance reparative readings of cultural sites of meaning-making that extend the insights of paranoid analyses.

Sedgwick's emphasis on the reparative potential of "local theories" (145), mirroring intersectional, postcolonial, and black feminist theorizations of the importance of subjugated, partial, situated, and local knowledges (Collins; Lorde; Mohanty), does not imply a dismissal of paranoid reading practices that highlight the structural forms of oppression within which reparative readings necessarily are located. My emphasis throughout has pursued the importance of balancing perspectives, of asking in what ways a low theory of audience engagement can speak to academic practices of knowledge production within the field of critical regionalism. Attempting to resist the attenuated cosmopolitanism of academic hermeneutics, a materialist critical regionalism that utilizes low theory and reparative reading practices can challenge the classism of much contemporary writing on reality television while remaining mindful of the larger intersectional systems of oppression, exploitation, and dispossession within which they are enacted.

## Works Cited

Aho, Tanja. "Active Citizenship, Liberalism, and Labor-Normativity: Queercrip Resistance, Sanist Anxiety, and Racialized Ableism in Viewer Responses to *Here Comes Honey Boo Boo.*" *Journal of Literary and Cultural Disability Studies* 12.1 (2018). Forthcoming. Print.

Butler, Judith. *Gender Trouble: Feminism and the Subversion of Identity.* 2nd ed. New York: Routledge, 1999. Print.

Catlin, Roger. "Reality TV's Explosion of Southern Stereotypes." *The Washington Post* 7 June 2012. Web. 9 June 2016.

Cavalcante, Andre. "You Better 'Redneckognize'!: Deploying the Discourses of Realness, Social Defiance, and Happiness to Defend *Here Comes Honey Boo Boo* on Facebook." *Reality Television: Oddities of Culture.* Ed. Alison F. Slade, Amber J. Narro, and Burton P. Buchanan. Lanham: Lexington, 2014. 39-58. Print.

Collins, Patricia Hill. *Black Feminist Thought: Knowledge, Consciousness, and the Politics of Empowerment.* 2nd ed. New York: Routledge, 2000. Print.

Combahee River Collective. "A Black Feminist Statement." *This Bridge Called My Back: Writings by Radical Women of Color.* Ed. Cherríe Moraga and Gloria Anzaldúa. Watertown: Persephone, 1981. 210-18. Print.

Cox, Karen L. *Dreaming of Dixie: How the South Was Created in American Popular Culture.* Chapel Hill: University of North Carolina Press, 2011a. Print.

---. "The South Ain't Just Whistlin' Dixie." *The New York Times* 17 September 2011b. Web. 9 June 2016.

---. *Pop South: Reflections on the South in Popular Culture.* n.d. Web. 9 June 2016.

Crenshaw, Kimberlé. "Demarginalizing the Intersection of Race and Sex: A Black Feminist Critique of Antidiscrimination Doctrine, Feminist Theory and Antiracist Politics." *University of Chicago Legal Forum* (1989): 139-67. Web. 17 October 2011.

Crew, Richard E. "Viewer Interpretations of Reality Television: How Real Is *Survivor* for Its Viewers?" *How Real Is Reality TV? Essays on Representation and Truth.* Ed. David Escoffery. Jefferson: McFarland, 2006. 61-77. Print.

Dainotto, Roberto Maria. "'All the Regions Do Smilingly Revolt': The Literature of Place and Region." *Critical Inquiry* 22.3 (1996): 486-505. Web. 21 April 2016.

Denning, Michael. *The Cultural Front: The Laboring of American Culture in the Twentieth Century.* New York: Verso, 1997. Print.

Foucault, Michel. *Power/Knowledge: Selected Interviews and Other Writings, 1972-1977.* New York: Vintage, 1980. Print.

Fralic, Shelley. "Television's Southern Fried Reality: Viewers Are in Love with 'Redneckognized' Stories Set in Swamps, Backcountry Moonshine Stills and

Duck Blinds." *The Vancouver Sun* 12 February 2013. Web. Not available anymore.

Friedman, May. "Here Comes a Lot of Judgment: *Honey Boo Boo* as a Site of Reclamation and Resistance." *Journal of Popular Television* 2.1 (2014): 77-95. Web. 9 September 2014.

Frith, Simon. "Art Ideology and Pop Practice." *Marxism and the Interpretation of Culture.* Ed. Cary Nelson and Lawrence Grossberg. Urbana: University of Illinois Press, 1988. 461-75. Print.

Garland-Thomson, Rosemarie. "Feminist Disability Studies." *Signs* 30.2 (2005): 1557-87. Web. 8 August 2013.

Glynn, Kevin. *Tabloid Culture: Trash Taste, Popular Power, and the Transformation of American Television.* Durham: Duke University Press, 2000. Print.

Gray, Herman. *Watching Race: Television and the Struggle for Blackness.* Minneapolis: University of Minnesota Press, 2004. Print.

Gray, Mary L. *Out in the Country: Youth, Media, and Queer Visibility in Rural America.* New York: New York University Press, 2009. Print.

Halberstam, Jack. *The Queer Art of Failure.* Durham: Duke University Press, 2011. Print.

---. *In a Queer Time and Place: Transgender Bodies, Subcultural Lives.* New York: New York University Press, 2005. Print.

Hall, Stuart. *Representation: Cultural Representations and Signifying Practices.* London: Sage, 1997. Print.

---, and Alan O'Shea. "Common-Sense Neoliberalism." *Soundings: A Journal of Politics and Culture.* Chapter 4 of the Kilburn Manifesto. Ed. Stuart Hall, Doreen Massey, and Michael Rustin. Web. 9 June 2016.

Harkins, Anthony. *Hillbilly: A Cultural History of an American Icon.* Oxford: Oxford University Press, 2004. Print.

Hatton, Erin. *The Temp Economy: From Kelly Girls to Permatemps in Postwar America.* Philadelphia: Temple University Press, 2011. Print.

Helsby, Wendy. *Teaching Reality TV.* Bedfordshire: Auteur, 2010. Print.

Herr, Cheryl Temple. *Critical Regionalism and Cultural Studies: From Ireland to the American Midwest.* Gainesville: University Press of Florida, 1996. Print.

Herring, Scott. *Another Country: Queer Anti-Urbanism.* New York: New York University Press, 2010. Print.

hooks, bell. *Where We Stand: Class Matters.* New York: Routledge, 2000. Print.

---. *Outlaw Culture: Resisting Representations.* New York: Routledge, 1994. Print.

Horowitz, Daniel. *Consuming Pleasures: Intellectuals and Popular Culture in the Postwar World.* Philadelphia: University of Pennsylvania Press, 2012. Print.

Hunt, Darnell M. (ed.). *Channeling Blackness: Studies on Television and Race in America.* New York: Oxford University Press, 2005. Print.

Jackson, Robert. *Seeking the Region in American Literature and Culture: Modernity, Dissidence, Innovation.* Baton Rouge: Louisiana State University Press, 2005. Print.

Jenkins, Henry. *Convergence Culture: Where Old and New Media Collide.* New York: New York University Press, 2006. Print.

Johnson, Colin R. *Just Queer Folks: Gender and Sexuality in Rural America.* Philadelphia: Temple University Press, 2013. Print.

Kilborn, Richard. *Staging the Real: Factual TV Programming in the Age of Big Brother.* Manchester: Manchester University Press, 2003. Print.

Lorde, Audre. "Age, Race, Class, and Sex: Women Redefining Difference." *Sister Outsider: Essays and Speeches by Audre Lorde.* Berkeley: Crossing Press, 1984. 114-23. Print.

Mahoney, Timothy R., and Wendy J. Katz (eds.). *Regionalism and the Humanities.* Lincoln: University of Nebraska Press, 2008. Print.

Memmott, Carol. "'Rednecks' Swamp TV as Viewers Seek Grittier Reality." *USA Today* 16 March 2012. Web. 9 June 2016.

Mohanty, Chandra Talpade. "Under Western Eyes: Feminist Scholarship and Colonial Discourses." *Feminist Review* 30 (1988): 61-88. Web. 9 June 2016.

---. "'Under Western Eyes' Revisited: Feminist Solidarity through Anticapitalist Struggles." *Signs* 28.2 (2003): 499-535. Web. 9 June 2016.

Muñoz, José Esteban. *Disidentifications: Queers of Color and the Performance of Politics.* Minneapolis: University of Minnesota Press, 1999. Print.

NPR. "Disappointing 'Redneck' TV Shortchanges the American South." *NPR* 7 December 2011. Web. 9 June 2016.

O'Connor, Barbara, and Elisabeth Klaus. "Pleasure and Meaningful Discourse: An Overview of Research Issues." *International Journal of Cultural Studies* 3.3 (2000): 369-87. Print.

Ott, Brian L. "(Re)Locating Pleasure in Media Studies: Toward an Erotics of Reading." *Communication and Critical/Cultural Studies* 1.2 (2004): 194-212. Web. *EBSCOhost.* 9 June 2016.

Ouellette, Laurie, and James Hay. *Better Living through Reality TV: Television and Post-welfare Citizenship.* Malden: Blackwell, 2008. Print.

Parkes, Geoffrey. "'He's Gonna Be a Little Gay:' Redneckognising the Queer American Family in *Here Comes Honey Boo Boo* and the Implications for Cultural Studies." *Peer Reviewed Proceedings of the 4th Annual Conference, Popular Culture Association of Australia and New Zealand (PopCAANZ).* Ed. P. Mountfort. Brisbane: PopCAANZ, 2013. 138-146. PDF file. Web. 7 September 2014.

Reichert Powell, Douglas. *Critical Regionalism: Connecting Politics and Culture in the American Landscape.* Chapel Hill: University of North Carolina Press, 2007. Print.

Romano, Tricia. "'Duck Dynasty,' 'Buckwild,' 'Honey Boo Boo,' and the 99 Percent." *The Daily Beast* 13 December 2012. Web. 9 June 2016.

Ross, Andrew. *No Respect: Intellectuals & Popular Culture.* New York: Routledge, 1989. Print.

Sedgwick, Eve Kosofsky. *Touching Feeling: Affect, Pedagogy, Performativity.* Durham: Duke University Press, 2003. Print.

Shumway, David. "Cultural Studies and Questions of Pleasure and Value." *The Aesthetics of Cultural Studies.* Ed. Michael Bérubé. Oxford: Blackwell, 2008. 103-16. Print.

Skeggs, Beverley, Nancy Thumim, and Helen Wood. "'Oh goodness, I *am* watching reality TV': How Methods Make Class in Audience Research." *European Journal of Cultural Studies* 11.1 (2008): 5-24. Web. 9 June 2016.

Slade, Alison F., Amber J. Narro, and Burton P. Buchanan (eds.). *Reality Television: Oddities of Culture.* Lanham: Lexington, 2014. Print.

Thomsen, Carly. "The Post-Raciality and Post-Spatiality of Calls for LGBTQ and Disability Visibility." *Hypatia* 30.1 (2015): 149-66. Web. 16 November 2015.

Torres, Sasha (ed.). *Living Color: Race and Television in the United States.* Durham: Duke University Press, 1998. Print.

Weeks, Kathi. *The Problem with Work: Feminism, Marxism, Antiwork Politics, and Postwork Imaginaries.* Durham: Duke University Press, 2011. Print.

Wood, Helen, and Beverley Skeggs (eds.). *Reality Television and Class.* London: Palgrave Macmillan, 2011. Print.

---. *Reacting to Reality Television: Performance, Audience and Value.* London: Routledge, 2012. Print.

# Notes on Contributors

**Tanja N. Aho** is a doctoral student and lecturer in American studies at the State University of New York at Buffalo and at the Friedrich-Alexander-University of Erlangen-Nuremberg. In her dissertation, she explores knowledge production and cultural practices under the current neoliberal paradigm. Her research interests include disability studies, gender and queer theory.

**Birgit M. Bauridl** is senior lecturer in American studies at the University of Regensburg. She is the author of *Betwixt, between, or beyond? Negotiating Transformations from the Liminal Sphere of Contemporary Black Performance Poetry* (2013). Her current research interests are performance studies, transnational American studies, and Americanization.

**Carmen Brosig** is a doctoral student in American studies at the Friedrich-Alexander-University of Erlangen-Nuremberg and is working on a project titled "Cultural Nationalism and Transnational Solidarity: Anti-Vietnam Protests by Ethnic Minorities and the Role of Tacit Knowledge."

**Katharina Gerund** is assistant professor in American studies at the Friedrich-Alexander-University of Erlangen-Nuremberg. She is the author of *Transatlantic Cultural Exchange: African American Women's Art and Activism in West Germany* (2013). Her research interests include African American cultural studies, reeducation, and affect studies.

**Cheryl Temple Herr** is professor of English at the University of Iowa. She is the author of *Critical Regionalism and Cultural Studies: From Ireland to the American Midwest* (1996). Her research interests are popular culture at large and, currently and more specifically, everyday social practices and the music scene.

**Klaus Lösch** is senior lecturer in American studies at the Friedrich-Alexander-University of Erlangen-Nuremberg. His dissertation is titled *Interkulturalität: Kulturtheoretische Prolegomena zum Studium der neueren indianischen Literatur Nordamerikas* (online publication 2001). His fields of expertise are Native American studies, cultural theory and interculturality.

**Amy Doherty Mohr** teaches American studies at the Ludwig-Maximilians-University in Munich. Her dissertation is titled *Reading American Self-Fashioning: Cosmopolitanism in the Fiction of María Cristina Mena, Willa Cather, and Nella Larsen* (1999). Current research interests are women's writing of the South and the West, regionalism, and modernism.

**Miles Orvell** is professor of English and American studies at Temple University. He is the recipient of the ASA's Bode-Pearson Prize of 2009 and the author of many canonical essays and books, among them *The Death and Life of Main Street: Small Towns in American Memory, Space, and Community* (2012). His fields of expertise are visual culture, urbanism, and technology in American literature and culture.

**Heike Paul** is professor of American studies at the Friedrich-Alexander-University of Erlangen-Nuremberg. She is the author of *The Myths That Made America: An Introduction to American Studies* (2014). Her current research interests are affect studies and public feeling, empire studies, and contemporary North American literature.

**Rachael Price** is assistant professor of English at Abraham Baldwin Agricultural College in Georgia. She is a recipient of the 2015 Fulbright Dissertation Award and is currently completing her dissertation titled "Beyond Main Street: Small Towns in American Literature since the 1960s." Her research interests are regionalism and $20^{th}$ century American literature.

**Claudia Sadowski-Smith** is associate professor of English at Arizona State University. She is the author of *Border Fictions: Globalization, Empire, and Writing at the Boundaries of the United States* (2008). Her research interests are Southwestern American literature, hemispheric American studies as well as, more recently, whiteness studies and the post-Soviet diaspora.

**Silvia Spitta** is Robert E. Maxwell 1923 Professor of Arts and Sciences in the Department of Spanish and Portuguese at Dartmouth College. She is the author of *Misplaced Objects: Migrating Collections and Recollections in Europe and the Americas* (2009). Her research interests are $20^{th}$ century Latin American and US Latino literature, material culture as well as border writing.